GODFREY'S GHOST

FROM FATHER TO SON

NICOLAS RIDLEY

First published in 2009 by Mogzilla Life
an imprint of Mogzilla

Paperback edition: ISBN 978-1-906132-98-9

A CIP catalogue record for this book
is available from the British Library

Prepared for publication by Aldridge Press
Designed by Christine Cox
Cover design: Kevin Ancient
Typeset in Minion Pro 11.5/15pt
Printed in UK by TJ International

www.mogzilla.co.uk/godfreysghost

Publisher's acknowledgements
We are grateful to the following for permission to include copyright material: David Croft
and Jimmy Perry for two extracts from *Dad's Army*; David Higham Associates for an extract
from the poem 'Do not go gentle' by Dylan Thomas; NI Syndication for an extract from *The
Times* (7/1/02); extracts from the Authorised Version of the Bible (the King James Bible),
the rights in which are vested in the Crown, are reproduced by permission of the Crown's
Patentee, Cambridge University Press.

Uncredited photographs and realia reproduced in this book are held either by the Ridley
family or in the Arnold Ridley archive at the University of Bristol Theatre Collection. Some
photographs either carry no identication or else their source has proved impossible to trace.
We have therefore been unable to credit them as we would wish. We will, however, be pleased
to incorporate any missing acknowledgements in future editions of the book.

*For Joç, Chris, Catherine & Lottie
with love and gratitude*

*Distant praise, from whatever quarter,
is not so delightful as that of a wife
whom a man loves and esteems.*
– Dr Johnson

*If a man is to wait till he weaves anecdotes into a system,
we may be long in getting them, and get but a few,
in comparison of what we might get.*
– Dr Johnson

Contents

Prologue

Godfrey's Ghost is, at its heart, a book about my father, Arnold Ridley, written for my son, Christopher.

Although my father died twenty-five years ago, my son, who was too young to know him, can see his grandfather whenever he chooses. Chris is, of course, aware that, while his grandfather was Private Godfrey, Private Godfrey was not his grandfather; but a well-drawn television character appears so complete that sometimes, I think, it may be difficult to distinguish the actor from the man. The thought disturbs me.

Yet there are worse ways to be remembered. As a character, Private Godfrey, the oldest member of the Walmington-on-Sea platoon, has always been a *Dad's Army* favourite. Gentle, fumbling, innocently willing, Godfrey was particularly popular among the very old and the very young. 'My sister cried last night when the bank manager was rude to you,' wrote a ten-year-old boy. 'He shouldn't have been because, although you're very stupid, you do try.' It was a part my father loved to play. 'A Bear of Very Little Brain'. But, as a picture of my father, the deferential, weak-bladdered bachelor residing with his sisters Dolly and Cissy in Cherry Tree Cottage will not serve.

Which is why – does this sound absurd? – I felt a need to rescue him. To prise Arnold Ridley from Private Godfrey. To free him from age and frailty. To revive and restore him. I wanted to paint a true portrait of my father for my son. For others, too, including – as I have come to realise – for myself.

I was born when my father was fifty-one. It seemed to me so much of his life had been lived already. His distant childhood in Bath. The horrors of the First World War. The astonishing success of his first play, *The Ghost Train*. The life of a celebrated playwright. Wealth and fame. Rooms at Garlands Hotel, winters in Nice or Juan-les-Pins. After which, an interval of alcoholism, a doomed affair, a first divorce, financial ruin, calamitous and complete. He returned to France to fight in another war. Shell-shock, blackouts, nervous collapse. And then – in some ways worst of all – the writer's block that robbed him of his confidence and his craft. Through most of my childhood he lived the hand-to-mouth existence of an ageing actor, struggling for small parts, harried by bank managers, bullied by bailiffs, pursued by implacable tax inspectors.

For me and for my mother, my father's triumphs were in the past. Ours was quite unlike the plush life he had known at the height of his success. As a family, we may sometimes have shared a wistful sense of what had been and was no more, but that was all. So that my admiration for my father had – and has – little to do with his public achievements. He was, for me, remarkable because he was my father; and because – faced with more than his fair share of life's vicissitudes – through love, courage and the kind of well-grounded philosophy that doesn't recognise itself as such, he lived his life so valiantly and well.

* * *

Writing about my father has brought him back to me. The loose change jingling in his pocket. His battered brown hats in the hall. I have seen him sitting in his turret at Lord's. I have watched him anxiously waiting by the window. I have heard his voice again as, I hope, one day, my son will want to hear mine.

CHAPTER ONE

Beginnings

I am standing at his bedroom door. Watching.

♠ *one / two / three / four / five / six / seven cards*

'What are you doing, Daddy?'

♥ *one / two / three / four / five / six cards*

He doesn't look up.

♦ *one / two / three / four / five cards*

'Oh,' he says. 'Thinking. Just thinking.'

♣ *one / two / three / four cards*

I am three, maybe four years old.

♠ *one / two / three cards*

'What are you thinking about, Daddy?' I ask.

♥ *one / two cards*

'Oh,' he says. 'Different things.'

♦ *one card*

He looks up and smiles.

I am too young to know what I'm seeing.

My father played patience endlessly. Daily, mechanically, joylessly. It was an inactivity my mother regarded with exasperation. She had no time for patience but – through most of my childhood – time was what my father had. In spades, hearts, diamonds, clubs. Flopping the cards untidily onto the wrinkled counterpane of his bed or our unsteady dining-room table.

'Thinking,' he would say. 'Just thinking.'

♣ *one / two / three / four / five / six / seven cards*

* * *

Chiswick, London W4.

Another father. Another son. You and me. Years later, on a half-remembered Sunday afternoon. You are at one end of the living-room, sitting in front of the computer; I'm on the sofa. How old are you? Twelve, thirteen? An unguarded age. You are quiet and content, but I am unsettled, restless, on the edge of irritation. Are you doing homework or playing a game on the computer? I feel the need to know. I want it to be homework but, from the sofa, I can't see the screen. I could ask you but I don't. You're perfectly happy. Why won't I leave you alone? Why shouldn't you be playing a computer game? After all, I am doing nothing more serious than reading the newspaper. Or looking over the top of it.

'Lord Chesterfield,' I say. I can't stop myself. 'Ever heard of him?' This is apropos of nothing; nothing at all. Although it's possible I have been thinking about fathers and sons. You don't reply. You're looking at the screen; concentrating. I twitch with irritation.

'Have you ever heard of Lord Chesterfield?' I am speaking slowly, deliberately. You say nothing. I feel myself tense. I put down the newspaper. At which point you notice that I've been speaking to you, and I notice that you're wearing headphones.

'Sorry?' you say, and you take off the headphones.

'I was just wondering if the name "Lord Chesterfield" meant anything to you.'

'No,' you say. 'Sorry.'

You replace the headphones.

'What about Lloyd George?'

Why am I doing this?

You lower one headphone.

'Lord George?' you ask.

'Yes. No. *Lloyd. Lloyd George.* Have you heard of him?'

'No,' you say.

And then, an afterthought, being helpful, you say, 'You could always ask Mum.'

I'm nonplussed.

'What?'

'Why don't you ask Mum? She might know.'

'I know who Lord Chesterfield is – was,' I say. 'And Lloyd George.'

Now you're nonplussed.

'I know who Lord Chesterfield and Lloyd George were,' I explain carefully. 'I wanted to know if you knew.'

'No,' you say. 'I don't.'

You lower the other headphone. You're puzzled but you're being very patient. You want to know why I want to know. I want to know why – as you don't know – you don't ask. We both wait to see what I'm going to say next. Thankfully I find it's nothing very much.

'Oh,' I say. 'I just wondered.'

You smile. And wait.

'Best known for writing letters to his son,' I say. 'Lord Chesterfield, that is. Lloyd George was – well – someone different. A prime minister.'

There's a pause.

'Nothing to do with the sofa then?' you say.

I regard the sofa with suspicion.

'What?'

'The sofa,' you say. 'Chesterfield sofa.'

Can you really have said this?

'Oh,' I say. 'No. I don't think so. Although I could be wrong.'

You wait a little longer but I don't say anything else. Which is just as well, because I have realised that I know nothing more about Lord Chesterfield and have certainly never read his letters. And Lloyd George? 'The Welsh wizard'. Or was that someone else? Did he have a mistress – or several mistresses? I don't know. That's the limit of my knowledge. You have replaced your headphones. Which means you don't hear me humming …

♪ *Lloyd George knew my father,*
  ♪ *Father knew Lloyd George.*

Although, in fact, he didn't. In his lifetime my father knew, or came into contact with, an extraordinary range of people. As a successful young playwright between the two world wars, he found himself in the company of celebrated painters, pianists, lawyers, journalists, surgeons, sportsmen. As a child, their names meant little to me. Later, as a teenager, I feigned indifference or contempt whenever they were mentioned. Not that they were brought in gratuitously; they were simply part of the story. My father wasn't greatly impressed by celebrity.

Except, that is, in the case of sportsmen.

* * *

I am six years old. It's Saturday morning and my father and I are in a small sports shop in the Strand. It's early summer. Outside, the noise and confusion of city traffic. Inside – a world apart – two pyramids of shining cricket balls, displayed like exotic fruit, lines of stiff white pads, batting gloves in boxes, an undertone of linseed oil and blanco.

The shop is owned by Sir Jack Hobbs, although I may not have known this at the time. We are there to choose a new cricket bat. My first bat with a splice; a rite of passage. I have in my hands a big bat, much too big, the schoolboy's temptation. My father and I examine it together. I know what he is going to say. It's my decision but the bat will go back in the rack. And then there with us in the shop is Sir Jack himself. Sir Jack Hobbs, Surrey and England; the most accomplished of English opening batsmen; 'The Master'. This is exceptional good fortune.

My father explains our mission.

'Don't buy a bat that's too big or too heavy,' counsels Sir Jack, endorsing my father's concern.

He hands me another and I take guard. I lift the bat and it rises, as it should, above the off stump. I can't do otherwise. My father's hours of patient coaching showing to advantage. Sir Jack approves my straight drive. There are kind words. We buy the bat and leave. My father is delighted, not for himself but for me.

As a boy, he had been presented by his own father to Dr WG Grace, the greatest cricket name of all. Then well advanced in years, WG and his brother, EM Grace, were regular visitors to Bath with the Gloucester village team of Thornbury.

6

'A big man with a squeaky voice,' my father remembered. He was not an uncritical admirer of Dr Grace who had a reputation for gamesmanship and bullying which meant that he would always reside at the outer edges of my father's pantheon of great cricketers. Whereas Sir Jack was a Gentleman; probably the greatest Gentleman among Players. And I had met him – Sir Jack Hobbs – and would tell the story to my son.

*   *   *

Time shifts. Scenes change. My father is back in the pavilion and I am alone and musing at the non-striker's end. A Gentleman? A Player? How would my father judge me, his son, now much the same age as he was himself that Saturday morning in the Strand? I know the answer, of course. He wouldn't need time to consider his decision. As the only child of an elderly father, I always knew how much I was loved. Well beyond my merits.

I fidget and tap my bat in the dust of the failings my father would never see in me. His decision will be generous – too generous – but I am grateful. I look up quickly, my eyes prickling, and see his grandson at the other end. How would he see you? In the same bright light. In an arc of love and affection. Would he see himself in you? Maybe not. But he should. Because there he is and there you are. Grandfather and grandson together.

*   *   *

A patch of grass on Barnes Common where my father and I play cricket. We use my father's folded tweed jacket to mark the wicket. We don't need stumps. No one is going to be out. I bat while he bowls his 'tweakers'. This is an odd, stabbing, bent-arm technique he has been forced to adopt because he can't bowl over-arm. A wound, an injury, arthritis? I don't know. It's something I simply accept. He walks back to the spot where I have left my school jersey and woollen tie. He tries to disguise his grimace. The first 'tweakers' of the morning cause him a stab of pain which I pretend not to notice. I play the strokes he has taught me; along the ground, not too hard. An elderly father and his young son. I don't want to make him walk too far to retrieve the ball or to have to search for it in the tangled bracken. He stoops to pick it up and, as he straightens, I hear the coins jingle in his pocket. I take guard, my father bowls again, and so we continue through the pale morning.

A shift. You have joined us. We are here together; my father, you and me. It's you who should be at the crease. We walk towards each other and I hand over the bat. Stepping outside the square, I take up a position at mid-wicket. Fielding becomes my task. I will watch my father bowl his 'tweakers' at you. Or perhaps now his shoulder has recovered and he can bowl as he did in his youth, forty years before he was a father. You lift your bat above the off stump and hit the ball. A sweet stroke, a fine drive with a full follow through. There's no need to hold back. I run to collect the ball and my father bowls again. I have found my position on the field. This is where I belong. My tension subsides. 'Sir Jack Hobbs. Have you heard of him? Or WG Grace? Do you know the meaning of 'apropos'?' There's no need for questions. My father bowls again. I must watch and learn patience. I must stifle my appeals. This is my role. To be a connection between you. There are things I believe my father would like me to say to you. And there are things I'd like to say to you myself. I believe you will be happy to listen to us both.

* * *

You're looking at me. I must have said something. What?

'Yes, Lord Chesterfield. He wrote letters to his son. His natural son, I believe. That's what he's known for. I've no idea what the letters said. I've never read them. I suppose his son did. Or perhaps he didn't. Who knows?'

'Perhaps his son replied,' you say.

'Yes, perhaps he did. I really don't know. I'm not sure why I mentioned him really.'

You smile and wait. But I say nothing, afraid of saying too little or too much. And so, not trusting myself to speak, I'll write. Not letters exactly. Notes maybe. Musings, memories, meditations. Something like that anyway. From me to you. From father to son.

* * *

So much of my father's story is so long ago. So far away. Another era. Another world. A grey-and-white photograph of him with my grandfather, walking together on the Riviera, more like two brothers than a father and son. Another photograph of my father's name in theatre lights in St Martin's Lane. A blaze of fame. Stage photographs, theatre programmes, one or two posters, the annual entries in *Who's Who*. Thirty plays produced in the West End. More than thirty. Distant history. Grist for an obituary.

But here beside me is the manuscript of *The Ghost Train*, handwritten in a series of school notebooks.

The Big Value Exercise Book
24 Pages
Ruled Both Sides
Superfine Paper Well Bound
One Penny

On the back of each notebook are the standard multiplication tables and 'Avoirdupois Weights (for all goods except Gold, Silver and Jewels)'. I don't think my father needed to weigh his words very much. He wrote *The Ghost Train* in just over a week. The handwriting is fluent, confident, unbroken. Very little has been scratched out or amended. He must have seen the waiting-room at Fal Vale station so clearly, heard his characters speak their lines, watched them make their moves. The dialogue flows from his fountain pen; lines of black handwriting crossing the ruled pages.

In the days of his prolific playwriting he always wrote longhand. The typewriter was for more material matters; proposals, revisions, short stories, agreements, business letters. Until – as he might have written himself – tragedy struck. After years of writing by hand, in the mid-1950s my father developed what was diagnosed as 'writer's cramp'. Two nerves in his right elbow were rubbing together, we were told. This would lead eventually to the complete paralysis of his hand and the withering of his arm. A wretched outcome for a writer; a truly terrifying picture for a child. My imagination played mercilessly with the ghastly image of the withered arm. The only hope was an operation at the Royal Masonic Hospital, Ravenscourt Park, where a pioneering surgeon was perfecting a procedure that involved moving a nerve from the elbow to the wrist. Neither of the first two operations had been successful but – my parents were told – they had been encouraging failures. Quite what this meant they didn't know, but my father had great faith in surgeons and in the Royal Masonic Hospital. It was therefore decided that he should undergo the third pioneering procedure in the hope – although not the expectation – that it might do some good.

Our raw anxiety was increased by the fact that my father's left hand was of very limited use. The wound he had received at the Battle of the Somme meant he could only use the thumb and forefinger. Normally he was able to disguise this quite successfully but the loss of the use of his right hand would cruelly expose the helplessness of the left. Not only would he be unable to write; his career as an actor would also be finished.

In the event the operation went well; or well enough to prevent my father's arm from withering and to give him some use of his fingers. As his hand recovered, my vision of the withered arm – a nightmare too fearful to be shared with anyone else – slowly receded, and only the memory of the dread remained with me.

In time my father regained much of the use of his right arm. Eventually, for short periods, he was able to hold a pen again. But something had been lost. He found he was able to use a ballpoint, but not a fountain pen. He needed to feel the nib on the paper, to follow the flow. This he couldn't now do. The faculty had gone and with it the fluency. He bought the first in a long line of typewriters with a lighter touch, a sickly, click-clicking Olivetti to replace the robust clack-

clacking Remington which he gave to me. From time to time he sat at his new typewriter, but the right words wouldn't come. He entered the long, numb years of his writer's block from which he never fully emerged.

Not that he stopped writing. I have pages and pages of his notes, drafts and treatments. But, without an audience, his became a lonelier and lonelier occupation. *The Ghost Train* apart, little else survives. His other plays – many of which he thought much better – were either forgotten or ignored. And, by the time that *Dad's Army* had become a success, it wasn't generally remembered that he had written anything at all.

* * *

There is little quite so heart-breaking as seeing someone you love fail. Not once. Not twice. But daily. Day after day. The elements of tragedy. Pity and fear. Pity for my father. Fear for myself.

My father's damaged hands meant that he couldn't shuffle a pack of cards in the conventional manner. Instead he dealt them out in groups of five and collected them up again; slowly, methodically. Then he would lay out the cards as before.

♠ *one / two / three / four / five / six / seven cards*

Waiting to begin. Waiting for a cue. Waiting to step onto a set that he could recognise. But when the handle turns and the door opens, it's his son standing there.

'What are you doing, Daddy?'

'Oh,' he says. 'Thinking. Just thinking.'

He begins again and I watch him – wordless – flopping down the cards, one after another onto the counterpane.

French's Acting Edition.   No. 780

THE GHOST TRAIN

A Drama in Three Acts

By ARNOLD RIDLEY

TWO SHILLINGS AND
SIXPENCE
NET

LONDON
SAMUEL FRENCH, LTD.
Publishers
26 SOUTHAMPTON STREET
STRAND, W.C.2

NEW YORK
SAMUEL FRENCH, INC.
Publishers
25 WEST 45th STREET

CHAPTER TWO

'The Book'

Notting Hill Gate, London W11.

We are standing in the hall of 62 Lansdowne Road, the house I associate with the happiest days of my childhood. It is a mid-morning in June, a few days after my fourth birthday. My first thank-you letter to Godfather Paul is propped up on the hall table ready to be placed in an envelope and posted. Godfather Paul is an old friend of my father's. Or has been. A wealthy businessman, he inhabits a different world from ours but, at one time, he and my father must have been close. Our families, however, don't mix. On one occasion we meet. It's not a success. Godfather Paul's son, also called Paul, doesn't like me and I don't like him. (I may dislike him because he doesn't like me.) We don't see each other again. But Godfather Paul does his duty (unlike my other godfather who irresponsibly drinks himself to death soon after my christening) and throughout my childhood I am sent, punctiliously, a postal order at Christmas and for my birthday. I am grateful and, twice a year, I write dutifully to Godfather Paul to say so.

My father picks up my thank-you letter and looks at its wobbly mix of pictures and script. Something is troubling him but I don't know what it is. On paper my father is a neat man; confusion and disorder cause him anxiety. Besides, his knowledge and experience of young children is limited to me.

'I was just wondering,' he says, tentatively, to my mother, 'if it could be a little – tidier.'

My mother reassures him. My letter is fine. My father is perfectly happy to accept this, but I am puzzled. There is something not right with my letter. I don't know what it is. I'm not upset. I'm not dismayed. But I take it away to try again.

* * *

My father's unpublished autobiography, *The Train and Other Ghosts*, known as 'The Book', begins with this *Prologue*:

Around about nine-thirty on the evening of November 23rd 1925, a young man in his late twenties was sipping brandy in the tiny circle bar of the St Martin's Theatre, London WC2. It was during the interval between the first and second acts of a new play of which he was the author – his first ever to be produced. He had just come back from the Gents where he had been violently sick and was hoping that the brandy would restore him sufficiently to return to his box in the auditorium. But he doubted it for, to put it mildly, the first act had been chaotic. The comedian had failed to get a single laugh and every dramatic situation had fallen flat.

The bar bells rang to announce the beginning of the second act and people finished their drinks and returned to their seats. All but two who remained in the bar to continue a business discussion which in the sudden silence the young man could overhear only too clearly. They were two impresarios, one of whom in later days was to become a close friend.

'The main difficulty,' said one of the impresarios, 'is that she has just gone down to the Riviera with her latest love and will kick like hell at the idea of coming back so soon.'

'We can but try,' observed the other. 'She must be damned hard up after her flop at the Comedy and probably needs the money badly. If we could get her back in London in three days' time, we could start rehearsing straight away. She's already played the part in a pre-London tour and we could open around about Wednesday week.'

'A bit short notice,' objected the first impresario.

'I don't think so,' replied the second. 'After all, it's a one-woman play. And,' he added, knocking the ash off his cigar, 'we shall have the advantage of rehearsing here day and night after Saturday.'

'You really think …'

'Of course. This thing will finish on Saturday. Not a hope in hell.

You mark my words.'

'I expect you're right,' his companion murmured. 'Coming back?' He nodded towards the door of the bar.

'What's the point? I've had more than enough of this already. Let's go over to the Ivy and discuss the rest of the casting.'

They drained their glasses and went out, leaving the young man with the dregs of both his brandy and his hopes. I was the young man. The play, certain to come off on Saturday, was *The Ghost Train*.

* * *

As a child I would ask my father, 'Why don't you write books?' I knew my father was a writer. It was a reasonable thing to ask. Books seemed to me more substantial – less dependent – than plays which I'd begun to sense were fragile, ephemeral creations that didn't always materialise. Books were solid. They didn't need theatres, producers, actors. They stood by themselves on the shelf. Or so it seemed to me then.

My father would smile but he wouldn't reply. He wrote what he wrote. Short stories, newspaper pieces, magazine articles, scripts. And plays, of course, although fewer than before. He didn't write novels. He didn't write books. He didn't think he could.

Later, after my years of sullen teenage deafness, I wanted to hear more.

'Why not write your autobiography?' I suggested, more than once.

'No one would be interested,' he'd reply.

'I'd be interested.' But this wasn't enough.

Later still – much later – in the closing years of his life, my father began writing 'The Book'. With the ending of *Dad's Army*, his life as an actor was coming to a close, but he could still write. Had the show's success restored some of his lost confidence? At my mother's prompting, he began tapping at the stained keys of the beige, soft-touch Olivetti – an ash-flecked, ill-willed machine with a slipping ribbon – and the pages began to fill.

15

My mother had great faith in 'The Book' which I'm sure she thought of in bold black capitals. For me – pedantically insisting that a book wasn't a book until it was published – 'The Book' remained in limbo between equivocal inverted commas.

It was my mother's belief that *Dad's Army* could be persuaded to lay one final golden egg and that Private Godfrey's autobiography would find an eager audience. Did she have in mind some frothy show business concoction filled with snippets and asides? If she did, she must have been disappointed. My father had no gift for gossip, no talent for scandal or tittle-tattle. But her chief frustration with 'The Book' was that it took so long to write. She recognised that television fame is particularly fickle; that the moment would pass; that it would soon be too late. But in fact it was already too late for the book I had hoped my father would write.

Five chapters follow the *Prologue*. They paint a picture of my father's family, his early childhood, schooling and youth, and provide a bleak, brief personal history of the Great War and its bitter aftermath. They detail the life of a young actor whose career is seemingly ended by a series of undeserved reverses, who turns to writing plays and then – at the end of Act One if you like – after a haphazard history of raised hopes and draining disappointments, the scene is transformed and his life is changed for ever with the first West End production of *The Ghost Train*. The writing is good – my father couldn't write badly – and the tone is his; unadorned, self-deprecating, gently humorous.

The *Interlude*, which follows Chapter Five and ends the first part of 'The Book', is a second flash forward and shows the successful playwright, producer and film director lifted up and dashed against the rocks of misfortune.

I'd often wondered how a man felt when he was told out of the blue that he was ruined. Now I knew. I was penniless, in debt and out of work …

And then? The hard truth is that *The Train and Other Ghosts* runs out of steam. Whereas the memories of childhood, youth and early struggles have been bright and alert, the account now becomes muddied, muddled, rambling. The chapters, which have given the story its shape, are discontinued and the pages which follow – numbered and re-numbered – start to lose their way. The narrative stumbles on in a colourless cloud from which – tantalisingly – sketchy characters and odd events occasionally emerge, only to fade away before they can be properly grasped, examined or understood. Pronouncements and opinions begin to pepper the text and lighter moments now become leaden. You can sense the writer aching for the end; you can feel his fatigue.

I have the typescript here in front of me. Or, more precisely, what I have in front of me is a poorly executed photocopy of the typescript. Odd lines are missing at the top or at the bottom of the page where the original has been misaligned on the machine. Where is the original? Who has it now? Sadly it doesn't really matter. *The Train and Other Ghosts*, my father's last laborious product, was unpublishable.

Not that this stopped my mother. She was entitled to ignore my advice and she did. 'The Book' was sent out again and again to publisher after publisher. Again and again – as I knew it would be – 'The Book' was returned. Did my father sense the humiliation? I don't think he did. He had done what he could and he let it go. But I felt it keenly. It seemed so pointless – so hurtful – at this stage of his life to invite further rejections. He had fought the good fight. He had finished his course. There was nothing more he needed to do.

After my father died, I made certain that 'The Book' stayed at home. My mother lost all interest in it, as she did in most things in the years that followed his death.

My father will accept what I have done with 'The Book'. He will approve my selection, my editing, my re-writing. He will understand. The father protecting the child. The child protecting the father. My father will trust me to do the best I can.

*   *   *

A child again; an older child. My role is to shave the back of my father's neck between haircuts. He bends his head, exposing the rough skin, the folds and fissures of an old man's neck. I stand behind him with a dry razor and scrape away at the tough grey bristles as tenderly as I can. I am happy to be doing this. I don't want anyone else to see him so exposed.

CHAPTER THREE

Only child

The first chapter of *The Train and Other Ghosts* begins,

> I was an only child, born at 4 Pera Place, Walcot, Bath, on January 7th
> 1896 to William Robert Ridley, a professional athlete, and to his wife,
> Rosa Caroline, whose maiden name had been Morrish.

Like my father, I am an only child and, like him, it might be the first
thing I'd say about myself. I might also say that I, too, was born in
Bath; a source of pride for both of us although naturally we had no
choice in the matter.

*   *   *

This was my mother's story. My father, when he was present, would
listen, gently assenting. The story pleased both my parents and
seemed to mean more to them than they could, or needed to, explain
to anyone else.

My mother, in her mid-thirties, wanted children. She was going to
have children. More precisely, she was going to have a son who would
then be followed by a daughter. My father, now fifty, had spent most of
his adult life avoiding young children. To him they were an unknown;
he had been happy to leave it that way. If he had been consulted, my
mother's plan would have alarmed him. He wasn't.

However, once my mother's pregnancy was confirmed, my father
courageously declared himself delighted. He knew what had to
be done, particularly as my mother was so confident I would be a
boy. Arrangements were made with a local doctor – an old friend

of my father's – and the Ormond Lodge nursing home was booked. My mother, eight-and-a-half months pregnant, was taken by taxi to Paddington where she was put aboard the train to Bath. In those early post-war days, a son's place of birth was critical; it was a prerequisite that I should be born in Bath. How else would I be qualified to play cricket for Somerset?

* * *

Another journey from London to Bath had preceded my father's birth.

My grandfather, Bob Ridley, was born in New Compton Street, Soho, in the shadow of St Giles' Church, where his father was a sidesman and he himself was a chorister. While serving a seven-year apprenticeship as a compositor with a firm of printers in Fetter Lane, Bob Ridley joined the world-famous London Polytechnic founded by Quintin Hogg. After completing his apprenticeship, he was offered the post of gymnastics instructor. This was a considerable achievement. A naturally gifted sportsman, Bob Ridley soon established a sound reputation and, in his spare time, started to give private lessons in boxing and fencing to an array of wealthy and distinguished clients. His future looked bright but – a recurrent motif in so many of my father's stories – 'everything took an unexpected turn'.

An impecunious relative – unnamed in 'The Book' but 'wicked Uncle Jack' whenever my father told the story – started to 'touch' my grandfather's rich clients for loans and handouts. Coming to hear of this, my grandfather was furious and vowed that, should it happen again, he would leave London for ever. As a child, it wasn't clear to me why this threat should have deterred 'wicked Uncle Jack' but I didn't ask in case I had missed the point of the story. Soon afterwards 'wicked Uncle Jack' repeated the offence. Bob Ridley had said what he would do and he did it. My grandfather was a man of his word.

He walked into the Reading Room that then stood at the bottom of St Martin's Lane and searched the *Situations Vacant* columns of the newspapers. A provincial YMCA was advertising the post of gymnastics instructor. The salary was low – less than half what he was earning – but it was enough to live on. A week later, he left for Bath and moved into lodgings there. Within a year he had married his landlady's younger sister. He never returned to London except for a few brief visits.

The family my grandfather married into, the Morrishes, was presided over by the fierce and formidably opinionated John Samuel Morrish. My father remembered him as 'a tubby bearded man, gentle by nature but of extreme verbal ferocity. All who disagreed with him "should be put against a wall and shot!"'

When my grandmother fell for the lodger – a handsome, red-haired gymnastics instructor – the family 'literally screamed their disapproval' and there was an urgent search for suitable walls. But my grandmother was – and remained all her life – a woman of steady resolution and she and my grandfather were duly married at the Congregational Chapel, Weston-Super-Mare, on Boxing Day, 1894. A painful period of family estrangement followed, but this ended with the birth of my father.

> The arrival of a grandchild – and a boy at that – in a family without male issue was too much for the bigoted but sentimental old man. All was forgiven. I was the last of the male Morrishes and so I remained until the birth of my own son fifty-one years later.

After my father's birth there were no further grandchildren.

> From the earliest age I was condemned to be an only child for, shortly after my birth, my mother fell seriously ill and was obliged to undergo an operation considered almost certain to prove fatal in those days when surgeons still operated in old frock coats, and although she survived, it rendered any further child-bearing an impossibility.

* * *

I don't know what age I was when my mother miscarried. Three years old, four. I remember her lying in her bedroom with the curtains closed for week after week. Or so it seemed to me then. She was pale, passive, withdrawn; utterly unlike my mother. And then suddenly she recovered. It was as if she'd come back from a long journey. I didn't know where she'd been and no one seemed able to tell me.

Fate, circumstance, whatever it was, had cruelly altered my mother's plan. She had been dispossessed of her daughter. She had lost the chance to reproduce the intensely loving relationship she had had with her own mother. For her, our family would not be complete. She continued to look for a daughter for the rest of her life. She didn't find her but she found young friends instead. Good friends, some of whom loved her in the way that a daughter might have done. But her own daughter – my sister – couldn't be substituted. She was an empty space in our lives. An empty place at the table. A gap on the mantelpiece where a photograph should have been. A birthday that we didn't celebrate. I was left – am left – with a feeling that something irreplaceable was lost to our family and that, in some way, I may have been to blame.

* * *

My father had the Morrish tribe to dote on him. But there were also his Ridley cousins.

> The blackest times of this period of my life were the all-too-frequent
> visits of the London cousins. Then indeed, I trod the stony path. They
> were noisy, uncouth, rough and lacking finesse in games. They did
> more damage to my carefully-preserved toys in a day than I would do
> in a year, in fact they appeared to glory in violent destruction. How I
> hated them!

This is the voice of the only child; the horrified response to the violation of one's ordered world.

I used to count the days against our visitors' return to London but it was nearly always postponed at the last minute. Indeed, I remember one party group who had been asked for a weekend, announcing on their arrival that they had monthly excursion tickets. At times, frustration and fury would break through and I once gave one of my cousins an awful hammering after he had 'murdered' one of my favourite tin soldiers. It must have been a distinct surprise for him to discover that a 'bumpkin' could pack a punch.

Unsurprisingly, my father's London cousins make no further appearance in his story.

* * *

Normally I go to the Round Pond with my mother. We take the 52 bus and walk from Kensington Church Street. Today I am with my father and we have arrived at Kensington Gardens by taxi. Taxis are a last leftover from my father's days of wealth. I am holding my sailing-boat – wooden, blue, solid – and we are going to sail it together, as other sons and fathers do. Although this is something we haven't done before. I am excited; my father less so. I don't know yet that my father and boats don't mix. He associates them with seasickness and uncertainty.

With my mother, I exercise caution. I place my sailing-boat carefully on the surface of the water and – despite her encouragement – am reluctant to release it. I concede she may have some understanding of wind and sail from her youth spent in New Zealand but I am not entirely convinced. At this age I am well aware that my mother has a carefree attitude to some of life's risks which I don't share myself. I know that my sailing-boat is nothing more than a crude wooden hull with a light cotton sail, but to me it is precious. I am at that innocent age where what I have is what I want and, although I admire them, I am not envious of the older boys with more elaborate craft. I watch them adjusting the trim, wading a few feet out into the water, holding their boats in position, waiting for the right gust to fill the sails. And away. I clutch my boat more tightly.

Today my father looks on as I steer my course as close as I can to the edge of the pond. I release the boat. It returns. Release and return. Release and return. Is it boredom that prompts him to suggest, very gently, that we could be a little more adventurous? I know he's right but I'm still anxious. Little by little I become bolder until we decide to head the boat across the pond to the far shore. The wind holds steady and we are there to meet it when our boat arrives. Which of us is it who suggests that we should try another voyage across the pond before we go home?

If you are expecting the story to end in disaster, it doesn't. There is a moment when the wind drops and changes direction, but it picks up again and my boat sails back to where we can retrieve it. I go home, happy and relieved.

My mother and I return to the Round Pond as before. It's an uncertain day of sudden squalls. I won't risk any further voyages across the pond and my mother is content to let me potter by the edge of the water while she reads her library book on a nearby bench. She doesn't witness the scene later in the afternoon. A boy with his father – each as helpless as the other – watch as their boat, water-logged and becalmed, sinks irretrievably in the middle of the pond. I knew this is how it might be. What I didn't know was that I would be more affected by the father's powerlessness than the boy's misery. I return to my mother; she closes her book and we go home.

Afterwards we return to the Round Pond very rarely. And then not at all. I keep my blue sailing-boat safe in my toy cupboard.

* * *

A father, mother and son. For my father, our family may have seemed complete, but my mother needed more. She wanted a wider family, a spread of connections. The problem was that we were regrettably short of immediate relations. My only surviving grandparent – Granny, my father's mother – still lived in Bath with Rose, her companion, and Mr Harper, her irreproachable lodger. Uncle Chris, my mother's adored brother, had remained in Auckland after she, and later her mother, had returned to England. The rest of the Ridleys were mostly untraceable. At least, my father showed no inclination to trace them. But my mother found that there was one cousin, Leslie, for whom my father had a certain fondness, and a week's holiday was arranged with Leslie's family in Selsey Bill. He was a large, apologetic, bullied man with a dislikeable second wife, a spiteful stepdaughter and a downtrodden daughter of his own. Their son, a year older than me, was a dull, lumpen boy who liked gadgets. The week in Selsey Bill was not a success (my father stayed two days before returning to London) and the rest of the Ridley family disappeared from our view.

It was as well that my mother could call on cousins of her own.

As it happened, I was much more fortunate than my father. To begin with my second cousins – Susan, Simon and Christopher – never threatened to disrupt my universe. My stuffed animals and tin soldiers remained intact. When the cousins came to London, it was only for a day or two. They didn't want to stay any longer. It didn't surprise me. The city had nothing to attract them. Sombre monuments, dull museums, idle hours in a mansion flat, the restrictions of 'indoors'. Whereas 'the country' was sunlight, adventure, escape. Why should they want to leave?

In the early years, my mother and I joined the cousins for their family holidays; the Isle of Wight, Devon, Bournemouth. My father might be with us for a day or two but would soon return to London to escape the noise. Later, when we could no longer afford holidays, my mother and I would stay with the family in the house that they'd moved to in Southbourne. I didn't miss the rented cottages or boarding houses where we'd stayed before. Far from it. I wanted nothing more than to be in the house at Southbourne. My cousins were family and my stays there were my intermittent glimpses of family life; unrestrained, quarrelsome, intoxicating. I didn't always understand what was going on or find it comfortable but it was the vigorous, varied life that I didn't have at home. Some part of me lived for the two or three weeks when I could go to stay. Susan, Simon and Christopher were the sister and brothers I didn't have. We weren't, I think, particularly close but this didn't bother me. I didn't know how close brothers and sisters could be. They were company, society, activity, excitement. It was enough.

I think I knew even then that for them I was never anything more than their London cousin. I wasn't unwelcome but I wasn't missed when I wasn't there. I came. I stayed. I went away again. That was all. This wasn't what I minded. But the last few days of each visit were painful. Listening to plans being made for the days ahead; outings, excursions, adventures. Days when I wouldn't be there; when I would be back in London on my own.

* * *

When is it, as a child, that you first learn life isn't fair? That what is and what ought to be aren't the same. That what you thought was yours can be taken away from you and that there is often no redress. How soon is it before the penny drops? Later, I suspect, for the only child than for others.

We are in a rowing boat – Susan, Simon, and their mother, Auntie Kate, and me. We are on holiday and Auntie Kate is rowing. (My mother has stayed behind to spend a little time with my father who will be returning to London that evening.) Wherever it is we have been, we are now rowing home. On the way out we were given a bag of cherries to share out between us – Susan, Simon and me. Susan and Simon's cherries are eaten speedily; two, three, four at a time. Theirs is a world where you take what you're given and hope that there's more. My cherries have been eaten more slowly and I have saved some for the return journey. I have removed the bag from my pocket and I am eating them, one at a time. I am not aware that Susan and Simon are watching me. I am not eating my cherries to provoke their envy. I am simply sitting watching the waves and listening to the gurgle of the water under the boat. Which is why, when Simon lunges for the bag, I'm caught off guard. Susan joins him in the struggle and the boat rocks and wobbles. Auntie Kate – mesmerised by the dip and the pull of her oars, lost in thoughts of her own – is brought back to the boat by a gust of howls. 'He won't share!' says Simon. 'It's not fair,' says Susan. 'But …' I say. It isn't difficult for Auntie Kate to see what's going on. 'Don't be selfish, Nicky,' she says. 'Share out the cherries.' I have confirmed her judgement. An only child. Unused to sharing. Spoilt. She returns to the oars. I am speechless with the injustice of it all. Susan and Simon take possession of the rest of the cherries. I have lost any interest in them. I'm bewildered but my picture of the world has begun to re-form. Life isn't quite what I thought it was.

Susan and Simon will remember none of this. But I can still see the black, shining cherries in the brown paper bag, and the seagulls circling overhead, mocking me.

* * *

Fifty years later. A roof-top beside the River Thames. A convivial family celebration. (Christening, birthday, anniversary?) Here we are. Susan, Simon, Christopher. And me. Around us, other cousins, nephews, nieces, family friends.

I don't see my cousins very often. I don't know how often they see each other. This evening they are recalling events from childhood. It's what I imagine most brothers and sisters do when they meet on such occasions. Outings, excursions, adventures. Bike rides to Hengistbury Head, camping in the New Forest, sailing near Swanage. Re-establishing memories, drawing closer together. One episode in particular has come to mind. An uproarious story. The afternoon when their cocker spaniel was sick on a bus. Interrupting each other, eager to add details, they turn to me. The narrative begins again. They want to share it with me. I have become their audience. 'Yes,' I say. 'The afternoon when Rip was sick on the Shamrock and Rambler bus to Wells.' They look at me blankly. 'I was there,' I say. 'Oh, were you?' I have spoiled the story somehow; the warmth has leaked away. A waiter fills our glasses and the conversation moves elsewhere.

I am such a small part of their childhood memories, whereas they are such a large part of mine. I am too shy to tell them this, either then or now.

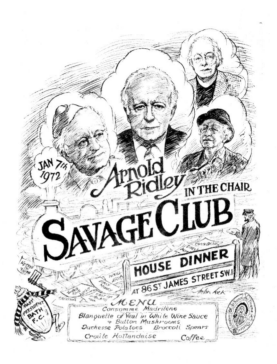

JAN 7th 1972

Arnold Ridley IN THE CHAIR

SAVAGE CLUB

HOUSE DINNER

AT 86 ST JAMES STREET SW1

MENU
Consommé Madrilène
Blanquette of Veal in White Wine Sauce
& Button Mushrooms
Duchesse Potatoes   Broccoli Spears
Croûte Hollandaise   Coffee

PAST PRESIDENT BATH F.C.

CHAPTER FOUR

God, the Father

I didn't find it difficult to believe in God, the Father; I was less sure about God Almighty. If, as a child, I'd understood them, omniscience, omnipotence and omnipresence would have been problematical. Because, from a very young age, I was certain of one thing. It's best not to ask for too much.

*   *   *

Lansdowne Road, Notting Hill Gate.

My mother is sitting on my narrow bed. I lie under the blankets, watching her and listening. My mother is absorbed in the book. She has a wonderful contralto voice and every evening she reads aloud to me. This is our ritual, a small performance, complete in itself. I may choose the book we read or she may have chosen it herself. If she has, I won't follow every word. This isn't important. I lie on my pillows and listen to the rise and fall of her voice. The notes, the tones. I am swimming in the rhythm of her words. I let them tumble around me, rolling across each other, like wavelets in the shallows. I know – I have faith – that in time all will become clear.

On Sundays we begin by reading a short passage from the Bible. There is nothing especially reverent about this. It is simply what we do on Sundays. This evening my mother is reading from the Gospel of St Luke.

If a son shall ask bread of any of you that is a father, will he give him a stone? or if he ask a fish, will he for a fish give him a serpent? Or if he shall ask an egg, will he offer him a scorpion?

I ask myself the question. And I am instantly – almost physically – enlightened. If I ask my father for bread – which I might do, or maybe a biscuit – will he give me a stone? Of course not. It's unthinkable. A stone? Why would he? I don't need to ask about serpents or scorpions. (Besides, it's very unlikely I would ask him for a fish.) To me the meaning of the passage is shiningly clear. God, the Father.

From that moment I came to believe in a beneficent, all-loving deity. Whatever terrors there are in this world – and I felt there might be many – the idea of a malevolent father was unimaginable.

*   *   *

St David's School, Elvaston Place, London SW7.

The Divinity lesson. Sitting in rows at cramped wooden desks, solitary and scared, we are reading aloud – one verse at a time – from a very different Bible. While we read, Mr Durnford, our headmaster, stands looking out of the window at the street below. To the unwary he may seem distracted but in fact he is listening, grimly attentive, for the next – the very smallest – stumble or hesitation.

'Next.'

And it came to pass after these things, that God did tempt Abraham, and said unto him, Abraham: and he said, Behold, here I am.

It is important – hideously important – not to falter. A single mistake unlocks the door to disaster. Mr Durnford, without turning his eyes from the window, will say, 'Again! Read it again!' A momentary lapse and you will be lost. You will become emmeshed, entangled, in a string of words. 'Again!' You will be exposed, stranded; a snake under a stone, a fish on the beach. 'Again!' The words will cling like cobwebs. 'Again!' The verse becomes inescapable. 'Again!' And though you may finally read it perfectly, it won't be enough. 'Again!' 'Again!' Until Mr Durnford, still looking down at the street below, has exacted his satisfaction.

'Next.'

And he said, Take now thy son, thine only son Isaac, whom thou lovest, and get thee into the land of Moriah; and offer him there for a burnt offering upon one of the mountains which I will tell thee of.

'Next.'

This time I have survived. I should be awash with relief but I'm not. The Old Testament is a stony desert of scrub and boulders; it's best to fix one's eyes on the next horizon and never look back. (Remember Lot's wife.) But I feel I must.

'Next.'

I re-read the words and try to absorb their appalling meaning. Have I understood them correctly? I am in grave danger of losing the place but I have to take the risk. I read the verse again. What is God asking Abraham to do?

'Next.'

And Isaac spake unto Abraham his father, and said, My father: and he said, Here am I, my son. And he said, Behold the fire and the wood; but where is the lamb for a burnt offering?

I find where we are. I'm thankful. This is Isaac, the trusting son. He has asked the right question. His father will now respond.

'Next.'

And Abraham said, My son, God will provide himself a lamb for a burnt offering: so they went both of them together.

Now, although my finger is resting on the verse, I am utterly lost. This is Abraham, Isaac's father, deceiving his son?

'Next.'

And Abraham stretched forth his hand, and took the knife to slay his son.

A father who is prepared to kill his son? I don't understand how Abraham has been tempted to do this. Or why. But I am as certain as I can be that he is about to fail God's test.

'Next.'

And he said, Lay not thine hand upon the lad, neither do thou any thing unto him: for now I know that thou fearest God, seeing thou hast not withheld thy son, thine only son from me.

I'm bewildered. I simply don't understand. How can this be right? It can't be right. Can it? Can it be right? There's no one to ask.

'Next.'

I'm still reeling. It will soon be my turn to read again but I don't know where we are. Where I am. I will be ridiculed and humiliated. Mr Durnford will tell me to read the same verse again. And again. And again. But I can't help it. I have lost my footing. I am floundering in the tide. A god who asks a father to kill his only son? A father who is prepared to do this and must be told to stop? Whose obedience is then commended, deemed right? I will have to face the consequences. I decide then and there. This god – the god of the Old Testament – is not one I want anything to do with.

* * *

The Morrish family creed was strictly non-conformist and my father's religious upbringing was unremittingly Old Testament. God was Jehovah, Yahweh; remote, jealous, demanding, unforgiving. The good news of the New Testament was to be read only if time allowed, which mostly it didn't. If gentle Jesus meek and mild figured at all, he was a near-unattainable reward reserved for only the most deserving. The established Church was anathema, and the beliefs and practices of other denominations were viewed in the same harsh light as those of the animists in the darkest jungles of Africa or the remotest corners of Borneo.

Grandfather Morrish had three great hates: Tories, publicans and the Church of England. 'I'd rather follow you to the grave than to the Church of England' was an oft-expressed sentiment. I don't remember him ever mentioning the Church of Rome. Possibly his mind boggled at the thought of it!

Most of my father's early schooling was religious instruction.

At the age of eight I could recite the Ten Commandments by heart, although I was somewhat vague as to their meaning. For many years I was under the impression that 'adultery' was in some way connected with the illegal watering down of milk. We started each day with prayers (often of a highly personal nature in which the individual minor sins of yesterday were disinterred), Bible readings and hymn-singing chanted to rather inaccurate pianoforte accompaniment. I shall always remember one hymn, 'Jesus wants me for a sunbeam', for the sole reason that Jack Horstmann, one of my fellow pupils, drew attention to the strange parallel of divine desire and the manufacturer's name engraved on his new bicycle. I quite thought that such irreverence would result in him being dragged down screaming into hellfire. For Hell was a very real place with a definite geographical situation in the centre of the big globe.

From time to time our Biblical studies were intensified by the fleeting visits of Pastor John Huntley, a successful grocer and unpaid minister of the neighbouring Ebenezer Baptist Chapel. These were terrifying days indeed, when the gates of Purgatory were kept shut by only the frailest of fastenings. A tall, gaunt man with a full black beard, John Huntley was a real Old Testament character and I was perfectly sure that on the awful Judgement Day we should find him on God's right hand, nominating the righteous for Heaven and pricking off the names of others destined to eternal damnation.

My father survived the terrors of Hell quite happily and retained the warmest memories of his time at Miss Silversides' Seminary. The hellfire teachings of his childhood were for him a source of gentle fun. One of his favourite stories was the Presbyterian preacher's sermon:

The wretched sinner has been cast into the deepest pits of Hell where, in indescribable agony, he writhes and burns through all eternity. Each day at noon when the fires are at their hottest, the Lord passes by high above him, and each day the sinner cries out piteously, 'Lord! Lord!

I didnae ken! I didnae ken!' But the Lord does not hear him. Each day the same. 'Lord! Lord! I didnae ken! I dinnae ken!' But the Lord passes on his way. Day after day, through all eternity. Until, one day, when the flames of Hell are hotter than ever and the sinner cries out more piteously than before, 'Lord! Lord! I didnae ken! I didnae ken!' The Lord pauses, looks down at the sinner and – in his infinite mercy – addresses the wretched man in the fires below. 'Well, you ken now!' says the Lord.

* * *

I disliked Sunday school and wouldn't go although I was happy enough to accompany my mother to the different high church services she attended. My father didn't come with us. Incense and genuflection were too theatrical for him. Also, as a man who had twice been divorced, he'd been informed he could no longer take communion. This may have given him the feeling that he had been disowned by the Church. Or perhaps he simply wanted an hour on his own on Sunday mornings.

Later, when we were living in Highgate, things changed.

At the age of nineteen, Bridget, my sweet-natured cousin, quite suddenly died. It was the school holidays and my mother was at work when my father heard the news. 'I think we should say a prayer, don't you?' he said, standing by my bedroom door. Together we crossed the road to St Anne's Church at the bottom of Highgate West Hill where we sat in silence for some time. What I remember most was my father's anger at Bridget's death. My father's anger was rare and reserved for injustice. Bridget, an illegitimate daughter at a time when this was still a source of shame, had been particularly fond of 'Uncle Bear' and he of her. Was my father's return to formal religion an attempt to make sense of what was otherwise senseless? Or was it more mundane?

The new vicar at St Anne's, Henry Whittingham, was a scratchy but conscientious Christian and an ardent follower of *The Archers*. My father, who for years played the part of Doughy Hood, the baker,

34

was Father Whittingham's conduit to another world which had hitherto been hidden from him. Whether or not Henry received the enlightenment he hoped for – my father wasn't over-reverent about *The Archers* – I can't tell, but a bond was formed between them. Henry Whittingham quickly dismissed my father's concerns about his entitlement to the Lord's Supper and my father was returned to the fold from which I don't believe he had ever really strayed very far.

In later years my father had a faintly baffling love affair with the new Polish Pope. Was it the pontiff's vigour, vitality and comparative youth that attracted him or was he seduced by the comfort of Catholic certainty? Although he never reached Rome itself, his spiritual journey had taken him a long way from the Ebenezer Baptist Chapel in Bath.

*   *   *

At the age of seventeen, on a journey of my own, docked in the port of Jeddah, my faith left me. If 'faith' is what I'd had. It had been straining at the ties for several weeks but here, standing at the bow rail of the *Jelsa*, the Yugoslav merchantman on which we were sailing anti-clockwise round the Red Sea, it – whatever it was by then – finally broke free. The last threads snapped and it bowled away like a tent down a hill in a high wind. I didn't give chase or try to retrieve it. I had reached an age when I thought I didn't need faith any more, or believed I could find it again if I did.

My travel diary stops two weeks earlier in Istanbul and memories of later visits mingle with each other. Was it then that we ate fish in a restaurant by the Galata Bridge while black rats, the size of kittens, scuttled between our feet; and watched the sunset from the Pierre Loti Café; and slept fitfully in a dormitory under the city while ancient cisterns gurgled between the beds? My travel diary doesn't help me. And it doesn't prompt me with the words I might have tried to form to describe whatever it was I experienced as I leant back against a pillar in the church, the mosque, the museum of Sancta Sophia. Because something happened there. A wrench, a twist, a tug, a sudden emptiness that unsettled me and that I couldn't explain.

I don't know what I had hoped for from the Holy City of Jerusalem (at the time still under Jordanian jurisdiction) but my visit to the Church of the Holy Sepulchre disgusted me; grubby brown monks scurrying about peddling candles, tracts and yellow relics; the smell of grease and stale incense, the shadows of tormented gullibility. I emerged from the dark and stood in the sun, feeling self-righteous and alone.

The *Jelsa* was unloading timber and tinned goods. Passengers had not been given permission to disembark and we were confined to the ship. I might have spent the time reading or playing cards with the family of missionaries who were due to disembark in Djibouti, but I was transfixed. For three days I leant over the rail and watched the ships at the quay opposite. Sheep were being unloaded – sheep in their hundreds, in their thousands – destined for Mecca. Quayside derricks hoisted the empty gun-metal containers high above the decks before swinging round to drop them rapidly into the ship's hold. A few minutes later the open containers would rise up out of the hold, swing back into position and drop down onto the quay. The stronger sheep would leap out of the containers and be herded into groups. Others would be pulled out by their heads, or their necks, or their legs. At the bottom of each container were what remained; the sheep that were injured or dead. The container would be raised a few feet and then tipped on its side so that they fell onto the quay; crushed, suffocated, broken bodies, twitching or limp. These were then thrown into piles and taken away later in trucks. The rest were herded away off the quay to play their part in Id al-Adha, the festival that follows the Hajj, the feast of sacrifice, the celebration of the willingness of Hazrat Ibrahim to submit to the will of God and to sacrifice his only son.

* * *

My journey ended with a charter flight home from Dar-es-Salaam in a turbo-prop Constellation; twenty-six hours with stops in Khartoum in the early hours of the morning and Malta in mid-afternoon. We landed at Luton and – disorientated and detached – I went back to school.

And I went back to St Anne's on Highgate West Hill. There were no yellow relics to offend my sensibilities and I could see no reason why I shouldn't. At Christmas, a server at midnight mass, I had a vision from the chancel steps. Did I believe I was seeing Mary Magdalene or the Blessed Virgin? Or maybe both together? I was transfixed. A student nurse, in uniform after an evening shift on the wards, was kneeling at the altar rail, her head bowed, her hands held up to receive the sacrament. She was – angelic. I knew I was in the presence of something profound and that my life was about to change.

It did. In the New Year. The initiation, when it happened, was less ethereal than I had imagined but this didn't trouble me. If I had been told that it had more to do with the body than the soul, I might have disputed it. I was, after all, in love.

* * *

An earlier Christmas scene.

My mother enters the dining-room. She is bearing the plate on which sits our turkey. (As always, it will be as dry as parchment but for my father and me this is the only turkey we know.) What she sees is my father with a knife in his hand, laughing and laughing, the tears rolling down his cheeks. This must have alarmed her considerably because my father is a man who smiles but does not laugh. And she sees me, her son, standing in front of him, aghast, horrified, in floods of tears. On the faded green carpet between us is a pool of blood.

I have been given a penknife for Christmas. I am delighted. It's exactly what I wanted, but I recognise that my parents will have had misgivings about such a dangerous present. I have been told to handle the knife with great care and I have promised that I will. The penknife is new, stiff, difficult to open and close. My father takes the knife from me. He will open it and close it a few times until it becomes easier. He is easing back the blade when it snaps shut sharply and cuts off the tip of his thumb. There is blood everywhere but it doesn't matter. My father is bleeding and laughing and thanking God. The knife has cut off the tip of his thumb but it could so easily have been mine. Or maybe my finger. He is breathless with relief and gratitude and retires to the kitchen to celebrate with a medicinal brandy.

Beliefs shift. Faith is unsteady. But I have had a fixed point. My father could not have taken me into the land of Moriah, whatever God said. And God, our God, my father's and mine, could never ask him to do such a thing.

CHAPTER FIVE

Father Time

We haven't been to Lord's cricket ground together, you and I. I would like it if we did. But you should know that, whenever I'm at Lord's, I see my father and hear his voice so clearly that I have an irrepressible need to talk about him to anyone who is willing to listen.

I can see my father in the distance, sitting high up in the right-hand turret – 'his' turret – at the top of the Pavilion. Away from the other members, Middlesex and MCC, seated in their rows of white benches below or crowding companionably about the Long Room. On his head he wears a discoloured, misshapen panama hat (which has made a number of television and stage appearances) and by his side sit his heavy wartime field-glasses. He is dozing alone in the afternoon.

And I see us together on one of the very many Saturdays we spent in the old 'Members and Friends' stand to the right of the Pavilion; I was, of course, much too young to be admitted to the sanctity of the Pavilion itself. With us we have our sandwiches in a brown paper bag, a bottle of pale orange squash and two scorecards. The first is for my father to scribble down the details as the wickets fall; the second is for me to keep unblemished, and to take home later.

'Lord's,' says my father, suddenly. 'The name has nothing to do with "lords", as in "lords and ladies".'

(What prompts him to say this? I have yet to hear anyone claim that it has.)

'Nothing whatsoever.'

(I know I am not expected to comment or respond.)

It's the opening morning of another three-day county cricket match. Middlesex has elected to bat first. The greatly underrated Jack

Robertson is opening. An elegant, unhurried, classical batsman, he is much admired by my father and therefore by me. Robertson will remain at the crease until just before lunch when, unluckily, he will be run out following a poor call from the other end. He will return quietly to the Pavilion to modest applause. A gentleman batsman.

'Mr Lord's cricket ground,' says my father. 'Mr Thomas Lord. Wine merchant and cricketer.'

I have heard this several times before. Over the years I will hear it many times more. Mr Thomas Lord. I roll the name round in my mind. I speculate that my father, as a young man, may have known Mr Lord. My father has known so many people. I don't ask him to confirm this. In his own time he will tell me about it – his youthful encounter with Mr Thomas Lord. Perhaps in the company of his father? Or so I speculate. In the meantime, we continue to watch the cricket.

'The second Lord's cricket ground in fact,' says my father, at the end of another over. 'The first ground was somewhere else. Dorset Square, I believe.'

I am six. I don't know where Dorset Square is. Or Dorset. But it doesn't matter. My father doesn't tell me that Thomas Lord was the son of a labourer who was forced to work on the estate which he himself had once owned but had lost because of his support for Bonnie Prince Charlie in the rebellion of 1745. If he'd told me this – if indeed he knew the story – I might still have wondered whether or not my father had spoken with Thomas Lord.

In my teenage years, my father's stories bored me into a seething spiral of fury but, as a child, I was perfectly content to hear them, aware that he was talking to himself as much as to me; a shared meditation to be enjoyed together. Which means perhaps that when we go together to Lord's, you – being nearer in temperament to the child I was than the teenager I became – will be able to let my memories pass gently by you like a silver summer breeze on a warm day in June.

* * *

It's the luncheon interval. We have eaten our fish-paste sandwiches – crumbly and slightly stale – and my father has had a light ale (although not at the Tavern which he dislikes because it's frequented by rowdies at weekends and resting actors during the week). We have walked to the Nursery End and watched the Middlesex apprentices practising in the nets. We are now making our way back, passing the office where other apprentices in Middlesex blazers are printing the scorecards on a hand press. I find the process compelling. (My father tells me that my grandfather was a compositor and that printing is in my genes.) It is the ceremony of reproduction. The smell of ink and the perfection of newly-printed scorecards – ivory, unmarked – laid out in lazy lines to dry before being gathered up and tapped sharply into neat stacks. I could stand there much longer but my father has moved on.

Away from the daylight, the passage under the Grand Stand is gloomy and grey. There is a smell of freshly scrubbed stone which faintly disturbs me. Above us, the Father Time weather-vane is motionless as it has been throughout the morning. We hear the sound of clapping which signals the return of the umpires and the players to the field. We increase our pace, heading towards the sunlight, when someone approaches us, walking in the opposite direction. This is one of my father's unnamed friends. He has many friends and acquaintances without names. 'Old so-and-so' in the third person. 'Old boy' in the second. The degree of acquaintance or friendship is never clear to me but it's not my concern. 'More fools know Jack Fool than Jack Fool knows,' my father tells me from time to time. 'An old Somerset expression.' It's one of his store of West Country saws and sayings. I accept that my father is Jack Fool and that this must be true. The friend stops, smiles and greets us. My father doesn't introduce me to old-so-and-so. He can't.

'And is this your grandson?' asks the friend.

It's a kindly-meant question expecting a proud response.

'No!' I say quickly. 'No!'

I'm furious, inflamed, ashamed. I can't speak. I can't see. I'm too angry. I'm too close to tears. My father smiles indulgently.

'No, old boy,' says my father. 'This is my son.'

41

We walk on but the June day has frozen over.

'Don't remember his name,' says my father, as he often does after such encounters. 'Charming chap. Heart's in the right place. A bit of a bore.'

The afternoon has clouded over. What do I feel? Outrage? Puzzlement? Fear? It's too difficult to explain to myself. Impossible to explain to anyone else. My father dozes. I sit and shiver, hot and cold with hurt.

'Idiotic,' says my father, towards the end of the afternoon. There has been an unexpected mid-order collapse and Middlesex have been bowled out. The Middlesex and England paceman AE Moss – and my father's special *bête noire* – is opening the bowling. 'No one needs a run of that length.' His irritation mounts as Moss approaches the wicket. 'Particularly when he slows down halfway through.' The batsman lets the ball go through to the wicket-keeper standing back. 'And it's not as if he's much more than medium pace.' I know my father is being unfair. 'No wonder he takes so long to bowl his overs.' This is the real complaint. 'I remember as a boy …'

But for once I'm not listening to my father's lament for the golden days when centuries were scored before lunch and four hundred runs were scored in a day. I'm not thinking about cricket at all.

The incident threads itself into the fabric of our family history. The day that I was mistaken for my father's grandson. My father smiles indulgently at each re-telling. My hot denial is pivotal to the story. My cold anger remains.

* * *

January 21st. The year is 1901. My mother is sewing under the oil lamp and talking to a friend who has called to bring me a combined Christmas and birthday present. The gift is a box of tin soldiers. I am playing with them excitedly when my mother suddenly says: 'Hush! That's Widcombe bell tolling.' She and the friend leave the room and go out on to the pathway in front of the house. I follow them. It is a bright frosty night and the ripple of the little stream across the road sounds clearer than usual. Yes, Widcombe bell is tolling. So is that of St Mark's and Bathwick. And in the far distance the heavy boom of Bath Abbey, the lantern of England. My mother turns to her friend. 'There's no doubt about it,' she says. 'It must be. The dear Queen is dead.' They are both so solemn that I begin to cry. 'You mustn't cry, dear,' says my mother. 'After all, she was a very old lady.' But the fact remains that I wept at the passing of Victoria the Good.

My father's was a long life, a wide span. It remains a source of mild wonder to me that he was born in the reign of Queen Victoria; that he was five years old when she died; that this was all so very long ago.

* * *

A memory of my own to bridge the years.

February 15th, 1953. My father takes me to Hyde Park on a grey winter morning to watch the funeral cortège of George VI pass by. The slow march, the officers' swords reversed. I am five years old but I understand the solemnity of the occasion.

That summer in June his daughter, Queen Elizabeth II, is crowned. We travel to Tring to watch the coronation on a family friend's television. We sit in a respectful group seeing history ceremonially enacted; flickering, black-and-white. I feel feverish.

Later we eat sandwiches and cake and my mother decides that I have chickenpox.

* * *

The knowledge that my father was old – so much older than other fathers – and the stark fact of death arrived together, like two grave umpires descending the pavilion steps. I watched them steadily and understood that there was nothing uncertain about death. You cannot carry your bat or remain unbeaten. Sooner or later, every innings will come to a close. A decision against which there is no appeal. And if you have occupied the crease for many years – however well you have played, however much you are loved – there must soon come a moment when the umpire's finger will rise and the batsman's spell in the middle will end. Father Time. There was nothing to be done about it. Except perhaps to pray.

I see myself kneeling by my bed. Behind me the light summer curtains in my bedroom are billowing gently in an evening breeze. Outside in the gardens, older children are playing. Older children with younger fathers.

Please, God. Let my father live another twenty years ...

I didn't pray for the defeat of death. Only its postponement.

Please, God. Let my father live another nineteen years ... Another eighteen years ... Another seventeen ...

Not knowing the power of prayer, I prayed as hard as I could, pushing my hands together, screwing up my eyes until they ached. *Another sixteen years ... fifteen years ... fourteen ...*

And I was honest with my prayers; mechanically honest. As the years passed – as the overs were bowled – I counted down.

Another thirteen ... twelve ... eleven ...

Every evening. Kneeling and praying. And then almost every evening, praying whenever a reminder of death had plucked at my sleeve during the day.

Another ten years ...

Long after we ceased going together to Lord's. Right through my years of frothing teenage rage. And when, at the age of seventeen, I lost my faith, I continued to pray. *Please, God. Let my father live another ...Please, God ... Please, ...*

Until twenty years had gone when it didn't seem fair to ask for more. If we'd had a bargain – God and I – He had kept his part. What could I do now? Be grateful. Which I was. Which I am.

* * *

'Before you were born ...'

Is it unusual to be so fiercely jealous of one's parents' youth? Is this what every child feels, or do children of elderly parents feel it more acutely? So much that can't be shared. Pictures of my mother as a young woman. Photographs of my father as a young man.

My mother, as a child, dressed as a Red Indian with a bow and arrow; a young woman, in fancy dress and glamorous furs; an actress in a gallery of classical and exotic parts. And then, quite soon, recognisably my mother.

My father, the soldier in his uniform; the actor, a very young Hamlet; heavily made up to play Methuselah; the successful director with his cast around him; the established playwright, posing, pipe in hand. The waves of success. The youth, the confidence, the vitality. The man I didn't know. Because my father was always middle-aged. And soon, he was elderly. And then he was old.

Family photographs. Black-and-white, coffee-and-cream, curling, stained, fading away almost as you look at them. As if, like the Shroud of Turin, they can only been be viewed on a limited number of occasions. After that you must rely on memory and imagination, and other clues which may lead or mislead you because now there is no one left to ask.

* * *

January 7th, 1972. St James's Street, London SW1.

The Savage Club House Dinner. My father is in the Chair. It's his seventy-sixth birthday and I am his guest of honour. It is a warm, convivial occasion. Everyone knows who I am. I am Arnold's son. I shake hands and smile. I know no one. Or those that I know I don't recognise. More fools know Jack Fool than Jack Fool knows. My father has turned away momentarily when I am approached by a famous novelist, madness shining from his bright blue eyes.

'I am greatly relieved,' he says, 'to learn that you have broken that filthy – that disgusting – habit.' He can barely suppress his icy contempt. 'It was destroying your life and causing your father such pain.'

I am briefly flummoxed. Which of my habits can have caused such distress? I start a swift list ... before it occurs to me that I've been mistaken for some other, more errant, son. I meet the novelist's wild stare with what I hope is a suitably contrite expression and nod sombrely. This seems to do the trick and he moves on.

I take the seat on my father's right.

MENU

Consommé Madrilène

Blanquette of Veal in White Wine Sauce

& Button Mushrooms

Duchesse Potatoes   Broccoli Spears

Croûte Hollandaise

Coffee

After dinner my father rises to speak. The audience is quiet, attentive.

'I would like to introduce someone who has known me all my life.'

All my life? My heart stops. No! That stab of panic when an actor dries. It is an opening line he has prepared for too long. He pauses. There's a sympathetic murmur and mild banter from a well-wishing audience who recognise it for what it is – an old actor's fluff. A pity but not a disaster.

'To someone I have known all *his* life,' he corrects himself. 'My son, Nicolas.'

CHAPTER SIX

Bearing the name

Names are tricky, aren't they? The names we give, the names we take, the names we leave behind. As parents we must furnish our children with names before we know who they are or who they are going to be; and, in some cases, before we know who we are going to be ourselves as parents.

Do we become our names or do our names become us? Do the names we give our children rule their destiny? Because, if they do, the act of naming is a sobering responsibility which, like matrimony, should not be enterprised, nor taken in hand unadvisedly, lightly or wantonly. The truth is that naming was a responsibility for which I had not prepared.

Borrowing shamelessly from 'Major Major Major Major' in *Catch-22*, my first suggestion was to call my son 'Ridley'. I thought it would be amusing, by which I mean I thought it would amuse me. Ridley Ridley, I told myself, would be an outstanding name that no one could forget. Or forgive? I didn't think about that. The suggestion was soundly squashed. I accepted the decision but gamely followed on with 'Mungo'. I could picture 'Mungo Ridley' – a sturdy traveller, a robust adventurer; broad, bland, untroubled by doubts, unaffected by setbacks. (Quite unlike his father.) Mungo wasn't squashed exactly. Your mother thought I was joking but I'm pretty sure that I wasn't. I would happily have come back with further suggestions but by this time she knew that your name was Christopher. And, when she told me, so did I.

* * *

We are attending your graduation ceremony. You are called up to receive your certificate. A small swell of applause. A word with the visiting dignitary. You return to your seat, smiling. High up in the auditorium your mother and I are beaming. Other graduands follow you. We continue to clap politely, but for us the ceremony is complete. We bask in our bubble of pride. Our son has graduated. It's both utterly extraordinary and just as it should be.

'Ridley!'

You have been photographed with your scroll in a borrowed mortar-board and now you are returning the gown you hired for the day. We are waiting for you to rejoin us and I'm trying to recall my own graduation ceremony. I'm disconcerted to find I can't. I try harder, snatching at pictures from the flow of memory, but when I hold them up to the light, I find there's nothing there. Did it never happen? Did I refuse to take part? Did I dismiss it as piffling, pompous flummery; a safe and fabricated rebellion?

'Ridley!'

I really can't remember, but I hope so much that I didn't deny my parents the pleasure that your mother and I are experiencing today.

'Ridley!'

A moment of guilty irritation. This is not the day for it. But I dislike being addressed by a bare surname. It brings back school or a bluff, clubby heartiness that sets my teeth on edge. Which is why I've been blocking out the shout in the distance. Although why anyone should be shouting at me …

'Ridley!'

But of course they're not. I'm back in the present. We're different. You aren't me. You are easygoing, untroubled, sociable. In your world you are known as Ridley. It's what you like to be called. It's what you call yourself. Besides, you can't shout out 'Chris' in a crowd. Which Chris? Where? There are Christophers whichever way you turn.

'Ridley!'

You stop and walk over to the group; boys who will soon be going separate adult ways. I am happy to wait; very happy to prolong the here and now.

Ridley. For the present we share the name. In future it will be yours much more than mine. And then it will be yours. I find the thought pleases me.

* * *

A thread runs through our four generations, pulling us together:
  William Robert Ridley (Bob Ridley, my grandfather);
  William Arnold Ridley (Arnold Ridley, your grandfather);
  Nicolas William Morrish Ridley (me);
  Christopher William Ridley (you).
All named William. None called William. A reserve name. A name-in-waiting. A hidden link.

My father disliked the name Arnold. In childhood it was the cause of much mockery. In later life it caused him considerable irritation and, he claimed, lost him jobs. From this distance it's difficult to see why my father's parents should have called him Arnold, an oddly pompous name for a modest family. The hated London cousins teased, taunted and tormented their country cousin 'Arnie' although I think he found this more wearisome than distressing. He didn't consider changing his name, although authors and actors often do. He accepted it as his. An inconvenience, an irritation, to be borne.

* * *

Ridley is a common enough name. There are Ridleys by the dozen in the telephone directory. But this was the age of chewing-gum.
  'Ridley, *not* Wrigley!'
  My father is standing with the receiver in his hand – he never sat when he spoke on the telephone.
  'Ridley.' (staccato) 'R-I-D-L-E-Y.'
  It is a curious fact that no one ever listens when one spells out a name.
  'Arnold. Yes, Arnold.'
  Every morning the envelopes flop on the mat. They are addressed

to Arnold Wrigley, Arthur Ridley, Arthur Wrigley. Contracts, bills, invitations, postcards, circulars and fan mail. A rotation of repeated irritation.

Only the Inland Revenue never errs.

* * *

My mother's name, Althea, was not unusual. It was, she insisted, unique. 'There are no other Altheas,' she would tell me. 'Aletheas, yes. But no Altheas.' Although I couldn't hear the difference, I didn't doubt her. How could I disbelieve what she believed so strongly herself?

In 1957, and again in 1958, Althea Gibson won the Ladies' Singles title at Wimbledon. 'Quite different,' my mother pronounced. 'It's spelt the same,' I objected. 'Yes,' said my mother, 'but the name is quite different.' And that was that. For my mother different was good. She never felt the need to apologise for her name. As far as I can remember, she never had to spell it out. No one called her Anthea. Or, if they did, they didn't do it twice. 'Althea means hollyhock,' my mother would say. A fact which pleased her. And which is very nearly true.

* * *

Family history was for my mother a source of legend. Her interest was colourfully imaginative more than drably genealogical. Facts, when they could be established at all, were building blocks to be set out to their best effect, but they would not be allowed to impede the story.

The Ridleys were always going to be a disappointment to her but she valiantly postulated a direct line of descent from the martyred Bishop of London (Nicholas or Nicolas Ridley) who was burnt at the stake in Oxford with Thomas Cranmer, or Hugh Latimer, or maybe both. The cast changed frequently.

'Be of good comfort, Master Ridley, and play the man,' my mother recited, 'for we shall this day light such a candle, by God's grace, in England, as I trust shall never be put out.'

I was deeply stirred.

'I have sinned, in that I have signed with my hand what I did not believe with my heart. When the flames are lit, this hand shall be the first to burn.'

And then moved to anxiety.

'So saying,' she continued, 'he held out his right hand until it was burnt to a stump, and made no further sound or movement other than to wipe the beads of sweat from his forehead with his left hand as the flames licked at his feet.'

Was this Cranmer or Latimer? Such details didn't trouble my mother. She adapted history to the requirements of drama and if two characters needed to be fused into one, it didn't worry her. But, being an actress, she didn't write dialogue. For her, therefore, it was a disappointment that Bishop Ridley had been given no lines (although a non-speaking part is better than no part at all). To me, my namesake's silence seemed perfectly understandable while, with him, I watched in spellbound horror and disgust as his friend's hand shrivelled to a shapeless, smouldering stalk.

On her father's side my mother's family – the Parkers – was solid but unspectacular; Royal Navy and British Raj. Her mother's family – the Gambiers – were more productive. The Gambiers themselves were Huguenots and boasted among their forebears the celebrated James Gambier – Admiral of the Red (although sometimes he was Admiral of the Blue) – who had been Governor of Newfoundland, had probably fought under Collingwood in the Lee Column at the Battle of Trafalgar (or may have missed the engagement) but had certainly commanded the Fleet during the bombardment of Copenhagen (although why Copenhagen had needed to be bombarded wasn't explained). As Lord Gambier he had also – rather remarkably it seemed to me – requested his own court-martial after a disagreement with Lord Cochrane, and had been acquitted. An odd bird, I decided. Alongside James Gambier – of whom there may have been more than one – was a considerable supporting cast of heroes and defenders of the Empire whose medals, letters, memoirs and buttons she produced to support their stories. There was too 'the Scottish connection' which existed through a skein of cousins and marriages with the clans Bruce and Rose. My trace of Scottish ancestry meant that I was entitled to wear the clan tie but not the kilt. I didn't regret the kilt and was happy to be bought the tie. Two ties, in fact: the hunting green and the dress red, reverently removed from the walls of labelled wooden drawers in a shop that smelt of tweed, dogs and pipe tobacco in Prince's Street, Edinburgh. I was also, my mother assured me, part-Jewish, although how this came to be couldn't be explained with any precision. But my mother's Jewish blood was a source of great pride and to it she ascribed the intellectual and artistic traits which she believed we shared.

It was my Huguenot ancestry that caused me to be christened 'Nicolas'. 'The family spelling,' my mother explained. 'The French name "Nicolas" not the English name "Nicholas".' And it was my father's wish to perpetuate his mother's Cornish family name which is why I found myself 'the last in the line of the male Morrishes'. Is it a name I should have passed on? Before deciding, listen to me speaking on the telephone.

'Ridley.' (staccato) 'R-I-D-L-E-Y.'

And …

'Nicolas. N-I-C-O-L-A-S. No. Without an "h", (lamely) the French spelling.'

And sometimes …

'Morrish. M-O-double-R-I-S-H. Yes. With an "h". It's a Cornish name.'

*　*　*

Like my father, I don't use the usual endearments, darling, dear, sweetheart. I find I can't say them. We must allow ourselves to express our affection as best we can.

I have three books on my desk: my father's confirmation Bible, the hardback edition of one of his earlier plays, *Keepers of Youth*, and the acting edition of a later play, *Easy Money*.

The inscription in the Bible in my grandfather's writing reads,

> *W A Ridley*
> *with love*
> *from Father & Mother*
> *In remembrance of*
> *March 24th 1911*

In the copy of his *Keepers of Youth* my father has written,

> *To Father & Mother*
> *With much love*
> *from*
> *Arnold*

'Father & Mother'. I am touched by the formality, the austerity. I close both books and open the acting edition of *Easy Money*.

> *For C, T & P*
> *with all my love*
> *from PB*

Which requires explanation.

Tradespeople such as the Morrishes, who lived above the shop, did not, I suspect, indulge in frivolous pet names. In my mother's family, however, they were – and always had been – the norm. If the practice of pet names was new to my father, it was one he adopted very readily.

My father and mother inhabited a richly-populated world of deep affection. When, where and how the cast of characters with their many idiosyncrasies first appeared I don't know. I was a welcome visitor but this was my parents' world, not mine. To her mother, my mother had always been 'Puss'. To my father, she became 'Puss Parker'. But naming was just the beginning. Puss Parker took on a life of her own. She and my mother coexisted in different universes that sometimes touched, like billiard balls on green baize, but more often bounced off each other in unpredictable directions. Puss Parker, I gathered, had considerable airs and graces and always stayed at the Dorchester hotel, the height of slightly vulgar luxury. It was plain that she had married beneath her but she soothed her disappointment with a relentless round of high living. As did 'C Lion', a sometimes interchangeable character, whose name derived from my mother's rather raucous laugh. There was a suggestion that when C Lion became too unbearably loud, Puss Parker would retire to her room above Park Lane. C Lion's family – the Lions – resided in Campden Hill, or Kensington Church Street, or Knightsbridge, and were especially snooty. 'T Lion', another family member, was a mystery whose role and character were not clear. If this sounds confusing, it was. But, as a child, I could see that there were mysteries here that were not for me to disentangle.

* * *

I don't remember calling my father 'Dad'. When I was very young I called him 'Daddy'. After that I always used his 'particular' name. My father was always – in one form or another – 'Bear'. The reason was said to be obvious. He looked like a bear and once – so the story went – when playing the part of a bear looked more convincing out of his costume than in. As a child, I accepted this resemblance as an absolute fact. If today I find myself asking how real this resemblance was, it doesn't matter. 'Bear' he was and always will be. Not that his name was immutable. Over the years it was blown about like a hat in the wind. The 'PB' of the dedication may have been 'Pooh Bear', a part that he doubled with Eeyore. Or possibly 'Poor Bear', reflecting either the many minor misfortunes that regularly beset him, or his perpetually impecunious state, particularly when gauged against the wealth of the Lions who, in addition to dining every night at the Ivy, sojourned languorously for much of the year in the sun of the SOUTH OF FRANCE (always capitalised).

A selection of other Bear incarnations:

- A pair of political bears, 'Bear Left' and 'Bear Right'
- The Job-like 'Bear With' (and his close associate 'Bear Up')
- The nautical, and usually seasick, 'Bear Away'
- The reluctant witness and unlucky batsman 'Bear Out'

– The thoughtful if ponderous 'Bear in Mind'
– The sadly down-at-heel 'Threadbear'.

When on tour my father left a list of dates, towns, theatres and digs, headed 'Bearabouts' and … but that's enough bears.

Later in life he was re-christened 'Old Bear' which became shortened to 'OB' and this became his 'particular' name and is how I think of him still.

* * *

The very helpful librarian at Chiswick library has found me a copy of *Who Was Who* and printed out an entry from the *Oxford Dictionary of National Biography*: 'Ridley, (William) Arnold (1896-1984) actor and playwright'. I skim it quickly and stop: ' … his third wife, Althea Parker, an actress; they were married in 1947 and had a son, Nicholas.' I resolve to email a correction. And then I know I won't.

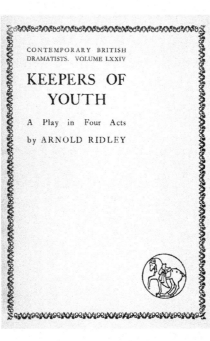

CONTEMPORARY BRITISH
DRAMATISTS. VOLUME LXXIV

KEEPERS OF
YOUTH

A Play in Four Acts

by ARNOLD RIDLEY

To Father & Mother
With much love
from
Arnold.

July 9th '29

CHAPTER SEVEN

Schooldays

The entire Morrish family concerned itself with my father's early education, their chief anxiety being to cushion 'the last of the male Morrishes' from the pernicious influences of the outside world.

There were several family conferences before it was decided that I should be sent to school. It was agreed that whatever happened I must not be contaminated by association with 'rough little boys' such as might be encountered at educational establishments under the control of the church or state. At all costs I had to go to a 'nice' school.

Eventually I was handed over to the daily care of Miss Eva Silversides then conducting a private seminary at Number 1, Prior Park Buildings – a choice probably due to the fact that my grandparents were now living at Number 6 so that my comings and goings to and from Number 1 would be under observation and I would be saved from molestation by 'nasty street boys'.

My unmarried aunt commissioned herself as a kind of permanent outpost, seeing me safely arrive in the morning and collecting me again in the afternoon. Thus did I escape much healthy pinching and punching which I'm sure my superior manner well warranted and which would have stood me in good stead in later days.

At Miss Silversides' Seminary – later to become Clarendon School – my father was introduced, in different permutations, to the mysteries, frustrations and terrors of sex, sport and religion. He survived the heavy diet of religion and the ever-present threat of damnation without any ill effects, but sport at Clarendon School was desperately unsatisfactory and left him with a persistent and unseemly urge.

Our athletic session, which took place one afternoon a week in the small railed gardens fronting the crescent, consisted of lawn tennis, which only four could play at a time, and croquet. Imagine small boys being compelled to play croquet! Even now, I never see a gaggle of croquet players without having to fight down a wild desire to leap upon the court, uproot their irritating hoops and smite their coloured balls into the surrounding bushes.

There were no male teachers at the school and boys were very much the minority. It was here that my father first encountered the female sex and developed a respect for women that may have been too wary to be completely satisfactory.

Scarcely an hour passed without it being pointed out to the male minority that they were of baser metal than the female majority and should consider themselves fortunate indeed to be tolerated in such superior society.

This was a game where 'sugar and spice' played 'slugs and snails' and the umpires were anything but impartial.

It had to be clearly understood that should a little girl put up her hand in class and express a wish to leave the room, it was merely an overwhelming and laudable passion for cleanliness that was urging her to 'wash her hands'. To suggest that she felt obliged to answer the call of nature was not only ridiculous but obscene. Only little boys had to do horrid things like that and I still remember the looks of disgust and whispered comments of female contempt whenever a male hand was raised hesitatingly towards heaven. I often wonder how many masculine bladders suffered permanently as a result of a determination to 'hold on' at all costs.

Absurd, of course, unless one remembers Private Godfrey's catchphrase, 'May I be excused?'. This kindly piece of scripting always gained sympathetic laughter in the *Dad's Army* studio although it was a trial when the programme was being screened and impertinent strangers shouted out the question in the street.

Clarendon School was, my father wrote, a backwater where he 'floated peacefully for seven years'. Perhaps he stayed 'five years too long from an educational standpoint' but he was happy and the school's influence seems to have been thoroughly benign. Later he concluded that he would find it 'hard to believe that any child who attended Clarendon School for a reasonable period of time could develop into a mean, brash or deliberately cruel adult'.

But in the summer of 1908 the time came to leave.

> I parted with Miss Silversides with genuine regret and walked down the garden path for the last time making every effort to feel what I considered to be appropriate sentiments. Unfortunately I found that I had left my slipper-bag behind and so had to go back and feel the whole thing over again.
>
> Most boys, on leaving Clarendon School, continued their education at the King Edward's School which provided tuition for the sons of successful tradesmen and lesser professional men of the city. I know that my parents were anxious that I should go there too, but I'd been unable to win a scholarship and the fees were beyond my father's purse. The next best thing was the Bath City Secondary School, where the charges were considerably less, and as my father was still a part-time member of the staff, it is probable that I was admitted at cut price.

Being the son of a member of staff, my father was initially regarded with suspicion by his fellow pupils. Life was made no easier by the headmaster who, instead of addressing him as 'Ridley', the normal school practice, insisted on calling him 'Arnold' as a misplaced courtesy to his father.

> As I was the only boy so honoured, the distinction was an unhappy one to say the least. If I had been a Jim or a Dick or a Harry, it might not have been so bad – but 'Arnold'! I felt obliged to prove my integrity by neglecting every task so successfully that for four years I occupied one

of the bottom places in every class and, at the same time, appointing myself a ringleader of general loutishness.

A few friends, who had been moved to admiration by some particularly cruel ragging in which I had indulged at the expense of an elderly French mistress unfortunate enough to be afflicted by a lisp, took pity on me and made me a present of a nickname, 'Tom'. I have no idea why, but it stuck to me for the remainder of my schooldays.

At this age, naturally, sport and relations with the opposite sex were of keen interest but, although croquet was now a thing of the past, in many respects Bath City Secondary School seems to have been just as odd and unsatisfactory as Clarendon School.

The playing field was at such a distance from the city that it could only be reached by a tramcar, the fare being far beyond the schoolboy pocket, or a three-mile trudge up a steep hill. The equipment provided was ridiculously inadequate. We started each cricket season with two bats – guaranteed heavy and unlikely to break – six stumps, four bails, two pairs of pads, a large and imposing score-book (apparently the accountancy branch of the game was the most important) and a ball. This ball had to last the whole season and by the end of June it was out of shape and had absorbed enough moisture to weigh a couple of pounds.

We were co-educational, there being an approximately equal number of boys and girls in each form. These were as carefully divided as the sheep and the goats, the girls occupying one side of the classroom and the boys the other. A wide gangway preserved decorum and decency. The apex of senselessness was a rule (strictly enforced) that no boy must speak to a girl and no girl speak to a boy in school, on the playing fields or in any other circumstances whatsoever. The penalty was instant expulsion.

For two days in the year the boys played the girls at cricket – the boys batting and bowling left-handed – and at hockey. All this had to be conducted in monastic silence. Just imagine! One hundred or more boys and the same number of girls, all passing through the tricky years of adolescence, kept for hours in each others' company without verbal contact.

Academically my father did not shine. 'During the entire four years of my attendance, I did no work whatsoever,' he confessed, and in later life would contentedly describe himself as being of very little brain. It wasn't true but it enabled him to put a comfortable distance between himself and the world of scholarship which, while he admired it, wasn't his. In this respect he was different from my grandfather, a self-taught man with a thoughtful library of literature and philosophy in several European languages, each book lightly and precisely annotated in soft pencil. Looking through these books today, there is nothing to suggest that my father read any of them.

Does my father's account of his schooldays give any indication of his future as a writer? Some, but not much.

I spent much labour on English essays but this was entirely due to the fact that I had discovered a style of prose which although 'within the law' was certain to arouse my tutor to a frenzy.

A source of irritation was a poppycockish school magazine published each term. Ninety percent of its pretentious balderdash was written by members of the staff although some of the girl pupils contributed a few sickly verses on such impersonal subjects as 'Spring's Awakening' and 'Thoughts Amongst the Buttercups'.

Only the other day I came across a copy of this publication with marginal notes and sub-editings in my schoolboy hand. And after all these years I found myself chuckling maliciously at some of the crude and wholesome debunking.

What appears throughout is a wonderful confidence that nothing that was taught at school would matter very much in later life, and that everything that would be needed could be learnt later on.

* * *

In any case, Samuel Morrish had provided for his grandson's future.

> When my grandfather died in September 1906, he bequeathed to
> me the sum of ten pounds so that, on leaving school, I might be
> apprenticed to a useful trade.

I try to picture my father following 'a useful trade'. And fail completely.
A less practical man it would be hard to imagine. My grandmother's
ambitions for her son were equally improbable.

> For a few days prior to my public examinations I put in hours of
> concentrated swotting and so managed to scrape a pass in both
> Junior and Senior Oxford locals, but I'm afraid this was done only to
> dumbfound those members of the staff who had publicly and loudly
> prophesised the certainty of my failure.
>
> At Christmas 1912, I left school and presented my long-suffering
> parents with the usual problem of my future. My mother had long since
> set her sights on the Inland Revenue department of the Civil Service
> which promised a safe and reasonably well paid job with a pension
> to follow. But I had proved during the last four years that I hadn't the
> slightest chance of passing the necessary examination. It was decided
> to make a schoolmaster out of me. On my seventeenth birthday, I
> started as a student teacher at East Twerton School.

Teaching might not seem the obvious choice of career for someone
who had shown such a marked lack of interest in scholarship, but
he must have performed his school duties well because, on the
recommendation of the headmaster, the Board of Education offered
him free tuition in the Education Department of the University of
Bristol. A happy period of his life followed before he was caught up
and swept away by the tide of events that would turn the world upside
down.

CHAPTER EIGHT

If we are marked to die

I am looking for Harfleur but instead I find Agincourt.

I have resolved to be bolder. At the school's end-of-term verse-speaking competition I will abandon the safety of the short poems I've recited in the past – John Masefield, Robert Louis Stevenson, Walter de la Mare, GK Chesterton – and take up the challenge of a speech from Shakespeare. The most obvious choice is 'To be or not to be' but I have been unimpressed by the renditions I have heard recited at school and feel that Hamlet's soliloquy lacks the drama I am looking for.

'Why not *Henry V*?' suggests my mother.

She and I have been stirred by Laurence Olivier's film which we have recently seen together. My mother once played Henry in a school production and, given any opportunity, would happily play the part again. She places in front of me her copy of *The Complete Works of Shakespeare* (inscribed 'Althea Parker Xmas 1942' in her mother's handwriting), a great blue brick of a book with tiny faded print and narrow columns. It takes faith to believe that great plays can swell from such cramped pages but this is a faith I have been born into and I am not affected by doubt.

I can hear the words but I don't know where I'll find them.

Once more unto the breach, dear friends, once more,
Or close the wall up with our English dead ...

My finger slides down the lines. And through the scenes. I turn each page with reverent care. I have reached Act IV but the lines I'm looking for have eluded me. And then another speech catches my eye.

O, that we now had here
But one ten thousand of those men in England,
That do no work today!

I read on.

What's he that wishes so?
My cousin Westmoreland? No, my fair cousin:
If we are marked to die, we are enough
To do our country loss; and if to live,
The fewer men, the greater share of honour.

I am suddenly certain I have found what I need. It's true I don't understand every word, but I'm sure that in time I will.

* * *

My father was hot in defence of his honour; to doubt his word was to risk defenestration.

In July 1914 while on teaching practice at a Bristol elementary school, I succeeded in imperilling my scholastic career. A particularly irritating headmaster so aroused my hot temper by doubting my word of honour and wagging a finger under my nose that I seized him by the scruff of his neck and the seat of his trousers and pitched him out of the open window into his own playground which fortunately was heavily grassed. Although I reported myself immediately to my university tutor, who was sympathetic as to the provocation, I hate to think what might have resulted had not the declaration of war thrown life in general into the melting pot.

* * *

Mine is 'the post-war generation'. We were defined by what we had missed; the hardship, the heroism, the sacrifice, the victory. As children, we were expected to listen respectfully to what we were told and we knew we should be grateful. As we grew older, we began to resent the debt it was said we'd incurred but which we had no means of repaying. Later, the problem resolved itself. War was wrong. MAKE LOVE NOT WAR! Love meant sex (and sex was generally good). War meant mutually assured destruction which self-evidently wasn't. There was no place for honour. The dreadful spectre that had shaped our lives before we were born could, at the touch of midnight's button, end them. And not only our lives but life itself in a boiling, billowing, thermonuclear mushroom cloud. For my generation, therefore, it isn't easy to conceive how war could be welcome or seen as virtuous.

* * *

At midnight on Bank Holiday, August 4th 1914, I was one of the cheering young men in Bath who welcomed the declaration of war with the utmost enthusiasm. Youth regarded war as a glorious adventure and I don't suppose many of them realised that they were heralding their own deaths. The streets were full of people. Any man in service uniform was borne shoulder high. Everybody had gone mad, myself included.

The next morning, together with six close friends, I tried to enlist in the local territorial regiment. My six friends were accepted, but to my utter dismay, I was rejected on medical grounds. A toe, broken playing rugby, had been badly set.

Strange to relate, my friends were all sent on garrison duty to relieve regular troops in India and remained there until 1919 without ever hearing a shot fired in battle. By the autumn of 1916, I – the 1914 reject – had been wounded three times.

By the summer of 1915, nobody – myself included – was so enthusiastic about the war as on the Bank Holiday of the previous year. Also, the physical perfection required of would-be infantrymen was very much a thing of the past. On offering myself again for enlistment I was received into the Somerset Light Infantry and, a few days later, despatched to Taunton to be fitted out. This was the first time that I'd been away from home but I soon got used to the new life and it seemed good news indeed when my name appeared among those to be drafted to the regiment's reserve battalion stationed at Crown Hill on the outskirts of Plymouth.

* * *

My father told two stories about Crown Hill. Only the first appears in 'The Book'.

We were quite a merry party that set off from Taunton at an early hour armed with kit bags and other impedimenta. When we arrived at North Road Station, Plymouth, it was raining just about as hard as it can rain in South Devon and our orders were to march to Crown Hill with rolled overcoats, carrying the rest of our belongings. By the time we arrived at Crown Hill village – approximately three miles mostly uphill – we were all pretty well exhausted.

But the village wasn't our destination. There was still another mile to go – up another hill to the wooden-hutted camp near the old Crown Hill Fort. It was still raining, we were soaking wet and our heavy overcoats, rolled and worn over the left shoulder, felt as if they weighed a ton. Exhorted to 'left – right – left' we staggered past the quarter-guard and were lined up facing the battalion headquarters.

There we waited for a further half-hour until the regimental sergeant-major emerged from the headquarters building, took up a position under cover of the balcony and called us to attention. From this point of vantage he welcomed us to the Third Battalion by cursing us at length, both collectively and individually. He ended on a cheering note which I still remember clearly after sixty years. 'Don't none of you think you're going to see your homes and mothers and dads no more 'cause you ain't. We sent out a draft to our First Battalion at Wipers three weeks ago and where are they now? I'll tell yer – they're all bleeding well dead! And that's where you buggers will be in a couple o' months time – all bleeding well dead!'

As a first class warrant officer, he must have been a few years older than me so I presume Regimental Sergeant-Major Chambers is now himself dead. If not, and he reads this, I'd like him to know that I wish him every possible evil!

The second story meant more to him than Regimental Sergeant-Major Chambers and his sadistic welcome to the raw recruits of the Somerset Light Infantry. It's very simple. Barely a story at all. One evening, wretchedly homesick, he climbed to a high point above the village and stood there looking in what he knew must be the direction of Bath. He waited while the light faded and stayed there most of the night. A true vigil. An attempt to anchor himself to the reality of his family and home in preparation for the horrors that would soon be tearing away at everything he had ever known. It was, he told me, the saddest point in his life.

*   *   *

Although he had fought in both world wars, 'the War' for my father was the First World War. The Great War, the 'war to end war'. Except that it didn't. Twenty-two years after being discharged wounded, Lance-Corporal Ridley, Prince Albert's Somerset Light Infantry (13th Foot) Number 20481, was back in France with the British Expeditionary Force and the rank of major. Fresh horrors to feed his nightmares of trenches; sucking, suffocating mud, rats the size of cats, repulsive, disgusting, inglorious death.

Like most actual combatants, he didn't talk much about 'the War'. He didn't write much about it either. 'So much has been written,' he says in 'The Book', 'that I don't think it necessary to give a fully detailed account of my 1914-18 war experiences.'

When I was young – the same age that he had been when he struggled back, an invalid, to Bath – I thought he was wrong. Wanting desperately to write myself but aware how little I had to write about, I felt it was his duty to use his experience. His was a different social class from the First World War novelists and poets, who were mostly subalterns. He could speak for and from the other ranks. He had, I argued, a rich store of unique 'material'. But however strongly I urged him, he resisted me gently. 'Oh, I don't think so, old boy. No, no. There are plenty of people with more to say than me.' This was a time when writing seemed to me more important than life itself. But I had never had to make the choice between life and anything else. When I was older, I began to understand that my father had to justify his survival, and that the only way to do this was to survive. In order to survive he had to train himself to forget. Or to remember less vividly, less unremittingly.

His nightmares he couldn't command.

For my own part, the mental suffering was far in excess of the physical. To anyone of sense and imagination it was quite clear that the vital question wasn't if I get killed but when I get killed. World War I was not a succession of battles but one long, continuous battle with periods of greater intensity than others. Battalions were wiped out, not once but time after time. What happened to survivors? Did they go home in glory? Not a bit of it. The best they could expect was that they might get a week or so out of the line, while the battalion was being brought up to strength again with drafts of fresh troops, before going back to yet another 'over the top'. One couldn't expect to be a survivor each and every time. It didn't make sense. One's only hope was that one might receive a 'blighty one' and that is why the war correspondents could rightly describe the wounded as being so cheerful.

In September 1916 during the Battle of the Somme, where 58,000 British troops lost their lives, my father, who had been wounded twice before, received his 'blighty one'.

I was badly wounded – particularly in my left arm and hand. As this particular attack failed and I was left for some days behind the uncaptured German front line, it was some time before I received medical first aid at Le Tréport where I was admitted by mistake into a Canadian hospital. That night I underwent the first of several operations I received there, quite certain that my hand would be amputated and I must confess that next morning I felt a strong measure of disappointment when I found that it hadn't been. The loss of a hand would, at the worst, reduce me to Home Service and save my life. I was twenty years old at the time. Rather young to welcome a prospect of being maimed for life!

* * *

I would prefer my father to relate these stories, but in 'The Book' he omits them which is why I must try to tell them for him.

Three nightmares from which to awake in horror.

He woke in the morning to find that he still had his left hand. The surgeons had saved it in the night. This was mortifying. He wept bitterly with rage, fear and utter frustration. For a time, he told me, he was inconsolable.

He woke in darkness with a terrible weight pressing down on his chest. Someone was kneeling on him, sewing him into a sheet. He had been sleeping so deeply at the field hospital in Le Tréport that it was assumed he had died in the night.

He woke to the sound of appalling screaming. He found himself in a shell-hole with the terrible shreds of a man who had been torn apart by shrapnel. The man – the source of the screaming – must have carried my father, unconscious, to safety. My father, lying on the other side of the shell-hole, had been sheltered from the later burst. Was his unknown companion – the comrade who had saved his life – able to form the words to ask my father to spare him further agony, or did the screaming become insupportable? The question was too terrible to ask him, but the screaming had to be stopped.

He succeeded in leaving the shell-hole and found himself leading a group of stragglers back through no-man's-land to the British front line. On their return, the members of the party were recommended for the MM – the Military Medal – but an officer, spotting that my father was a lance-corporal and thus nominally in command, recommended him for the DCM – the Distinguished Conduct Medal. The other members of the party duly received their MMs – during the course of the war 115,600 MMs were awarded to other ranks – but my father was turned down for the DCM and received nothing. He told the story ruefully, with little bitterness. This was simply how things were, he said. But I knew how hurt he had been; the MM was the only recognition he had hoped for.

When my father was awarded an OBE in the New Year's Honours List of 1982 'for services to the theatre' it was for playing Private Charles Godfrey, a conscientious objector, who had been awarded the Military Medal for his actions as a stretcher bearer during the Battle of the Somme. (A photograph of Godfrey wearing his medal hung above his bed at Cherry Tree Cottage, Walmington-on-Sea.) My father's OBE seemed to me a poor, overdue reward for his service to his country, but he was happy to forgive past oversights and pleased to receive his decoration at Buckingham Palace. I didn't go to the investiture. It wasn't my battle, but I was still angry for him.

* * *

In the event, the army didn't require my father to sacrifice his left hand. From Le Tréport he was sent to the Woodcote Park Military Hospital, Epsom, where he was judged 'unfit for further military service' and returned to his depot for 'final adjustment of discharge'. His wounds had saved his life, but before he was released there was another episode to play out.

All seemed set fair when I was ordered to appear before a travelling medical board.

Wherever in 'The Book' my father writes 'All seemed set fair when …' or anything similar, the reader may expect something dreadful to happen. As in this case it duly did.

After being kept stark naked for over an hour in a very well ventilated stone corridor on a bitter January morning, I found myself in the presence of an excessively corpulent surgeon general.
'Well – what's the matter with you?' he demanded.

Anxious to get the matter settled with all speed, I held out my shattered left hand, which was the most obvious of my injuries. He took it and twisted it in an agonising grip.

'How did you do this?' he demanded. 'Jack knife?'

Probably this was meant only as a heavy joke but I was still suffering from shell-shock, blue with cold, and in considerable pain.

'Yes, sir,' I replied. 'My battalion is famous for self-inflicted wounds. And just to make sure, I cracked my skull with a rifle butt as well, and ran a bayonet into my groin.'

The general's normally ruddy countenance changed to a deep shade of purple. He gave my hand a twist in the opposite direction.

'Treatment at command depot,' he barked.

So instead of returning to civilian life, I was granted a further experience of military matters at Number 2 Command Depot, County Cork. The command depot consisted of leaky and badly-heated wooden huts strewn over a mountainside. Rations were at near starvation level, the number of medical officers hopelessly inadequate and 'the treatment' consisted of physical training conducted by sadistic column-dodging instructors from Aldershot. Add to this the fact that it snowed three days out of four and that the camp was suffering a permanent epidemic of scabies and impetigo; there was considerable support for a theory that we had been sent there to die – as many did – and thus relieve our grateful country from having to pay our disability pensions.

I decided I must get away at all costs. But how? In my physical condition it was impossible for me to 'volunteer fit'. I resolved to commence a war of attrition. I reported sick on every conceivable occasion and paraded my injuries before the senior medical officer. He cursed me with the greatest fluency and frequency and threatened to put me on a charge. This I knew was a bluff as, in my ample spare time, I had read the King's Rules and Regulations. From this I'd learnt it was impossible to accuse me of malingering but, if I was so charged, I could demand a court martial. So I persisted. One of us would have to crack some time and it was the senior medical officer who did. He returned me to my Taunton depot with a note that I had been found unsuitable for further medical treatment.

71

I came back to England on one of the worst nights of the Easter gales in which a number of ships were lost with all hands. My travel voucher provided for third class rail and steerage only. I found that part of the boat packed full of Irishmen on their way to England to join labour squads. Most of them were already drunk and milling around in the most frightening manner. Neither had they any love for an English tommy. It could hardly be expected that they would after the barbarous treatment meted out following the Easter Rising. I must admit I was pretty frightened at the thought of crossing St George's Channel in their company on a voyage that promised to be one of the worst ever. I decided that despite the wind and the rain I might be better off on deck. I gathered my kit together and set off up the companionway. On a landing near the top a door stood ajar. I peeped in. It was a kind of smoking-room. I entered, shut the door and stretched myself out on one of the settees. Sanctuary indeed! I was just dropping off to sleep when the door was opened, the light switched on and I was confronted by a large and extremely formidable-looking stewardess.

'What are you doing here?' she demanded.

I tried to explain but she continued to glare at me.

'I can't help that,' she said. 'You can't stay in here.'

Clearly my luck was out. She seized my kit bag and ordered me to follow her. Presumably I was to be taken before some authority, possibly to be put in irons. She led the way along a narrow passageway, stopped and opened a door.

'Get in there,' she said, her voice as fierce as ever, 'and don't come out till we dock at Fishguard.'

It was a first class cabin. She dumped my kit bag and went out, locking the door behind her. I can't say I had a peaceful night. There were times when I thought I'd survived Arras, the Somme and the command depot only to be drowned on my way home. But in the morning she brought me an excellent breakfast. Appearances can be deceptive. Without that grim woman's kindness, I doubt if I should have reached Taunton at all.

At Taunton I found myself on a good wicket. The young medical officer was a Bristol University man I'd played rugby with. He assured me that I'd get my discharge in a few days' time. Then another panic. My return had coincided with another visit of a travelling medical board and I should have to appear before it. Judge my horror when I found myself before the same surgeon general as the last time. Fortunately he didn't recognise me and seemed in much better humour. He examined me with considerable attention, intermingled with sympathetic 'tut-tuts' and enquired where I had been for the past few months.

'Number 2 Command Depot, County Cork,' I answered.

'Good God!' he exploded. 'What bloody fool sent a man in your condition to a place like that?'

* * *

Although my father wrote little about the First World War, he wrote – and spoke – less about the Second.

Within hours of setting foot on the quay at Cherbourg in September 1939, I was suffering from acute shell-shock again. I don't mean that I was sweating, trembling and stuttering. It is quite possible that outwardly I showed little of it. It took the form of a mental suffering that can best be described as an 'inverted' nightmare.

I suffered badly from nightmares between the wars. They always took the same form. Somehow or other my discharge had gone wrong and I was back in the army again. Not amidst shot, shell, bayonet and other horrors, but merely back in France awaiting orders to go up to the front line once more. These dreams never varied and were so real and undramatic that sometimes it would take me an hour or more to persuade myself that what I had dreamed was impossible. Now it was no longer impossible. The fact that I was wearing a staff-major's crown and not a lance-corporal's stripe made no difference. My dream had caught up with me. My real and conscious life was now my nightmare – a nightmare from which I had no awakening.

To recount the events of this time I would have to relive them. I have no intention of reliving them. I am too afraid.

20481 L/Cpl William Arnold Ridley
Somerset Light Infantry

Served with honour and was disabled in the Great War.

Honourably discharged on 27th August 1917.

George R.I.

Wishing you a very Happy Christmas

France 1939.

CHAPTER NINE

Unarmed combat

It's a pleasant day in early April and we are learning how to kill people. Or disable them. Maybe both. I'm not sure yet.

Together we chant the sergeant's mantra:

One-two-three-four,
Step-on-his-jaw,
Just-to-make-sure.

'Next!'

Last winter we slept in our boots on Dartmoor. We learnt the lesson on the first morning. If you leave your boots outside the tent, they freeze solid. The answer is to keep them on all night. This means lying on your back in your sleeping-bag with your feet pointing upwards which is awkward at first but you get used to it. When you're fourteen years old, sleeping isn't usually terribly difficult.

One-two-three-four,
Step-on-his-jaw,
Just-to-make-sure.

'Next!'

This spring the school's Combined Cadet Force is camping in the Thetford battle area. We have spent much of the week crawling through damp bracken and sheep's droppings but we've camped in worse places before and we expect we will again.

This afternoon a group of us has volunteered to undergo training in unarmed combat. It sounded more fun than signals, mortars or map-reading. We are in the care of our instructor, square, unhurried, amiable, Sergeant Jones.

Methodically, almost languorously, Sergeant Jones disarms, maims and dispatches us by numbers.

'You take the arm. You break the arm. You twist the wrist. And over he goes.'

It's oddly hypnotic.

'You take the arm. You break the arm. You twist the wrist. And over he goes.'

One at a time, we rush at Sergeant Jones with a wooden weapon. Step-by-step he goes about his business.

'You take the arm. You break the arm. You twist the wrist. And over he goes.'

I'm not certain what we're learning except that Sergeant Jones is the master of his craft. If we have to watch him doing it for the whole afternoon, we may become restless but, for the present, it passes the time.

One-two-three-four,
Step-on-his-jaw,
Just-to-make-sure.

'Next!'

The sun shines down on us benignly and tonight we will sleep peacefully in our socks.

*   *   *

Remembrance Day.

As each year they do, public figures have paraded their poppies for more than a week. I put my coins in the tin but I won't take a poppy. At the age of nineteen – rows of headstones still fresh in my memory – I decided I wouldn't wear one. I didn't then; I don't now. No one notices. No one cares. Why should they? There are poppies enough in the congregation. Although – should I be ashamed to admit this? – one part of me would like to be challenged. I want to demand whether we are engaged in an act of commemoration or an act of celebration; whether we are honouring the dead or glorifying their deaths. I want to utter my anger. But this isn't about me. Except that, through my father, in a way I can't justify, I feel that it is.

♪ *Onward Christian soldiers, marching as to war ...*

Fresh-faced cadets march through a county town. Tattered regimental colours hang limp, like limbless tunics, in the corners of the cathedral. The well-heeled congregation, glowing with righteousness, trumpet their hymns.

♪ *With the cross of Jesus, going on before ...*

The Church militant. The Church triumphant. The Son of God, a subaltern with pipe and puttees, leading his disciples over the top. The priest intones ambiguous prayers. Service, sacrifice, glory, guilt. The Church troubled, the Church muddled, the Church in broken retreat. We spill out into the churchyard. The red-faced and bellicose; the pale and pious. Our duty done.

One year I attend a Quaker Meeting. It seems a good place to be on a Sunday in November. The silence ends with notices and news. The Friends file out of the meeting room. The sound of china cups and saucers; the smell of brewing coffee. There are white poppies for sale laid out in a basket. I put some coins beside the basket but I find I can't take a white poppy. As if wearing one would be another betrayal. Of what? Of whom? I don't know. But a betrayal nonetheless.

* * *

MAINWARING You mean you didn't want to fight?
GODFREY No, not really, sir.
MAINWARING I can't believe it, Godfrey. I really can't.
                                        – *Branded, Dad's Army Episode 23*

* * *

In 1917 in Torquay my father was handed a white feather – the symbol of cowardice given to men who were not in uniform – by a tall young woman wearing a fox fur.

♪ *Oh, we don't want to lose you*
   ♪ *But we think you ought to go.*

He accepted the white feather. ('I wasn't wearing my discharge badge. I didn't want to advertise the fact that I was a wounded soldier, and I used to carry it in my pocket.') He said nothing to the woman in the fox fur. He felt, I believe, the aching guilt of those who survive; the wretched knowledge that they, too, should have died.

* * *

What did you do in the war, Daddy?

What did the war do to you?

In the afternoon my father 'reads'. He borrows books from the public library – books by generals, historians, politicians – about the First World War. They lie open, scattered about his armchair, as he sleeps; like boys laid out in a field, exhausted or dead. I don't know if he reads these books or what comfort they bring him. My mother and I try not to disturb him in the afternoon.

Once, as a child, I wake him suddenly, tapping him urgently on the shoulder as young children do. He springs to his feet and has his hands round my throat before he sees me. It is an incident we don't discuss. The instincts of trench warfare didn't leave him. The horrors couldn't be forgotten. If we need to wake him, my mother and I, we knock gently with the door between us and wait until he remembers he is safe.

* * *

This is how I remember it. It is 1966 and I am nineteen. I haven't been back, I may be mistaken, the details have faded but the scene is as sharp as it was.

Private Albert Frome
Aged 18
Lest We Forget

It is the university vacation and we are driving a battered blue Dormobile through Germany, Austria and Yugoslavia to Greece and Turkey. We have watched a wedding party processing in pairs, men in black, women in white, enchantingly formal, along a promontory to a church on an island in the Ionian Sea. We have slept in warm olive groves and bathed in rocky mountain streams. We have discovered feta and dolmades, ouzo and retsina. We are very young and the world is still new to us.

Lance-Corporal Charles Hemington
Aged 20
Lest We Forget

We have gazed, awed, at the monasteries perched on rocks at Meteora. We have made a tour of the Peloponnese. We have crossed the Corinth Canal. We have inspected the Acropolis in the very early morning. We have climbed Mount Olympus and, reaching the summit in the afternoon, seen the clouds part all the way down to the sea. We have driven through Thessaloniki and on through Thrace towards Turkey. We have eaten yoghurt and wild honey in earthenware bowls on the Turkish border while waiting for our documents to be returned to us. From time to time we have heard news of England's continuing progress in the World Cup from people we meet, but we are now in country where other travellers are rarely encountered and mass tourism won't arrive for several years.

Private Edgar Mells
Aged 19
Lest We Forget

Which is why, when we cross the narrow strait to Çanakkale and then stand on the beach at Gallipoli, we find we are alone. Our knowledge of the campaign is sparse but we don't need a guidebook to tell us what we are seeing. High above us are the cliffs from which Turkish troops fired down on the soldiers landing from the sea. There is no cover. There is nowhere to hide. Our appreciation of military matters may be limited to what we learned in the Combined Cadet Force, but the picture is shockingly clear.

Private Frederick Radstock
Aged 19
Lest We Forget

'The odd thing about the Dardanelles Straits,' says our geographer, who has provided us with a stream of facts for more than four weeks, 'is that the water flows in both directions. From Asia to Europe and Europe to Asia. From the Sea of Marmara there's a surface current to the Aegean Sea, and from the Aegean Sea to the Sea of Marmara there's an undercurrent.' No one says anything. This is a moment when history would be more useful than geography.

Corporal David Vobster
Aged 21
Lest We Forget

We find that there are stone steps from the beach. We climb them. At the top we emerge from behind a stand of trees and low bushes. We look out at an expanse of white headstones, stretching far in front of us, row after row. We cross the field, reading inscriptions as we pass, and climb more steps. Another expanse of headstones, wider than the first. A perfect parade, a faultless disposition, row after row.

Private Bernard Wells
Aged 20
Lest We Forget

More steps and a further field, greater than the other two; row after row, row after row, stretching into the distance, row after row. We turn back and retrace our steps soberly through the headstones. By the trees and low bushes we encounter a soldier, a Turkish military policeman, white tin helmet around which is a red band, light khaki uniform, black webbing, immaculate. He halts, salutes us solemnly and walks on. His function is to guard the graves of the fallen enemy. We return silently to the beach.

'Churchill's greatest folly,' says my father, when I describe the scene to him. 'Among his many great follies!' he adds grimly. The rest of the world may have forgotten but my father could not bring himself to admire a man who had broken his parole – his word of honour – during the Boer War.

* * *

I finish with a flourish.

> *And gentlemen in England now abed*
> *Shall think themselves accursed they were not here,*
> *And hold their manhoods cheap whiles any speaks*
> *That fought with us upon Saint Crispin's Day.*

Mr Durnford raises his chin to clear his throat. I return to my bench. I am exhilarated. I know I have done well and that my boldness has been rewarded. This is the first term that I win a cup for verse-speaking. In the future I will win more.

Next term I return to *The Complete Works of Shakespeare* and *Henry V* and I find the speech right away. It leaps out at me; rousing, robust, martial.

> *Once more unto the breach, dear friends, once more,*
> *Or close the wall up with our English dead.*

But the time has passed. After urging my troops so subtly on the eve of Agincourt, I can't step back to exhort them to a bloody, frontal assault before the gates of Harfleur. I look again at *Hamlet* and see some merit in it.

THE
CASABLANCA AMATEUR DRAMATIC SOCIETY
PRESENTS

ost
train
GHOST
TRAIN
gho
ghost
train

A DRAMA IN THREE ACTS

BY ARNOLD RIDLEY

CHURCHILL CLUB   8.00 P.M.
CASABLANCA   26 NOVEMBER 1965

CHAPTER TEN

Live sport

In 'The Book' my grandfather is described as 'a professional athlete'. This isn't strictly true, but it is meant as a homage to his sporting prowess.

> A clear memory of my father. I am standing at the bottom of the stairs as he is about to descend. He sees me there, completes a half-somersault and comes down the stairs walking on his hands with his feet pointing skywards. I roar with laughter and hurry to pick up the money which has fallen out of his trouser pockets.

Sporting talent was for my father an incomparable blessing. Religion had its place; law served its purpose; the arts were worthy callings. But, in his eyes, sport meant more.

Bob Ridley was a truly gifted sportsman. He excelled at hockey, football, fencing and gymnastics; he held middle-distance records for the mile, the half-mile and the steeplechase and gained an international trial at water polo. He paid for his subscription to the famous London Polytechnic by fighting (under an assumed name to protect his amateur status) in the brutal boxing-booths of Soho where the purse for the winner was half-a-crown and the loser received nothing.

After an illness which left him an invalid, he took up bowls and won a succession of championships and medals. The evening before he died, he and his partner, Charles Francis, played a friendly match at the local Bloomfield Bowling Green against the current holders of the Somerset Pairs Championship. They won. Bob Ridley, it was said later by those who were present, played as well as he had ever done.

* * *

Whereas Bob Ridley is 'a professional athlete', my grandmother is described in 'The Book' as 'a Sunday school teacher' and 'probably the least athletic woman who ever lived'. (Is it unkind to suggest that my own mother might have run her close?)

> It was to be a minor tragedy in my life that I should inherit from my mother a distinct ineptitude for playing games and from my father a fanatical desire to excel at them. My minor successes resulted only from interminable practice and my disappointments were frequent. All my life I've envied the natural athlete and ball-game player. Yet, despite my ducks, dropped catches, double-faults and holes-in-nine, I think I've had more than my fair share of pleasure.

* * *

An afternoon in Richmond before a winter kick-off. We favour this pub because it has a paved garden and a wooden bench where we can sit together, my father with his pint of beer and I with my orange squash. We are in reflective mood.

'When it comes to sport,' says my father, 'being third class is a great boon.'

(As so often, nothing has prompted him to say this.)

'Take golf, which can be a particularly cruel game.'

(At the age of six I have not played golf. More than fifty years later this remains true. But I recognise gravity in his voice and I listen solemnly.)

'Let's suppose you are a first-class golfer,' says my father. 'You go round your local course in even par and return to the clubhouse. There's no celebration. There's no reason to celebrate. You're a first-class golfer and you expect to round in even par.' (I don't know what par means but this doesn't seem important.) 'You have a glass of light ale and you go home. There will be some days when you go round in one under par but again you won't celebrate. In fact you may ask

84

yourself why can't you go round in one under more often. You expect it of yourself. You are, after all, a first-class golfer. And then there are other days, perhaps not many, when golf – and life – being what it is, you drop a shot. Maybe two. It's a disaster. You shun all company. You sit alone with a glass of scotch which, as despair takes hold, may be followed by another. You are a first-class golfer and you have dropped a shot. You are filled with self-disgust which tomorrow's round – when as usual you go round in even par or better - won't entirely dispel.'

I sip my orange squash and my father drinks his beer. A sparrow hops expectantly on the paving stones in front of us.

'Being second class is no better,' my father continues. 'Worse, in fact. For the very simple reason that you're not first class. You're so tantalisingly close to being first class but you're not. You work so hard at your game but it makes no difference. Oh, there are times when you can almost believe that you're better than you are, but they're there to taunt you. A hole, two holes together, that you play perfectly. As well as they can be played. Is this, finally, a sign that you are destined for greater glory? The question no sooner forms itself in your mind than you find you've dropped a shot. And another at the next hole. And one more at the hole after that. Later you share a joke with other members at the bar but inside you're contorted with bitter disappointment. You try to brush it aside but the thought haunts you. What would life be like, you ask yourself, if I were first class? You know the answer, of course. It would be wonderful, joyful, triumphant. Your life would be complete.'

My father returns with a second pint of beer and two limp cheese sandwiches which we eat happily enough because our thoughts are really not on food.

'Whereas the third-class sportsman can only win,' my father pronounces. 'He is used to losing. His life is, after all, a catalogue of minor disappointments. A dropped shot here, two dropped shots there, and sometimes worse. The third-class golfer smiles ruefully as he recounts the story of his last round. If he sometimes secretly permits himself to wonder what it would be like to be better than he is, the thought doesn't detain him. He'll play again tomorrow happily enough. Next week, too. Yes, there may be a day when – magically – everything goes right. There will be no reason for it; it just happens. His drive soars the distance of the fairway; he misses the bunker that always ensnares him; he sinks an impossible putt. He goes round – no, not in even par – but several strokes better than his best. In the clubhouse he buys a bottle of champagne and shares his triumph with everyone present. He won't expect to repeat the performance tomorrow but he will certainly repeat the story to anyone who cares to listen. The day when everything went right. When he had a glimpse – a momentary taste – of what it might be like. Yes, being third class is a great boon.'

I have been told something profound although I'm not precisely sure what it is. What I know, however, with great certainty, is that in 1965, twelve years from now, the club's centenary year, I must play scrum-half for Bath at the Recreation Ground.

The sparrow darts backwards and forwards pecking at the crumbs from our sandwiches, and we allow ourselves a moment's further silence before finishing our drinks and heading for the ground.

* * *

My father's association with Bath Football Club was lifelong.

> On winter Saturday afternoons, I sometimes extracted an extra penny from my father in order to support Bath Football Club, playing under Rugby Union rules with much ferocity on the Recreation Ground. My chief heroes were Frank Cashnella, a pallid, black-moustached and utterly ruthless forward who could be counted on to have the best of numerous fights, and an albino of great physical strength with frizzy snow-white hair known to the populace as 'The Silver King'. In 1908 I became a member of the club, paying, I believe, half a crown for a boys' membership ticket. I have been a member ever since …

In later middle age, a much-loved, greatly-respected past president and life member of Bath Football Club, it was said by some that, had it not been for the wounds he received in the First World War, my father would have played stand-off for the club, for Somerset, quite possibly for England. It wasn't true. The myth was perpetuated by well-wishers who had never seen him play. When the story was recounted within our hearing – a kindly codger keen to praise a father to his son – my father would shake his head to deny it, but it was difficult for him to do more without seeming ungracious.

'I was never much good,' he would say to me later. 'I didn't have the talent. As simple as that.'

Although he never played rugby for the club, he served Bath well in other capacities.

In 1928 I took over the post of fixtures secretary of Bath Football Club, and set out to make improvements to the fixtures list obtaining dates with London clubs such as Harlequins, London Scottish, Blackheath and Richmond. To make room for these, I dropped games with clubs who habitually played dog-fight, spoiling rugby. As many of these were near neighbours, I wasn't very popular in the district. But the difference between first- and second-class clubs depends upon the company they keep and I was determined that Bath should be graded with the best.

It was always an uphill struggle.

On Saturday afternoons in winter my father and I watched rugby. Harlequins, Blackheath, London Welsh, Richmond, Rosslyn Park, Saracens, Wasps … We took buses and trains to most parts of London and sometimes further afield. In a single season, we'd see Leicester, Northampton, Coventry, Sale, Bristol, Bedford, Birkenhead Park …

Before the game, if the pub had no garden, I often waited for twenty minutes – no hardship at the time – while my father drank his lunchtime pint. Or maybe two. Because, although he was punctilious about not drinking in the afternoon, the afternoon didn't begin until just before kick-off, whatever time kick-off happened to be.

We might watch the game from the touchline or the stand, wrapped up against the wind or the rain; damp grass, the smell of pipe tobacco, light fading through the afternoon. Sometimes we were joined by one or two of my father's rugby acquaintances, men whom we didn't see anywhere else. Few of them seemed to have names and to me they were mostly indistinguishable. A possible exception was a man my father christened 'Moomin'. Moomin, a Finnish troll, featured for years in a popular strip cartoon in the *London Evening News*. My father was particularly pleased with the name which he thought was wonderfully apt. Moomin himself, although not notably responsive, didn't seem to mind. To my eyes – and I felt disloyal to be thinking this – Moomin looked no more like Moomin than many of our other rugby acquaintances, and I found myself wondering – a still more disloyal thought – if, unknowingly, my father might have applied the same soubriquet to more than one of the ponderous, pipe-smoking figures whom we regularly encountered looming out of the mist at Sudbury, Sunbury or Old Deer Park.

These were relaxed afternoons when we could watch the game with the easy detachment of spectators who owed no allegiance to either side. Our instinct was to support the underdogs – generally the visiting team – but the final result didn't concern us greatly. This was just as well because, no matter how close the score, my father liked to leave a game five minutes before the final whistle. His plan was, he explained, to avoid 'the crowd'. We would hurry from the ground to arrive at the bus stop or the railway station at exactly the moment that an empty bus or train was pulling away. A five-minute wait would follow, my father pacing about impatiently until we were joined by 'the crowd' who then jostled with us onto the next bus or train in the direction of home.

These were happy, untroubled Saturday afternoons; but the precious days when Bath played in London were different altogether.

* * *

On Sunday mornings my father and I went to Paddington station where we stood on the concourse listening to the brass band that played there dressed in shocking pink uniforms. My father liked trains and stations and Paddington station in particular. Paddington was the home of the Great Western Railway, 'God's Wonderful Railway', the pride of the West Country. These were the days of steam. Billowing smoke, shrill whistles, the guard's green flag, stepped exhalations as the train pulled away from the platform. We watched them depart. One hundred miles of permanent way from Paddington to Bath, a city both nearer and further away than simple geographical distance.

More prosaically, Bath is our destination when we visit Granny in her modest terraced house in Wellsway where she lives with Rose and Mr Harper. While we are in Bath I am happy to be shown the Pump Room, the Royal Crescent and Pultney Bridge, but I know that Bath is more than this. I can't express it at the time but Bath for me is an ideal; an inspiration and a cause. It is sacred and the source of its sanctity is the Recreation Ground. The Rec. This – the most beautiful rugby ground in England, overlooked by Georgian buildings with the Abbey in the distance and the River Avon flowing behind the stand – is where Bath plays rugby on alternate Saturdays.

We only go once to the Rec. A dark afternoon in November with the lights of the city pricking the gloom. I am overwhelmed to find myself here. I am transported. Later, in the front room with Granny and Rose – the egg-green gas fire hissing, Mr Harper upstairs, busy being unseen – my father asks me if I enjoyed the game. It's the sort of question that other adults ask but not my father. He is, I suppose, filling a silence while Granny picks the currants from her currant bun and Rose sips her tea. I find I can't answer him. I don't have words to explain; the wonder, the elation but also my realisation. That although Bath is in some deep sense 'home', I don't belong here. My father and I are the city's loyal sons but we must serve abroad. A day may come when we will be recalled but, for the present, our place isn't here. We are visitors – I much more than my father – and we have our purpose. We are Bath's London supporters. We have our role. We know what we must be and what we must do.

* * *

Usually we meet the Bath team at the ground but there are some wonderful Saturdays when we meet them off the train at Paddington station. Warm greetings from committee members and senior players; firm handshakes and gruff laughter. We are the Londoners – Arnold and his son – there to bring them luck. We sit by as they eat their lunch at a Paddington hotel; white napkins tucked in at the chin, brown meat, brown vegetables, brown gravy, washed down with bottles of light ale. We board the coach ('Plenty of room, Arnold') that takes us to Old Deer Park or Richmond Athletic Ground, everyone in high spirits. Laughter from the back of the coach, gentle ribaldry ('Language, boys, language') my father's Bath accent returning. We travel through the streets of London, suddenly foreign, and then we're there. A stern silence; the serious business of the afternoon. Each man collects his kit; the trainer and the coach follow, carrying between them a four-handled bag as big as a stag; spare kit, plasters, 'the sponge', odds and ends. Half-an-hour before kick-off we visit the changing room. 'Good luck, boys,' says my father. 'Thanks, Arnold.' We leave. The door is locked behind us for the mystery of 'the team talk'. When the players reappear, each man is noticeably bigger than he was before; a blur of blue, black and white stripes; the smell of embrocation in the autumn air. 'Good luck, boys,' my father says again, but this time they don't respond. Studded boots clacking awkwardly on grey concrete before sinking into green grass; polite applause from the home crowd. We take our place in the stand where we are joined by the reporter from the *Bath & Wilts Chronicle*, a twitchy rabbit of a man with his little yellow notepad, stopwatch and self-propelling pencil. His cheerless match report will appear on the back page of the sports edition of the newspaper, the front page being reserved – to my father's weekly fury – for a fulsome account of Bath City's latest game in some lowly soccer league.

The rugby of the era is a player's game. There are few concessions to spectacle. On dark afternoons in the driving rain the ball disappears from view for minutes at a time. It emerges briefly, is swallowed into a ruck, appears again and is kicked to touch. A line-out follows and the ball is gone once more. By half-time – when white china plates

My grandmother, 'a woman of steady resolution'.

My grandfather, 'a damn fine watch with a broken mainspring'.

My father at the ages of seven and twenty-one.

Above left My father, the celebrated West End playwright.
Above right With his parents outside 4 Sunny Bank, Lyncombe Vale, Bath.
Left My father and grandfather in Juan-les-Pins, 'more like two brothers than a father and son'.
Below My grandfather's shop at 14 Manvers Street, Bath.

Above left and right Private (later Lance Corporal) Ridley, Prince Albert's Somerset Light Infantry Number 20481 in 1915. *Below* Major Ridley with the British Expeditionary Force, 1939-40, 'a nightmare from which I had no awakening'.

My father as a young man in a variety of parts from Hamlet at Bristol University to Little Aminadab in *She Stoops to Conquer*.

bove 'My mother was certain to be an ctress'. As Britannia, at the Navy League all, Auckland, New Zealand, 1932.

Above Althea Parker, 'the glamorous actress pursued by a string of suitors'.
Below Playing Cleopatra in the West End.

Above Chris, my son, at the helm.
Right 'The boy who travels' in
Egypt in 1964 and Macao in 1978.
Below The family in 1990:
Catherine, Jocelyn, Nicolas, Lottie
and Christopher.

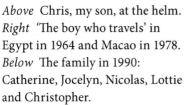

The framed photograph that always hung in my father's bedroom. KEEPERS OF YOUTH. 'His name in lights in St Martin's Lane.'

At night in the dismal waiting room at Fal Vale, 'a station on a branch line of the South Cornwall Joint Railway Company'. Two scenes from *The Ghost Train*.

of quartered oranges are brought onto the field – the forwards on both sides are indistinguishable while most of the backs are laundry-fresh. It doesn't matter. For me this is drama enough. I don't look for entertainment. All that matters is the result.

We lose.

Not always, but enough for defeat to be the rule and victory a rare exception. The wind, which all afternoon has been blowing down the field in our faces, changes direction at half-time and blows in our faces again. The London Society referee – a solicitor, accountant or member of some other profession mistrusted by my father – can be relied upon to favour the home side whenever a decision is in doubt and often when it is not. A drop goal attempt misses by inches; a pass is dropped or deemed to have gone forward; a boot slips into touch. We are used to such things. There are times when the game has run away from us long before the end and others when a last-minute penalty or a breakaway try undoes the afternoon's endeavours. It is hard to bear but not unexpected. The final whistle. We return to the changing-room. 'Well played, boys,' says my father. 'Better luck next week.' Black mud and grass on the changing room floor; steam rising from the players' bath. 'Thanks, Arnold. See you in March.' We leave the ground. On our way home we are sombre but not despairing. We have done what we could. No more could be asked of us. We didn't expect to win.

Except that sometimes we do – which brings a test of a different kind. At Bath games we never leave before the final whistle; we take our chances with 'the crowd' (and still miss the bus or train). We wait in the final minutes for the undeserved penalty or the injury-time interception that reverses the result. But there are one or two matches when miraculously this doesn't happen. When we win. And when we win, our routine changes.

'Let's go home, shall we, old boy,' says my father. 'No need to wait around.' There is to be no visit to the changing-room. 'We don't have to tell them that we're pleased,' he says. 'They know that already. And there'll be plenty of people to help them celebrate.' I don't protest. I know that this is my father's philosophy. We are supporters. In times of disappointment and defeat, we are there. In times of victory and success, there are fair-weather friends who will hold the victors aloft.

It's still hard.

*　*　*

A few months after my father's death, Bath made a first appearance in the Twickenham final of the John Player Cup. Their opponents, the holders, were Bath's long-standing West Country rivals, Bristol. Throughout my childhood Bristol had always beaten Bath both at home and away. That day at Twickenham Bath won, 10–9.

Soon after the final whistle has blown, an old friend of my father's calls from the ground to give my mother the news. How overjoyed Arnold would have been, he says. How very sad that he wasn't able to share in the club's success.

'I'm sure he was there,' my mother tells me.

'Yes, I'm sure he was,' I say.

And we both agree that he would have celebrated with a second gin. And maybe a third.

But the next morning, and in the seasons that followed, I fancy he might have felt a little lost. The John Player Cup was the start of a succession of triumphs. The Courage League, the Pilkington Cup, the Heineken European Cup. For almost a decade Bath reigned supreme as the dominant club in English rugby. I am not suggesting that my father would have wished it otherwise but he might have found it disconcerting. He would never abandon the club that he'd supported for seventy-five years but I can see him stepping back a little, distancing himself from the clamour and 'the crowd'.

*　*　*

The 1992 Pilkington Cup Final. Bath are playing Harlequins. I have been to very few Bath games since my father died, but today I have been given tickets, for myself and my son, and we have come together. You haven't been to Twickenham before and naturally you're excited.

It's a close match which could go either way. At full-time the score is 12 points each and two periods of extra time follow. With one minute left, the score remains tied. I am disconcerted to find how painfully important it is to me that we win. I so badly don't want you to be disappointed. I have flashbacks to the dark afternoons when penalties went against us and breakaway tries brushed aside our victory. I am holding my programme so tightly that my fingers are numb. A last line-out. We win the ball. It goes back to Stuart Barnes, our stand-off. Barnes kicks. The ball soars, hangs and passes between the goalposts. It is an immense, a prodigious, a legendary drop goal. The crowd is on its feet. Around us Bath supporters are cheering wildly but I am stuck to my seat. 'Have we won?' you ask anxiously. 'Yes,' I say. 'Yes, we've won.'

We stay on to watch the cup being presented, the trophy being passed back to each player in turn. We leave the ground with everyone else but I find we are walking away from the rest. It's not a conscious decision but I need to be alone, to hold on to the moment, to find my bearings. It takes me some time to realise that we have been walking too long and that you're beginning to tire. I don't know where we are but you're not old enough yet to think I could be lost. We see a bus that's going some of the way home. You've revived and chat happily about the game. I want to share your cheerful joy but my feelings are complicated. It seems I have no gift for triumph.

BATH
FOOTBALL
CLUB

(Affiliated with the Rugby Football Union
and Somerset County R.F.U.)

VICE PRESIDENT

**Members are requested to show their tickets
on entering the Ground and Stand.**

Limited car parking for Members Only inside the
Recreation Ground

SEASON

1983-84

(118th year)

**THIS TICKET ENTITLES THE MEMBER
TO USE THE PRESIDENT'S LOUNGE**

CHAPTER ELEVEN

Tailenders

We have been brought together – family, friends and neighbours – for a party to be held at Auntie Tara's house, 'Carsona'. Auntie Tara's sons, my older cousins Michael and Mark, have recently returned home on leave – Michael from East Africa, Mark from the West Indies – and the party is in their honour. Before it begins we are invited to attend a cricket match on the local village green.

Michael and Mark are unmistakably brothers but in most respects they are very different.

Michael has always been a glamorous figure, much admired by his younger cousins and older relations. At the Royal Masonic School he was head boy; at the start of his national service he was commissioned and served in Africa; at Cambridge he won a hockey Blue; and now, destined it seems certain for a shining future, he is a district officer in the Colonial Service. Handsome, popular, solid, assured, Michael displays the relaxed confidence that some men have about them from their earliest years, and others do not.

Mark is generally described – often within his hearing – as a 'worthy plodder'. It is kindly meant, almost a compliment; and Mark seems to accept it with good grace. He didn't excel at his school, Christ's Hospital, and it was decided he should join a bank; throughout his National Service he remained in the ranks but his promotion to lance-corporal was noted with approval; he now works in an overseas branch of the bank where the pace of life is slower and more suited to him. Since early childhood Mark has worn thick glasses and a gentle, bemused smile.

Hearing that Michael will be home, the captain of the local cricket team has invited him to play for the village this afternoon. An invitation has also been extended to Mark although this may have been an afterthought. It is the prospect of the cricket match that has persuaded my father to attend a family event which otherwise he might have employed one of his well-practised stratagems to avoid.

It is a glorious mid-summer afternoon; the village green is a picture postcard. My father stations himself in a deckchair at some distance from the pavilion where gentle background chatter is interrupted intermittently by a mild flurry of clapping. I remain with my mother, for whom cricket is a distant tableau of very little interest, but she is surrounded by members of her family and is enjoying the warmth of the sun.

The village has elected to bat. Michael comes in at the fall of the first wicket. He plays a classic innings; watchful at first, waiting until he has re-acquainted himself with the pace of an English pitch, before opening up with a series of bolder strokes through the covers and mid-wicket. He has just made his fifty and looks set for more when he is given out by the opposition's umpire, a dubious decision which, naturally, he doesn't query. He returns to the pavilion, briefly raising his bat to acknowledge the applause. The overs have been bowled, the innings has ended and a respectable total has been achieved. Mark, who was due to come in at number nine, will not be required to bat.

The opposition's openers take the field and I join my father, sitting cross-legged next to his deckchair. Neither Michael nor Mark are bowlers. For most of the afternoon Michael fields at cover point while Mark, who doesn't have the eyesight to be a close fielder, stands on the boundary. Once or twice a ball is hit in his direction and Mark gets down on one knee, as he was taught at school, and fields it watchfully. It has become a gentle, drowsy, uneventful afternoon.

And then a lurch. The batsman, intending to hit a six, has mis-timed his shot and the ball is soaring high into the cloudless sky. It's plain that it won't clear the boundary rope where, a few yards from us, Mark is fielding. The ball hangs hypnotically above us. Time stops. I can see with a terrible, impotent clarity, what is about to happen. The rest of the world watches the ball; my father and I watch Mark. From the pavilion this will seem such a simple catch. The fielder has nothing to do except get in position and see the ball safely into his hands. Mark squints up painfully into the sunlight, peering through his pebble lenses. I can't bear to look. The sharp shame when the catch is dropped; the instant of disbelief; the moment of humiliation. It will be quickly forgotten, of course. These things happen. Except that sometimes they don't. A shallow ripple of applause. I open my eyes and see the ball safely in Mark's hands. My father, most unlike him, has risen from his deckchair to clap. His delight is undisguised. 'Well held,' Mark's captain shouts across. No more than that. The ball is back with the bowler and the game resumes. It was, after all, a pretty straightforward catch. My father is still clapping although Mark doesn't notice; he is, I think, still slightly stunned. 'A very fine catch,' my father tells me, resuming his deckchair. 'All too easy to drop a catch like that.' There's no one else near us to share this with which means that he tells me again. 'A very fine catch'. I nod, very ready to agree.

At the party that follows my father stands by an open window, away from what he describes as 'the throng'. He repeats his praise for Mark's catch to family members and others who come within range. 'All too easy to miss a catch like that.' He might like to reach a wider audience but this would mean mixing with the crowd. Everyone he tells is happy to indulge him although they may wonder why 'Uncle Bear' is making quite such a fuss about Mark's catch while barely mentioning Michael's stylish fifty. I know that this, too, has delighted him, but in a different way.

* * *

A print of a photograph taken for a local newspaper. My father, wearing Godfrey's smile, is coming in to bat, an old cricketer, comfortable in pads and gloves. Although on this occasion he isn't playing Godfrey; fact and fiction have become cross-laced.

Cricket was a passion shared by several members of the *Dad's Army* cast. Both John Le Mesurier and Bill Pertwee were fine cricketers, and Arthur Lowe was president of his local club as his father had been before him. They must have enjoyed making *The Test*, an episode in which the Walmington-on-Sea platoon plays Bill Hodges' team of air raid wardens which includes a fictional fast bowler, Eddie Egan, played by the legendary Freddie Truman. The match ends when Private Godfrey, coming in last, joins Sergeant Wilson at the crease and, despite dropping his bat, miraculously hits the winning six.

But the photograph I have in my hands was taken six years later, on Sunday, 9th August 1976, at Arthur Lowe's Hayfield Cricket Club in Derbyshire. The *Dad's Army* stage show is on tour and members of the cast have agreed to take part in a charity match. On this occasion my father, then seventy-nine, has been given a runner and a chair to sit down on from time to time. Joining Bill Pertwee in the middle, he plays one or two strokes before – in Bill's words – 'becoming rather excited'. He hits a full toss into the outfield and, forgetting he has a runner, starts to run himself. 'We all finished up in a heap at one end,' says Bill, 'and it was deemed that I was out.'

An over or two later my father will retire. He will sit in a deckchair while my mother kneels on the grass to unfasten his pads. Later they will drink tea from a thermos flask and enjoy a buttered bun. My parents together in the late afternoon. A happy picture.

I return the photograph to its cardboard-backed envelope. Stamped in red: PLEASE DO NOT BEND.

* * *

My son and I been invited to a friend's fortieth birthday party, a family event with entertainments throughout the day. The highlight – our friend is a great lover of the game – will be the match between the itinerant cricket club of which he is a member and a scratch team composed of other guests. I am flattered to have been asked to play and I have borrowed white flannels and cricket boots for the occasion. I'm also a little apprehensive; it's several years since I last played cricket.

It's no surprise to find that, when the time comes, both teams are one or two players short. There's a flurry of recruitment during which it's decided to invite you to join our team. Aged eleven, you are many years younger than everyone else but you're keen to play. You can field somewhere safe and bat at number eleven. It should be fun.

Our captain has the portly authority of someone who still plays the game. At present he is trying to identify the members of his team and gauge their capabilities. While we're waiting, I pick up a bat and invite you to throw a ball to me. I hit it back to you along the ground. You throw the ball again. My bat rises, as it should, above the off stump. I can't do otherwise. I'm unaware that the captain has stopped to watch us and has noted my batting style.

'Would you like to open?' he says.

'I'm afraid I haven't played for years,' I reply.

The captain doesn't take this as an answer and waits.

'I think I'd better bat lower down the order,' I say.

'Fine,' says the captain. 'I'll put you in at six.'

I thank him, and you and I resume our practice. We've played a little cricket in the park but I haven't tried to coach you.

In the changing-room the captain reads out the batting order. I am down at number nine. It's unlikely I'll have an innings. Which is just as well, I think, although I begin to regret my timidity. As it happens, our openers are less accomplished than we might have hoped and they're both dismissed before they score. Our number three looks the part but does little better and is plainly furious to be given out while still in single figures. To avoid a collapse our captain promotes himself up the order to number four. It's a sound decision. He's untroubled by the bowling and quickly begins to put together an innings. At the other end, however, his partners either swing wildly at the air or fail to move their feet. The result is the same. Our wickets fall steadily. With six wickets down it looks as if I will be called upon to bat. I put on some pads that I find discarded in a corner with some damp batting gloves. A new bowler has come on and quickly has our captain in trouble. He plays and misses. He plays and misses again. There is a loud appeal. Our captain is out.

As I pass him on the way to the wicket, he says, 'Do your best'. I have the feeling he isn't confident my best will amount to very much. As I approach the stumps, I nod affably at the close fielders. No one smiles back. The match, it seems, is more serious than it appears from the pavilion. I take guard. The bowler runs in. I plant my front foot firmly down the pitch to play a forward defensive stroke. My bat does not connect with the ball which hits me squarely on the toecap of my boot. The bowler shouts a loud appeal. I stand quite still. It seems probable that – in my father's phrase – I am 'plumb out'. The umpire looks at me and I meet his eyes. It's a long moment. I wait for his finger to rise but instead he shakes his head. 'Not out,' he says. The bowler, justifiably, is outraged and returns to his mark muttering darkly. This may be a friendly game, but for a fast bowler cricket is cricket. His next ball is faster but wide of the off stump. I play it instinctively – inside the line of the ball, soft hands, angled bat – and my partner calls for a single. It's the last ball of the over and the field changes. 'Thanks,' I say quietly to the umpire as he walks away to square leg. He smiles. We both know how generous he's been. At the other end, the bowling is gentle and short. I play a stroke or two and at some point a piece of misfielding enables me to take two runs. Over.

My partner faces a flurry of ferocious balls from the aggrieved fast bowler who, with his fifth, a vicious Yorker, bends back the middle stump. I am joined in the middle by our number ten, a plump young man who, for some reason, is wearing a pink tie and seems unhappy to be here. He stands stock still as the ball passes close to his shoulder and then, without warning, runs at me. We cross. I should be out but the ball has been flung to the bowler's end. Run out. Our number ten returns, beaming, to the pavilion.

The last man in is you. For me it's a magical moment. Here we are, father and son, batting together. You seem quite comfortable although I don't think you can have worn pads and gloves before. The bowler tosses down some gentle balls at you which you deal with perfectly well. You are, like your great-grandfather, a natural ball player. Perhaps we score a single each. I can't be certain. I'm in a sort of dream. Over. It's my turn to face the bowling again. All my anxiety has gone. I play a series of solid defensive strokes down the wicket. I am seeing the ball onto the middle of the bat. I could stay here for hours. The bowler glares at me and I realise I am frustrating him, which strikes me as unsporting. I resolve to be more adventurous and I swing at his next ball which comes off the shoulder of the bat and describes a pleasant arc into the hands of the fielder at point. I'm out. The innings is at an end.

We walk back together, you and I. I smile to myself and think how lucky I am. I have not been given out first ball and I have played an innings with my son. Something I didn't dream I'd do, something I never did with my father. Something I would like to have done.

There are times, I conclude, in sport – as in life – when things go right.

PROGRAMME

"WOVEN WIND"

(A Drama in 3 Acts by Helen M. Parker)

THE ALTHEA PARKER FAREWELL

CONCERT CHAMBER, Town Hall

Thursday, 30th July

Under the Auspices of:

THE AUCKLAND LITTLE THEATRE SOCIETY.
AUCKLAND OPERATIC SOCIETY.
BRITISH DRAMA LEAGUE.
CATHOLIC REPERTORY SOCIETY.
GRAFTON SHAKESPEARIAN SOCIETY.
LYCEUM CLUB.

Price 3d.

CHAPTER TWELVE

An ill-requited profession

My mother was certain to be an actress, there had never been any doubt about it. Rosalind, Shylock, Cleopatra, Abanazer, Helen of Troy, Henry V. There are photographs of her in costume throughout her childhood. This wasn't dressing up; this was theatre. At every opportunity she staged performances. Family, friends and guests were either her audience or played supporting roles. My mother was always the lead. Following a string of triumphs in the vibrant amateur theatre of New Zealand, money was raised by a public subscription to send her 'home' to England where she trained for the stage at the Old Vic.

My father's choice of career was much more unexpected.

* * *

As far as the Morrishes were concerned, the theatre was not respectable.

> I was fourteen before I saw a play enacted by a professional company, my mother allowing that Shakespeare was 'different' and permitting me to witness Mr Frank Benson and his company depict *Hamlet*, the set play for the year's Oxford Junior Examination.

Although in the late nineteenth century the theatre had begun to acquire some degree of social acceptability – a year before my father's birth Sir Henry Irving became the first actor to be honoured with a knighthood – in the eyes of teetotal, nonconformist Bath tradespeople such as the Morrishes and the congregation of the Ebenezer Baptist

Chapel, it remained 'a den of iniquity', inseparable from low morals, loose living, heavy drinking and every sort of unspeakable vice.

The formidable actor James Quin is buried in Bath Abbey. An engraved stone lies in the nave and his bust sits to the side of the St Alphege chapel to the east of the high altar above a fulsome eulogy by David Garrick. Until Garrick's debut on the London stage, Quin had been the leading actor of his age. He was a substantial figure; more than twenty stone, a prodigious drinker (a 'six-bottle man'), a rake, a duellist, who had been convicted of manslaughter, and, reputedly, a philanderer, although he was too bulky ever to be a beau. When asked by the Duchess of Queensbury, 'Pray, Mr Quin, do you ever make love?' (meaning do you ever play lovers), the great actor replied, 'No, Madam, I always buy it ready made.'

Although my father had been a keen playgoer in his London days, he bowed to my mother's convictions. But I remember walking with him up Manvers Street (it must have been in 1905) and seeing a striking-looking man with long white hair blowing from under his silk hat, striding ahead of us. 'Take a good look at that gentleman,' my father said. 'When you grow up you'll be proud to remember that you saw him!' It was Sir Henry Irving, on his way from the station to unveil a memorial plaque to the actor, James Quin, at the Bath Literary Institute – now pulled down to provide a site for a public convenience.

* * *

According to my father's account, it was the decision to award a recitation prize at Clarendon School that sowed the first seeds of his theatrical ambitions.

It may seem strange that Clarendon School should have awakened in me an interest in the histrionic art but such was the case – although I'm pretty sure that neither a member of the staff nor a pupil had ever entered a theatre which, as we all knew, was an outpost of Satan.

My father not only urged me to enter but coached me. My chosen piece was *The Battle of Blenheim* and I can remember declaiming it with particular enthusiasm for 'the thousand bodies that lay rotting in the sun'. Apparently, by Clarendon School standards, my 'Lyceum rendition' was so surprising that, before she had recovered from the shock, poor Miss Silversides had named me as the winner.

A year later Clarendon School staged a rendering of Browning's *Robert of Sicily* as an action piece without historic costume. This representation was so successful that it was repeated on the platform of the Jubilee Hall in Broad Street before an audience of relations and friends. We had a feeling that it was all just a little bit sinful.

* * *

An aside. Verse-speaking was compulsory at St David's School. For many it was an agonising, stuttering, stammering test of nerve; for me it was a hurdle that I found I could clear with comfort.

My father didn't coach me and neither did my mother. She once or twice suggested a piece I might learn, but that was all. Would I have liked them to listen to me speak my verse? I don't know. I didn't ask them. My parents had no wish to encourage in me any thoughts of being an actor. I was, they said, too 'sensible' to dream of having anything to do with the stage. This assumption was more powerful than any prohibition could have been.

Early in his career Sir Henry Irving was advised that the theatre was 'an ill-requited profession'. It was a view to which my parents subscribed. Not to accept it would have seemed somehow disloyal.

* * *

From October 1913 my father attended the University of Bristol where he became a member of the university dramatic society 'at a time when, fortunately for me, it was terribly weak in male talent, to such an extent that, after minor successes in Synge's *The Well of the Saints* and Wilde's *The Importance of Being Earnest*, I was cast for the title role in *Hamlet*.' This led to the offer of a part in an Arthurian play with a long list of male characters that was being produced at the Bristol Theatre Royal.

> In one scene I had to fall down a flight of stairs backwards clothed in a suit of armour – a procedure far more difficult and bruising than appeared in the script! But, presumably this brought me to closer notice, to such an extent that I was asked if I would care to accept a part-time professional engagement at a pound a week when cast. I accepted and in consequence of this made my first professional stage appearance in a tiny part in Laurence Housman and Harley Granville Barker's play *Prunella,* using the name of John Robinson to disguise my non-scholastic activities from the university authorities.

Shortly afterwards he wrote his first play, a one-act tragedy in verse, in collaboration with Idris Jenkins, a Welsh poet and fellow student, who had become a firm friend.

> I had always shown a marked individuality in my school essays which had earned me nothing but censure. But Idris opened up a new and exciting world for me … The most important lesson I learned from him was that the arts were well within the reach of ordinary people.

Their play was due to be produced by the University Dramatic Society in 1915, but by then the war had disrupted what might have been the beginning of my father's theatrical career.

* * *

Returning from the war, my father reverted to 'schoolmastering' while he recovered. He spent a very happy year as a games master in Torquay but the disappointment of a first, unrequited love affair caused him to resign and, at the end of the summer term, he found himself back in Bath. 'With my limp less pronounced,' he wrote, 'my left arm more useable and my general health largely restored, I decided I was now fit enough to go on the stage.'

The letter he wrote to the Bristol Theatre Royal was forwarded with a warm recommendation to the Birmingham Repertory Company, which had been founded by Barry Jackson and John Drinkwater in February 1913. As a result, he was invited to join the company in August 1918.

John Drinkwater welcomed me with great kindness, reassured me on several points that were bothering me, handed me a copy of *Milestones* and told me I had been cast for the pleasant enough part of Young Lord Monkhurst. I went to sleep thinking that all might yet be well. This proved to be optimistic.

On arrival at my first rehearsal I was to discover that the stage director, AE Filmer, who was also producing the play, had taken an instant dislike to me. I never discovered why, although I'm quite prepared to admit that probably I thought a bit too much of myself. Anyway, the part of the young lord was quickly wrested from me and exchanged for a double – a silent footman in Act Two and an unloquacious butler in Act Three. It was evident that I was unlikely to play many Hamlets, Othellos or Macbeths for as long as Filmer was in charge.

My father, scrupulously fair, refers to Filmer as 'an excellent stage director and producer'; a generous description of a man who might be said to have blighted his career as an actor.

Esme Filmer was an odd character – small, dark and saturnine with a vitriolic tongue. He once asked me (and before the whole company too!) if I could oblige him by walking across the stage looking more like a man and less like a constipated rat. Another pleasantry consisted in asking me to do something my physical disabilities rendered impossible. He would then apologise profusely, murmuring something about having to make allowances for 'our brave fighting men'.

I shall never know if Filmer had deliberately set out to break me as an actor. If he did, he very nearly succeeded. He destroyed my confidence in myself to such an extent that, even after over sixty years, it hasn't completely returned. To this day whenever I see my director in whispered conference with the author or manager, I always feel that they are planning the best way to get rid of me.

Filmer was never forgotten. My father knew himself to be a good actor technically but he felt that he might have been more. He carried with him a sense of something unfulfilled as well as a memory of hurt and puzzlement. Having no cruelty or malice in his own make-up, he found it impossible to understand it in other people.

Despite Filmer, it was at the Birmingham Repertory Company that my father learnt his craft and played a variety of parts. In October 1918 the first production of John Drinkwater's *Abraham Lincoln* put the theatre firmly on the theatrical map. Unfortunately the play's opening was closely followed by the outbreak of Spanish influenza which was to kill more people than had died in the First World War.

I was one of the first to go down with it and went down pretty thoroughly, collapsing at the side of the stage. I was dispatched by cab to my digs in Varna Road where my landlady took fright, refused to come near me and left glasses of milk at the end of the corridor leading to my unheated room. After a week, a frantically overworked doctor managed to visit me and advised that, as I was getting no attention, it would be better if I got up and risked the journey home to Bath. With tramcars and taxis almost completely stopped by the epidemic, the journey from Varna Road to New Street Station posed a problem, but I reached home and began to recover. However, my convalescence was cut short by a telegram from John Drinkwater. If I was fit enough, would I come back as things at the theatre were desperate. Despite my mother's protests and foreboding, I did so.

I well remember the days following my return. My landlady, despite her precautions, had caught the pestilence and died of it. The stage doorkeeper was dead and so was a member of the company. Most of the others were in various stages of illness. The wholesale undertaker was working overtime and unvarnished coffins were piled high in Hinckley Street.

The cast of *Abraham Lincoln* is a very long one with practically every member of the company playing two parts at least. The epidemic had played such havoc that many of us were obliged to appear in far more than that. One night I played as many as seven, donning and whipping off uniforms, beards and moustaches in the wings. There were moments when I felt that, as I rushed on for the next part, I might meet myself hurrying off from the last!

But the theatre can be a cruel profession and my father's loyalty and service during the two seasons he spent at Birmingham were not rewarded as they might have been.

It was an unpleasant shock when in June 1920 I received a note warning me that I wouldn't be offered a contract for a third season. I was one of several players who were told that, with the return of servicemen who had been senior to us, the company was becoming too big. Despite this I think I might have stayed on, but for my pride.

On the last night of the season, I went to see Barry Jackson in his office to thank him for his kindness and to wish him goodbye. I don't know if he had any idea that I'd suffered quite a bit from Filmer but he looked hard at me and then, after quite a long pause, said: 'I'm particularly sorry about you leaving us, Ridley. You've been most loyal and always given your best.' I thanked him again and he continued: 'Have you fixed anything for the future yet?' 'Oh yes, sir,' I lied. 'I'm terribly glad to hear that,' he said. 'Good luck to it.' I still wonder what would have been the result if my vanity hadn't prevented me from speaking the truth.

Here I think my father is being particularly hard on himself. Vanity is one thing; self-respect another. A dignified acceptance has much to commend it although this doesn't mean it will be rewarded.

There were some depressing months after leaving Birmingham. I wrote scores of letters to managements and made numerous trips to London. I went from queue to queue, often meeting the same artists seeking 'a shop' several times a day. The war was over, demobilisation speeding up and the shortage of young male actors had ended. Nobody seemed to want me. Then, in December 1920, I received a telegram offering me an engagement to join the Plymouth Repertory Company. It also said that, if I accepted, I was to come at once. I did so.

On arrival at the theatre I discovered that I was to replace an actor who had been sacked on the spot for drunkenness and that I was to open on the Monday. This gave me two days in which to learn and rehearse a pretty long part. I was told by the stage manager, who was also the producer and always conducted rehearsals wearing an overcoat and bowler hat, that there would be no Saturday rehearsal as there was a matinée, and that all I would get was a run-through on the Monday before facing the audience. To add to my apprehension, instead of a full script, I was given what was then known as 'a part'. This consisted of half-sheets of paper on which were printed the character's speeches and the line or half-line preceding it but with no indication of which actor spoke it. When I told the stage manager that I didn't know the play and asked him what kind of man my character was, he replied, 'I don't know, dear boy. The script doesn't say.'

On Monday night I managed to stammer through in a high state of nervousness and went back to my dressing room anticipating the congratulations and thanks for saving the day. But there was no sign of Mr George S King, the manager, until the next morning. He was wearing a cloth cap and smoking a self-made cigarette which at all times hung from his lower lip at such an obtuse angle that it appeared to be defying the forces of gravity. I smiled a greeting but his face remained grim. 'Last night, he said, 'you called Sir Daniel Carteret "Cartwright"'. 'Did I?' 'Yes,' he replied. 'Twice!' In the circumstances these seemed to be trivial errors but I didn't say so. I apologised and said that I had been very nervous. 'Yes,' he said. 'You were.'

The Christmas I spent at Plymouth could hardly be described as a merry one. I wasn't popular with my fellow artists and remained uninvited to several parties taking place. I found out later that there was nothing personal about it. I had replaced a much-liked actor who, the company felt, had been dismissed harshly and they

weren't particularly anxious to make welcome his successor. I ate
my Christmas dinner, steak and kidney pie, alone in my bedsitter in
Catherine Street.

Plymouth completed the first act of my father's professional career.
At the end of the season the theatre closed and he was back where he
started in Bath.

* * *

A postscript. In life – as in the theatre – you must try to play the parts
that suit you and avoid the parts that don't, but it isn't always obvious
which is which.

Some years afterwards I thought I'd been presented with a chance of
getting my own back on Filmer. It was towards the end of 1926 just
after *The Ghost Train* had celebrated a year's run in the West End. I
was in Oxford on the eve of rehearsals of a new play of mine, *The God
of Mud*, which was to be produced at the old Playhouse Theatre in
Woodstock Road. That Monday night *The Seagull* was playing and I
was invited to attend. On arriving at the theatre, I saw from the posters
that the production was directed by AE Filmer. I smiled to myself and
thought, 'This is going to be fun, meeting Filmer again. No longer
a small-part actor but a successful West End author.' But I hadn't
bargained on his skill in dealing with the situation. When I entered
the theatre, Filmer was there waiting for me. Before a word could be
spoken he had bowed to me deeply and graciously and, with his hand
on his heart, said, 'Ah! The great Mr Arnold Ridley. How perfectly
splendid!' There was nothing I could say.

My father was not made to play the revenger. It wasn't in his nature.
There is very little satisfaction in revenge and no sweetness at all.
What Filmer had done to him couldn't be undone. As a result, there
were parts he would never play. But throughout his life he remained a
working actor – a courageous and worthy calling.

* * *

There is no memorial for my father in the nave of Bath Abbey and no bust in a side chapel, but guides taking visitors on walking tours of the Bath Abbey cemetery sometimes stop at his parents' grave where his ashes are buried to read his headstone.

CHAPTER THIRTEEN
The story of Lechmere Worrall

After his season with the Plymouth Repertory Company, my father returned to Bath. He was back where he started from and his prospects seemed bleak.

> Then something turned up that, on the face of it, appeared a piece of wonderful luck. Unknown to me, there were two well-known dramatists living in Bath: Lechmere Worrall, author of the famous *The Man Who Stayed At Home*, and Charles McEvoy, author of *David Ballard* and *The Likes of Her*. Quite out of the blue, I received a letter from Worrall asking me to call and see him.

My father was an optimist; a description which would have surprised him. But optimism is often misunderstood and shouldn't be confused with self-deception or blind faith. Optimism isn't characterised by platitudes about glasses, half-empty or half-full. Optimism is an innocent state of hope.

* * *

This is my father's story and I must let him tell it. I see the two of us at the kitchen table facing a bottle of my mother's homemade wine. The bottle of drinkable Beaujolais that I have brought with me stands unopened beside it. Although I may be sometimes tempted to interject I have, as an adult, learnt a little patience. I know that, if I say anything, my father will lose the thread or jump to another much less remarkable story. I will therefore content myself by asking a simple question before you read on. Would you willingly put your trust in a man with a name as improbable as 'Lechmere Worrall'? Now I'll sit back with a glass of my mother's homemade wine and listen to his story.

It was high summer and we had raspberries and cream for tea in the garden of his house in Cavendish Place. I remember that Worrall was wearing a magnificent white serge suit and smoked Turkish cigarettes from a long holder. McEvoy was also present but seemed content to remain in the background.

After some questions regarding my experience at Birmingham and Plymouth, Worrall told me that he and McEvoy had decided to start a repertory theatre company at the Bath Assembly Rooms. I had been suggested to him as the stage and general manager and he had been greatly impressed at meeting me. He offered me a salary of ten pounds a week which seemed princely, especially as I should be able to continue to live at home. All seemed set fair and it was quite some time before I discovered the 'snag'.

The 'snag' was Lechmere Worrall. He was a most charming man, always gay and perfectly dressed, and a wonderful host. But he was afflicted – in his case 'afflicted' is the correct word – with an optimism which, in the end, reached the point of mania. People who had been asked to contribute to the financing of his new repertory company and had declined to do so were entered on his list as having accepted with large sums placed against their names. Each and every wish of his became true. If he had a good idea for a new play, it was already written, produced and had run for a year in London. All that remained to be done was the spending of the royalties.

I think that Charles McEvoy must have realised his partner's 'peculiarity' a long time before I did for he withdrew from the scheme and published a statement to this effect in the local newspaper. This struck me as shocking disloyalty on his part and I stuck to Worrall more firmly than ever – despite the fact that I wasn't to be paid until the money for the scheme was firmly in the bank. Worse than this, in my capacity as manager I ran up quite a number of debts on his behalf for printing, typing and stationery.

Then came the day when Worrall had to appear before magistrates to obtain a licence for his new theatre. This was opposed by the owners of the Theatre Royal and the Palace. The magistrates refused to grant the essential licence but Worrall remained undaunted. He would open his theatre in another town. By this time I was becoming a little anxious regarding Worrall's stability but, when he invited me to accompany him to London for the day where he was going to sell a new play to the Vedrenne and Eadie management, I was given proof positive of his 'peculiarity'.

Eadie and his partner Vedrenne had offices in the Royalty which then stood in Dean Street, Soho. We entered the outer office where Worrall greeted the receptionist as an old friend.

'Mr Vedrenne in?' he asked.

'Yes,' she answered, 'but it's no good asking to see him, Mr Worrall, because he won't.'

'Don't be so silly, my dear,' laughed Worrall. 'You know he will.'

The poor girl was obviously embarrassed by my presence.

'I'm not being silly, Mr Worrall,' she answered. 'I've told you before that neither Mr Vedrenne nor Mr Eadie will ever have anything to do with you again.'

'But I've brought them my latest play,' he protested.

The receptionist continued, 'It's not the slightest use, Mr Worrall,' she said, 'and I think it would be better if you were to go away.'

'Oh, very well,' said Worrall. 'Then I'll leave the script.' He placed it on her desk.

She tried to return it to him saying, 'It's a waste of time, Mr Worrall. You know it won't be read.'

He refused to take it back. 'Of course it will,' he declared. 'Give Mr Vedrenne my best regards.'

He took me by the arm and led me to the door. Outside in Dean Street he said, 'Well, that's that. Now we've sold the new play, we'll have lunch at the Troc to celebrate.'

My lingering doubts were then a certainty.

Shortly after this trip to London, Lechmere Worrall left Bath suddenly. This was a blow to me as the bills I had run up in his name remained unpaid. The total sum wasn't a large one but too large for an actor who had been working three months and more without pay. I suppose I could have disclaimed all responsibility but some of the creditors were personal friends and all of them my father's fellow tradesmen. So with his assistance I managed to pay up. This left me penniless and, to add to the difficulty of the situation, I had just become engaged to be married.

At this point, can I ask you to put yourself in my father's place? After a series of painful setbacks you are presented with an extraordinary opportunity. You seize it gratefully and work for several months without pay. During this time you incur debts on behalf of your employer who then reveals himself to be a fraudster or, at best, a fantasist. Without a word of warning or apology he disappears and leaves you in the lurch. You have no money. You have no job. You have nothing except, rather unexpectedly, a fiancée. You feel sorry for yourself, of course. This is to be expected. But what about the agent of your misfortune? What is your verdict on Lechmere Worrall? Do you curse him as a crook and a buffoon, or can you find it in your heart to forgive him?

The sad thing about Lechmere Worrall was, although he was afterwards convicted of a minor fraud, he was as honest a man as ever lived. There was nothing of the confidence trickster about him. Neither did he lie. Every word he uttered he believed to be true. I understand his imprisonment was very short. Some old friends persuaded the authorities to have him medically examined and he was released to enter a home.

In this – as in so much else – my father was a better man than I will ever be. Having recognised this fact once again, I sit and stare a little glumly into my glass of wine.

* * *

116

Once again, the theatre had proved a miserable disappointment. This left my father one option – the boot trade.

> My father came to my aid. There was an empty shop at the High Street end of the Corridor in bad repair with collapsed ceilings and broken floorboards but it could be put in reasonable condition cheaply. He offered to open a branch of his Manvers Street business selling 'job lines' at cheap prices if I would manage it. I agreed to do so. I could do little else. But it felt to me like a confession of my failure as an actor.
>
> I was far from happy and loathed every minute of it, particularly the tiresome elderly female customers of which Bath seemed to have a super-abundance. Some of them could be particularly irritating. An 'old trout' – a name I bestowed on most of them – would say she took size 4. Then, after one had succeeded in getting her foot into a size 6, she would say: 'Of course I always take size 4 in good shoes.'

For four years he sold boots and shoes, but the theatre was still in his blood.

> In my spare time, I started writing plays in a small, unfurnished room above the shop. There was a broken window, covered with cardboard, and plaster was falling from the walls and ceiling. A large packing case was my desk and a smaller one served as a seat. Lighting and heating had to be supplied by an oil lamp and an oil stove.

He was, as he says, 'pretty prolific at the time' and bombarded London agents with his plays, most of which remained unread. 'Then,' in my father's words, 'Fate took a hand.'

I raise my glass and eye my mother's homemade wine optimistically. I am hoping that the bottle is now half-empty and that we will soon be able to drink my own bottle of Beaujolais.

Astra Cinema

Manager - Eric E. Livingstone.

MONDAY, SEPTEMBER 29th, 1941.

At 19.30 Hrs.

E. N. S. A.

Presents

"The
Ghost Train"

(By ARNOLD RIDLEY).

By permission of Air Commodore J. C. Quinnell, D.F.C.

Officer-in-charge Entertainments -   - Rev. T. Madoc-Jones.
Station Stage Manager   -   L.A.C. Rowley.
Assistant Stage Manager   -   - A.C.1 Bees.

Programme...

BARRY OZELLS LTD.

CHAPTER FOURTEEN

'The Goat Train'

Neither the story of *The Ghost Train* nor its plot is straightforward which is why – without having my copy of 'The Book' to hand and a much-marked Samuel French acting edition of the play – I would struggle to recount either.

The action of *The Ghost Train* takes place at night in the dismal waiting room at Fal Vale, a station on a branch line of the South Cornwall Joint Railway Company. The curtain rises on a most depressing scene. The fire is smoking and a single gas-jet burns faintly, throwing gloomy shadows about the room. Outside the rain falls heavily. Everything is damp and clammy and strips of wallpaper hang from the walls.

A train enters the station. There are cries of 'All change!', 'All change!', and the sound of carriage doors slamming. The whistle blows and, through the waiting room windows, lights from the railway carriages can be seen as the train moves slowly out of the station.

Enter Saul Hodgkin, the stationmaster, who turns up the gas and exits. Enter, in turn, the rest of the cast. A man and a woman whose marriage is going through difficulties; a honeymoon couple who will soon have to part; Miss Bourne, an elderly lady carrying a parrot-cage, who at the beginning of the second act empties a flask of brandy, becomes tipsy, falls asleep and misses the rest of the action; and Teddie Deakin, a dandified young man with an eyeglass and cigarette holder, who is quite plainly an idiot except that, equally plainly, he is not. After that things become complicated.

There are comings and goings, a great deal of 'stage business', high drama and gentle comedy, moments of tenderness, an influx of additional characters, the stationmaster's fall at the end of the first act and Julia's fall at the end of the second, the sound effects of the train itself. If, at the end of Act Three, like Miss Bourne, we find ourselves uncertain how we've come to be here, it's not important. We don't need to know. This is theatre. We have been propelled by the plot. We are where we find ourselves and very shortly we'll be in the pub across the road, saying how much we enjoyed the show. Tomorrow tonight the curtain will rise again. The sound of the train arriving at Fal Vale station, slamming doors, cries of 'All change!', 'All change!' and Saul Hodgkin will make his entrance.

> During my second winter at the Birmingham Repertory Company
> I was courting a girl in Bath, and from time to time, when I could
> scrape up the train fare, I used to go down to see her, travelling by a
> night train on Saturday and returning from Bath at crack of dawn on
> Monday in time for rehearsal. Leaving New Street by a 2.30 a.m. train,
> I was obliged to change at Mangotsfield Junction – a few miles short
> of Bristol – at around 4.00 a.m. and there wait for a local Bristol train
> which arrived at 6.30 to take me on to Bath. Mangotsfield Junction was
> just about as lonely and gloomy a dump as one could possibly imagine.
> There were no nearby houses, the platforms were long and the only
> shelter was a kind of combined waiting room and ticket office with
> paper peeling from the damp walls, out-of-date posters and a fireplace
> containing the ashes of a fire that appeared to have gone out during the
> days of broad gauge. There was rarely a member of staff on duty and,
> more often than not, I was the only passenger condemned to wait two
> and a half hours for the Bath connection. It could be cold, very dismal
> and just a bit eerie. If I managed to doze off on one of the backless
> benches, I was usually awakened by some freight train chug-chugging
> through or by a Bristol to Birmingham express rip-roaring past with a
> flash of lights and scream of whistle.

During his visit to London with Lechmere Worrall, my father had been introduced to Bernard Merivale who was at that time in charge of the drama department of the Hughes Massie agency in Fleet Street. Taking advantage of this useful contact, my father began sending him a succession of three-act plays. Bernard – who was to become my father's collaborator and closest friend – had been unimpressed and, as he later admitted, had left most of them unread.

But then Fate took a hand. One of Bernard's clients arrived at the Hughes Massie offices one afternoon and found that Bernard had been delayed. He was shown into Bernard's office to await his return. For want of anything better to do, he picked up a play amongst a pile on the desk and started reading it. It was a comedy drama of mine entitled *His Majesty*. On Bernard's return to the office the client said, 'I've been reading a play by a chap I've never heard of. Who is he?'

'He runs a boot-shop in Bath,' Bernard replied. 'He sends me a play about once a fortnight. In fact he's getting to be a bit of a nuisance.'

'Have you read this one?" the client asked. "I think you should. It's very good.'

Bernard took his advice. The next day he sent it to the actor-manager Arthur Bourchier who was looking for a new play.

Prior to this I had sent a copy of *His Majesty* to Horace Hodges, a well-known actor-manager, who had visited Torquay in my schoolmastering days with his celebrated play, *Grumpy*. I had been so impressed by his performance that I'd dared to go round to the stage door to congratulate him. He had been so courteous and kind that I'd sent the script to him. To my astonishment and delight, I received a letter from Hodges saying that he liked the play and was prepared to take it out on tour. Would I come to London to discuss the details?

I set off with the most pleasant anticipations and presented myself at his flat in Avonmore Road near Olympia. Hodges opened the door to me himself and I saw in an instant that he was upset about something. 'I'm afraid I've bad news for you, my boy,' he said. 'I find I shan't be able to do your play after all.'

Hodges, it seemed, had made an earlier promise to another management to take the lead part in a certain play if it should ever be decided to stage it. That morning he had learnt that the play was about to go into rehearsal.

This was a terrible blow and he was so genuinely upset at my ill-concealed disappointment that I left as soon as possible. I had booked to stay the night at a cheap hotel in Bloomsbury and in the evening I decided to go and see a play in the West End.

I was in a pretty depressed state and it may be that I wasn't in the right mood but I didn't like the thriller I saw at all. All the characters seemed unreal, the situations largely impossible and the denouement unconvincing. 'All right!' I thought. 'If this is the sort of tripe London managers put on, I'll write a thriller myself – only I'd like my characters to resemble real people in which one can believe and the place where it all happened somewhere familiar to most. But where?' It was then that those cold and dreary hours spent on Mangotsfield Junction came back to me. Right – off we go – passengers stranded on a lonely railways station. Station haunted. Obviously haunted by the shades of passengers killed in a smash. Why not the ghost of the train itself? Why not indeed!

From this point the story moves forward, although not without new delays and disappointments.

A copy of *The Ghost Train* reached Bernard Merivale on the same morning that *His Majesty* was returned to him by Arthur Bourchier saying that he liked the play but thought that the leading part of the gentle exiled little king reluctant to return to his throne unsuited to his more robust style of acting. He added that he would be grateful if Merivale would give him a first refusal of the next play written by the same author. Without reading it himself, Bernard had *The Ghost Train* delivered to Bourchier within the hour. Late in the afternoon Bourchier phoned to say that he would like to discuss a West End contract and would Mr Arnold Ridley partake of lunch with him at Romano's in two days' time?

After an elaborate lunch at Romano's, the formidable but gracious actor-manager Arthur Bourchier announced that he planned to draw up a contract for the production of *The Ghost Train* and outlined the terms he proposed. My father, a little apprehensive about the effects of the nine-inch cigar he was now smoking, readily agreed. It was a verbal agreement only and the formal contract was not received for another three months. When it arrived, the only difference from the terms outlined at Romano's was a single clause in my father's favour. However, changes to the script were required.

Bourchier wanted to play the part of the stationmaster himself, but his wife was anxious to appear in the production as well and there was no suitable part for her unless one of the three characters who came into the play in the second act was changed into a woman.

This was certainly a problem but it had to be faced and I set about it straight away. I soon decided that the victim of the change would have to be a character called Floyd who had to be replaced by a very artificial young woman, Julia Price. The part when written was a very showy and dramatic one and fitted into the story all right but I had the feeling (and still have) that the play lost a lot of its realism.

No sooner had I made this change than another vital one became imperative. The reason for the running of the train was that its trips were connected with the smuggling of cheap continental cars into England to undercut the market. Then the first Labour government was elected with the Liberal Party, which advocated Free Trade, and the import duty on foreign cars was scrapped. This meant that there was no further need to smuggle! The solution was the substitution of the smuggling of arms by a hostile nation and so it remains today (although the 'hostile nations' have varied according to the political situation of the time).

More delays followed, by which time Bourchier's plans had changed. As it happened, neither he nor his wife, for whom the part of Julia Price had been written, ever played in *The Ghost Train*, but by now the production had gained a momentum of its own. A short 'try out' provincial tour was booked, starting at the Brighton Theatre Royal.

On Sunday June 20th 1925 I set off from Victoria with some members of the cast bound for Brighton in a carriage labelled: RESERVED FOR THE GOAT TRAIN COMPANY. I seem to remember little of the actual first night. I must have been in a pretty jittery state as I spent most of Monday in one or other of the lavatories in the Old Ship Hotel where I was staying with my father and mother and my fiancée. One of the few things remaining in my memory is that of a feeling of surprised awe when I realised that real professional West End actors and actresses were actually speaking the lines I'd written in the small room above the boot-shop to an audience who had paid to see my play and who were listening to it.

The Ghost Train went reasonably well on the first night at Brighton and the reception was quite enthusiastic. The Brighton press was beastly, as it always was in those days, and the Brighton public apathetic. Those who came were enthusiastic but 'the Wood family' (empty benches) were much in evidence. The second week of the tour was at Golders Green where we did even worse than Brighton. It fared little better at Glasgow and Birmingham, and Brixton would have none of it. It was always the same story. Those who came liked it tremendously but there were so few of them.

Despite poor business, the management had faith in the play and a new tour was booked.

The second provincial tour did no better than the first. The Manchester press tore the play to shreds, it failed at Aberdeen and a second visit to Birmingham was as unsuccessful as the first. After a final week at Eastbourne the company was disbanded and the scenery was sold. *The Ghost Train* was dead and would have remained so for all eternity but for another set of circumstances and coincidences.

Harry Cohen, a young theatrical manager from New Zealand, had rented the St Martins Theatre in the West End for three months but the play he produced there had been a catastrophic failure and closed in a fortnight. Cohen was left with a theatre but no play.

The director of the play that had 'flopped' happened to be Lionel Howard who had been stage manager of *The Ghost Train* during its unsuccessful tours and still believed it to be a potential winner. He urged Harry Cohen to take a chance on it and Bernard Merivale added his support. I was back in Bath living at home when, while attending an Armistice Night Ball in the Bath Pump Room, a telegram was brought to me. I was to go to London at once. *The Ghost Train* was to open at the St Martins Theatre on November 23rd – less than a fortnight ahead.

Which brings us back to the small circle bar in the *Prologue*, and the young playwright sipping brandy and listening miserably to two impresarios confidently predicting that *The Ghost Train* would close in a week. As it happened, the press notices were generally friendly and, although business wasn't brilliant at first, *The Ghost Train* began to make a small profit. The problem was that the lease on the St Martins was running out. The question was whether or not Harry Cohen would take the risk and transfer the play to another theatre. He would and he did.

The Ghost Train transferred to the Garrick in January and business jumped amazingly. This may have been due to the fact that the Garrick had a far larger number of seats at popular prices or it may have been due to Cohen's flair for publicity. He was an expert at this and his audacity was astonishing.

I remember walking down Charing Cross Road one night in February and being delighted to see that the Garrick had HOUSE FULL boards out. They were stretched imposingly along the whole front of the theatre: GALLERY FULL, PIT FULL, UPPER CIRCLE FULL, STALLS FULL, PRIVATE BOXES FULL, HOUSE FULL. The next morning when my agents received the box office returns I learned that, although the house had been a very good one, it was quite a bit short of capacity. Was an attempt being made to cheat me of royalties? At the theatre I tackled Harry Cohen. 'No, it wasn't full,' he admitted. 'But it was full enough for the boards to go out, and they didn't go out until just before the rise of the curtain.' He went on to explain. Nine-tenths of disappointed latecomers would come again later and, in the meantime, spread the news that *The Ghost Train* at the Garrick was a sell-out.

Another of Harry's stunts was masterly. The pit and the gallery queues stretched down a pathway to the north of the Garrick and sometimes – particularly on Saturday nights – overflowed into Charing Cross Road in front of a tobacconist shop. Cohen persuaded the tobacconist to bring an action against him on the grounds that this queue was obstructing the entrance to his shop and losing him business. The tobacconist won and Harry paid cheerfully. He had full value too. There was no particularly outstanding news that day and all the evening newspapers printed the story on the front pages.

In mid-January the first of many provincial tours started. By the autumn there were four tours on the road, arrangements were in place for the play to be produced in Australia and the United States and a contract was signed with an Anglo-German company to shoot a silent movie of the play in Berlin. As my father writes, 'the old train had certainly puffed itself successfully out of the dark tunnel.'

CHAPTER FIFTEEN

True accounts

When my father was wealthy, he didn't think about money; it didn't concern him. When he had no money, it was impossible to ignore it. Money worries nagged at him unremittingly, a shrill tinnitus he couldn't shake off.

I don't know how his account books served him. They seemed to produce no tangible results. Perhaps they were soothing; an alternative form of patience. The account books themselves he purchased from the post office at the bottom of Highgate West Hill. They were either red or black and fitted comfortably into his jacket pocket although he usually kept them in the drawer of the desk in his bedroom. It was there he would sit transferring figures from the back of several envelopes into three neat, well-ordered columns of numbers.

| Pounds | Shillings | Pence |

A cigarette hanging from the side of his mouth, concentrating sternly, ash dropping unnoticed on his trousers, my father would run his finger steadily down the columns of figures, adding them up in his head. He wrote nothing down except the final totals. A knack he said he had inherited from his father.

* * *

Farthings, florins, guineas. Old money. Halfpennies, pennies, thruppenny bits. The coins that my mother and I saved in a glass sweet jar for eight and a half years until we were able to buy a red and cream record-player. A currency as puzzling and foreign today as a rouble, a sou or a centime and, year by year, becoming more remote to me so that adding 3s 2d and 6s 4d and 9s 6d, once a simple schoolboy sum, has become a brainteaser.

* * *

My mother and I catch the 52 bus to Kensington High Street.

'A tuppenny and a penny, please.'

The conductor takes my mother's money, extracts two tickets from the wire springs of the ticket-holder, clips them and hands them to me. Most small boys collect bus tickets – blue, pink, white, green – and I hold them until the end of the journey when I hand them to my mother for safe keeping.

'Pontings, Barkers, Derry and Toms.'

There was a time when my mother went shopping in Kensington High Street. Not now. Instead we visit her branch of Barclays Bank on the corner of Kensington Church Street. There are hushed conversations with a cashier and sometimes my mother leaves me sitting on a chair while she goes up to an office on another floor. This is where I first hear the whispered word 'overdraft'.

My mother and I are both relieved to be out in the street again and heading together towards Kensington Gardens and the Round Pond.

* * *

My father's money worries were more to do with income than expenditure. He was not profligate. On the contrary, he seldom bought anything. 'Things' didn't interest him. The only 'things' I can remember him buying were hats, of which he had an extensive collection. Why he bought more hats is a puzzle. His hats were indistinguishable from each other and yet – how can I explain this? – his latest hat always seemed to be shabbier and more battered than the one before. But although he barely spent money at all, it contrived to leave him. It was almost as if my father's money spent itself. This may have been partly because his loose change was looser than other people's. He kept his coins – a shifting, clinking symphony – in his trouser pocket and his notes somewhere vague inside his jacket. If he had a wallet, I never saw it. He certainly didn't possess a purse. The cash he had about his person was therefore free to come and go as it liked. Most of the time it liked to go.

* * *

A thought experiment to prove the magic of money:

Step 1 – I will invite my father to empty his trouser pockets and count out one pound in small change, including at least one sixpence.

Step 2 – I will hand back the coins that I have counted out, and ask him to walk once round the block.

He will descend the steps of 62 Lansdowne Road and turn left, as if going to the pillar box on the corner to post another speculative letter to a theatre management, an apology to his bank manager in Bath or a token payment to the Inland Revenue who always demand more. He will walk up Lansdowne Rise, a short slope, and turn left into Lansdowne Crescent. He will walk along Lansdowne Crescent to Ladbroke Grove where he will turn left again. (This is a walk he often takes in the evening to calm his anxieties.) Ordinarily he will walk down Ladbroke Grove and on to the *Elgin Arms* but today he will turn left when he reaches Lansdowne Road and return home. He will not have stopped. He will not have spoken to anyone. He will not have done anything except walk once round the block. There is no hole in the pocket of his trousers.

Step 3 – I will ask my father to empty his trouser pockets again and then count the coins he gives me.

Step 4 – I will ask him to check his pockets carefully and count the change again.

The result is this. The value of the loose change in my father's pocket will be nineteen shillings and sixpence. (On some days it will be a few pennies less.) How can this be true? There's no explanation except that there is a magic about money, and my father's talent was to make it disappear.

* * *

A more practical proof if one is needed.

On Sunday evenings we play Monopoly. It's a weekly ritual. After supper we sit at the table with the unsteady extendible leg, the warped flap and the peeling veneer. I set up the board and sort out the property cards. My mother, who is always the banker, counts out the money. My father (getting into the part?) lights a noisome cigarillo and sits thinking.

Each week he tries a new tactic: to buy every property he lands on, to buy no property at all, to buy only the cheapest properties in the vicinity of Old Kent Road, to restrict himself to Mayfair and its environs. Some weeks he buys stations and utilities, other weeks he invests everything in houses and hotels. It is odd how seriously he takes a game that he dismisses as being no more than a matter of luck. It's true that he seldom passes Go or collects £200, that he lands in gaol when he doesn't want to and fails to find sanctuary there when he does, that he is forced to pay tiresome fines and supertax, and that finally he finds himself facing a demand for rent that he cannot possibly pay. All this is true, but there must be more to it than luck.

Two hundred million sets of Monopoly have been sold in eighty countries and there are estimated to be 500 million players of the game. I contend that no one has ever lost at Monopoly as consistently as my father.

Every Sunday evening, the three of us – my father, my mother and I – sitting at the table with the unsteady leg. In just under an hour there are two of us – my mother and I. My father has gone to bed. Bankrupt.

* * *

Even at the height of my father's success, my grandmother distrusted the theatre. It's not hard to see why she hoped her son would choose a steadier profession. When wicked Uncle Jack's disgraceful conduct forced my grandfather to leave London, Bob Ridley was abandoning a promising career at the London Polytechnic and embarking on a new life in Bath where he knew no one; but his optimism and resilience were rewarded so that, by the time of my father's birth, he was well established in the city and his future looked bright.

My father was doing very well for himself. To his nightly classes at the YMCA he had added appointments at Bath College, Bath Grammar School, Bath Secondary School and the School at Bruton. In addition to this, he managed to find time to give fencing and boxing lessons to private pupils and was probably earning as much as seven to ten pounds a week which in those days, was wealth indeed. We had moved into a pleasant semi-detached villa in the peaceful valley of Widcombe. Then came disaster of such magnitude, and so unexpected, that it seemed an impossibility.

There was little public transport at the beginning of the century and my father made his long journeys over the high hills of Bath, between schools and pupils, either on foot or by push-bike, and such was his amazing vitality that he saw no danger in working at top physical pressure for as much as sixteen hours a day. A neglected chill was followed by rheumatic fever. For many weeks his life was in the balance and, during convalescence, his doctor told him what my mother already knew. He had contracted valvular disease of the heart and would never work again – at least, not as an athlete or in any capacity that involved physical energy.

What was to be done? There was no welfare state in those days. Illness not only meant loss of earnings but the heavy expense of doctors and medicines. Savings had been spent. My father's health had gone and also his means of livelihood. He had a delicate wife and a young child to support. It was a situation that could be faced only by the bravest of men. He faced it.

Ever optimistic, he decided to go into business and open a sports shop, confident that he would receive the support of his many friends in Bath. Eventually premises were found in Manvers Street just opposite what was then the Great Western Railway station. The dismal empty shop had a sinister reputation. Three previous occupants had

131

gone bankrupt and the last one had departed in such haste that he had
left a few miserable relics of his stock to bear witness of his failure. The
shop stood in a gaunt and grim house reputed to have been occupied by
Isambard Kingdom Brunel during the extension of the Great Western
Railway from Bath to Bristol – four floors, steep stairs, no bathroom
and a dark underground kitchen liable to flooding when the nearby
Avon was in winter spate. The pretty villa in Lyncombe Vale was sold
and, after the payment of debts accumulated during his illness, my
father was left with a bare £100 to stock his shop.

Life began anew. My father was able to retain a part-time
appointment at Bath Secondary School and my mother decided to take
in lodgers. At one time she had seven! After a terrifyingly slow start,
the sports business entered a period of minor prosperity.

My grandmother remained acutely anxious about money for the
rest of her life and my father's changes of fortune did nothing to calm
her fears. In her later years she relied on the advice of her lodger, Mr
Harper, in financial matters. This amused and irritated my father in
equal measure. Whenever the topic arose, we agreed – my father, my
mother and I – how foolish Granny was in this respect. But now I
allow myself to wonder.

* * *

With the success of *The Ghost Train* and his later plays my father was
suddenly rich. He rented rooms in London, travelled first class on the
train to Bath, ate in fashionable restaurants and took taxis – a habit he
found hard to break – but it was hardly high living.

Looking back I think the greatest pleasure I enjoyed through my
change of fortune was that of being able to send my father and mother
to the Riviera and thus enable my father, who was suffering from
cardiac asthma, to escape the cold months. I decided to holiday in
Juan-les-Pins where my father and mother were spending the winter.
My dear father – who was inclined to take my success as a playwright

more seriously than I did myself – insisted on my staying in the Provençal near the Cap d'Antibes, the only large hotel in the district. Actually, I didn't care for it much and would have preferred the modest guest-house where my parents were staying.

I find it difficult to imagine anyone less suited to wealth than my father.

Returning to Bath I became a little anxious as to my financial state. My latest play, *The Wrecker,* was still playing to good houses and *The Ghost Train* tours and foreign productions continued but it seemed to me that recently I had been spending a lot of money. During my weeks at Juan-les-Pins I had been pretty extravagant, hiring cars to take my father and mother on afternoon drives, visiting the opera at Nice and the casino at Monte Carlo. Had I been overstepping the mark?

I found a number of letters awaiting me. Amongst these was one from the manager of my bank. As there were matters needing immediate attention, would I please call and see him as soon as possible. I was quite scared and had a bad night.

In the morning, I called as requested and was admitted to his room with what appeared to me as undue haste. After a brief spell of casual conversation he got down to the point. 'The reason I've asked you to call, Mr Ridley,' he commenced, 'concerns your account. I'm rather worried about it.' 'Yes?' I murmured apprehensively. 'I really feel it's time you did something about all this money,' he continued. 'You shouldn't have a large sum like this lying idle. It should be put into some safe investment.'

Since that day I have had many discussions with a bank manager regarding my account but none of them has ended as pleasantly as this one did.

It isn't difficult to see why.

George Bernard Shaw once wrote that the playwright's job was to take money out of the theatre and never in any circumstances to put money in. I followed this advice for many years, even refusing to participate in ventures which I considered would make money, and more often than not, did ... In view of this, it must seem odd that the first time ever I put money into a show it was – at a few minutes' notice – to back a play I hadn't read. It may seem almost incredible that when I sat down in my seat prior to the rising of the curtain on the first night of *The Lord of the Manor* at the Apollo, I knew no more of the play in which I had an interest than the rest of the audience. But such was the case.

Two lines from the play might have given him a clue about what would happen: 'Nothing goes smoothly for long nowadays!' and 'You can't tell me that's a good sign!' *The Lord of the Manor* closed after four weeks. But although he lost his money, it was a relatively small amount and his continuing West End success spared him any financial embarrassment.

However, having broken his rule never to invest in the theatre once, it seems to have been easier to break it again and to invest in films where the risks and the sums involved were both much higher.

Around 5.30 on an evening in December 1938 I was directing a film at the Sound City Film Studios, Shepperton, and feeling pretty pleased with myself. It was very much a one-man show for, not only was I directing, I had also written the story and the script myself. This was my second excursion into film production and direction. The first had achieved minor success and my partner and I had got our money back and made a small profit.

The film now being made involved a far greater outlay of capital but we were batting on a good wicket. We had an excellent distribution contract and had arranged sound backing from a firm of highly reputed brokers. The only snag was studio time. Studios had to be booked in advance. This meant beginning filming two weeks before the start of our contract, with our own money and credit. Now we were in sight of being in the clear. In two days' time our contract would become operative, the city brokers would release the money required and I would receive payment for a large sum of money due to me for my story and services. Everything seemed set fair.

I was lining up a last shot and consequently was a little annoyed when my personal assistant appeared on the set and told me I was to phone our office in Jermyn Street at once. Still pretty irritated, I went to our studio production office and dialled the number. 'Why am I being called off the floor in the middle of a shot?' I demanded. My partner's voice was quiet but grave. 'Because you're to close down everything right away. Our distribution company has gone broke for several hundred thousand.' 'It can't be true!' I gasped. 'It can and it is!' he said and the phone went dead.

The outbreak of war in 1939 meant that my father had no time to put things right. He was advised to go bankrupt but that wasn't something he could bring himself to do. Over many years he paid off his creditors until only the Inland Revenue – relentless, insatiable, implacable – remained.

* * *

It's an odd conclusion but what was probably my father's costliest financial decision was, at the time he made it, the right one. After two failed provincial tours, with the company disbanded and the scenery sold, *The Ghost Train* had ground to a halt and there was no reason to believe that it would ever run again.

It was at this juncture that Messrs Samuel French offered me £200 for the amateur rights of the play. I accepted the offer, thereby sacrificing many, many thousands of pounds. Numerous people have tried to stir me into a sense of grievance over this but I positively refuse to have one. It was a perfectly straightforward proposition. The play had failed and the chances of it going on in the West End were nil – and I badly needed the money. In fact, I was lucky. Had Samuel French offered me £500 for the entire world rights, I should have accepted joyfully.

For 'many, many thousands of pounds' may be safely read 'many hundreds of thousands of pounds'; maybe more. *The Ghost Train* is still performed by amateur theatre companies all over world – the play is said to be staged somewhere every night of the year – and royalties from the play would have transformed my father's and mother's life together. But throughout his periods of financial despair my father remained steadfastly philosophical about his decision. He could not have foreseen the success of *The Ghost Train*, he insisted, and the decision was the right one. He refused to regret it and that, he said, was that.

* * *

My mother didn't marry my father for his money. When they met, he had none and it didn't matter. At the time she was no more interested in money than he had been although, coming from a different social background, she may not have known quite what it meant to have no money at all. During the war there were other things to worry about and my mother's concern was more for the present than the future. Later, when the practical realities of income and expenditure showed themselves more starkly, her thoughts would turn to the past.

My mother was a strong woman but she had a weakness for regret. If only things had been different. If only she'd met my father before he lost his money. If only he had not invested in films. If only he had not sold the amateur rights of *The Ghost Train*. If only. An unprofitable lament that provided neither of us with any comfort.

I must have been very young when my mother started discussing money with me. She talked to me because she couldn't talk to my father. She knew that talking to him would increase his anxiety and make him wretched. She needed to share her worries with someone else and I was all she had. In moments of particular desperation she would say, 'Sufficient unto the day (pause) is the evil thereof.' I didn't know what this meant – I'm not sure I know what it means now – and it brought her precious little comfort. I wasn't aware we lacked very much. We seemed to have most of what we needed. But I had a sense that nothing that we had was properly ours and that it could all be taken away. With my mother, I began to worry about money. And it didn't stop.

I remain financially timid. I imagine the worst. At times of self-dramatisation I see myself wrapped in old newspapers on Hampstead Heath. If ever I am asked to explain my fears, I relate the story of the bailiffs' visit.

*   *   *

Hammersmith, London W14.

We have left behind the sunlight and space of Notting Hill Gate and are now imprisoned in the gloom of a Victorian mansion flat opposite Olympia. It is not a happy time.

The doorbell rings and two large men in light brown coats announce themselves. They walk round the flat taking notes while my mother and I follow meekly behind. We are both aware that, humiliatingly, my father is hiding in the cupboard in his bedroom. The bailiffs take their leave and, on this occasion, nothing else.

My story generally arouses some sympathy which is, after all, its purpose. But did it really happen? Did the bailiffs come to 23 Palace Mansions or did I imagine it? I can see the cupboard where my father is hiding. It's empty except for the linen jacket that he wore in the summer which hangs limply on a peg. Could he have fitted into the cupboard? I try to see it but the picture won't form. It's unimportant. The truth is that there was never anywhere for us to hide. Our money worries sought us out like the dust and fumes from the Hammersmith Road that seeped through the windows and begrimed our lives.

*   *   *

A true story: fiction.

Among my father's papers is a bleak short story based on his personal experience. It features a man who has fallen on hard times and, after much agonised deliberation, contacts a wealthy friend hoping he will offer him some financial assistance. The friend is delighted to hear from him and at once invites him to lunch. The restaurant that the friend chooses is hideously expensive. The man cannot taste the food. He is terrified that somehow he will find himself being asked to pay for the meal. But the friend is full of delicacy and understanding and, before ordering a brandy for each of them, insists that this is his treat. The man takes the opportunity to broach the subject of his financial embarrassment but the friend stops him short. There is nothing to worry about, he assures him. He understands perfectly. Everything is in hand. Relieved, the man enjoys his brandy and permits himself to accept a second. The friend suddenly remembers that he is late for his next appointment. There is another agonising moment when the man wonders if his friend will remember to pay the bill. He does. He then hands over an envelope with a no-need-to-thank-me smile and is gone. The man postpones opening the envelope until he is outside the restaurant. When he does, he finds in it a single five pound note – a fraction of the cost of the meal. The shock is appalling. The man in the story finds the nearest pub and spends the five pounds drowning his humiliation.

* * *

A true story: fact.

I have no reason to doubt this story except that it seems so improbable. When he was at his lowest ebb financially, my father received a brown paper parcel in the post. He wasn't expecting anything except perhaps the return of a hat that he'd left in a railway carriage, but even in those dark days my father had enough hats and he set the parcel aside. It was a few days later when he finally opened it to find that it was filled with banknotes to the value of several hundred pounds. He never discovered where the parcel came from. It was, he said, a godsend.

* * *

A last story: part fiction, part fact.

While on tour together in the early days of their marriage, my father and mother visited a second-hand bookshop in Cambridge. There they came across an old account-book. Its delicate pages and careful entries attracted them and they bought it. Taking it back to their digs they discovered that the entries in the account-book painted a detailed picture of a young man's life. From his accounts it is clear that he is careful and conscientious; he spends his money sensibly and saves regularly. Late in the book there is an entry showing that he has bought a motorbike. This is what he has been saving for each week. The entries continue with regular amounts entered for petrol. A few weeks later there are no more entries. Blank pages remain at the end of the book. My parents' assumption was that the young man had been killed while riding his motorcycle. A melancholy story which touched them both.

Looking through my parents' papers, I wondered if I would find the young man's account-book among them. I didn't. Instead I found my father's account-books again.

* * *

Pounds, shillings, pence. Twelve pence to the shilling. Twenty shillings to the pound. A little exercise. I try adding up my father's figures, but I find I can't. My totals are wrong. It's not as easy as I thought. Where have I gone wrong? I try again but my totals still don't match my father's. These aren't additions that can be easily checked with a decimal calculator. I add the pence and divide by twelve. I add the shillings and divide by twenty. Finally I realise. My father's totals are wrong. Not all, but most of them. I see him again, steadily running his finger down the columns, adding up the figures in his head. A knack he had inherited from his father. But maybe not.

Money is puzzling. Money is magic. It poses complex questions. But sometimes the answer stares you in the face. My father wasn't good with money.

NEW THEATRE

London: The WYNDHAM THEATRES, Ltd.   Licensee: Lady WYNDHAM (Miss Mary Moore)

EVENINGS at 8-30.   MATINEES: Wednesday and Saturday at 2-30

By arrangement with Miss MARY MOORE
E. J. CARROLL and HARRY I. COHEN

present

THE

WRECKER

(ANOTHER TRAIN MYSTERY)

By ARNOLD RIDLEY
AUTHOR of "THE GHOST TRAIN"
and BERNARD MERIVALE

G. H. MULCASTER

GEORGE ELTON   JULIAN ROYCE   KENETH KENT
EDNA DAVIES

Play Produced by SEWELL COLLINS

"Twice as good as 'The Ghost Train'"

DAILY MAIL—25th October, 1927.

CHAPTER SIXTEEN

Smart Alec, poor fish

'Bernard Merivale.' Whenever my father spoke his name, he smiled. 'Bernard Merivale.' A pleasing name. A lost smile.

> Bernard's gravity of manner was a most useful asset to him when planning a practical joke. He once induced me to enter a surgical appliances shop in the Strand with him. Unknown to me, he took the assistant in charge aside and imparted the whispered information that I was shortly to suffer an amputation of a leg and desired to inspect a false one in advance of the operation. I was much puzzled when the assistant approached me and, bowing sympathetically, asked which leg it was that I required, right or left?

I lose count of the times my father tells the story. It isn't helped by the fact that he begins chuckling as he starts to tell it. I don't find it funny; I don't laugh; I seethe with teenage irritation. I can't see the point of the story; I find practical jokes ridiculous and can't imagine my father enjoying them.

'Bernard Merivale,' he begins again, 'was a wonderful raconteur with a fund of splendid stories. The great joy with all Bernard's stories was that he was always the "poor fish" and never the "smart Alec".' (The 'smart Alec' was a regular member of life's cast of characters that my father would do everything in his power to avoid.)

'A typical story of Bernard's was the time that he rushed in late to a wedding party. Seeing a group of guests standing round in a solemn circle, he shouted out gaily, "Why are we all so gloomy? Anyone would think that someone's dropped down dead!" It was then that he saw the bride's father lying on the floor!'

My mother had the actor's knack of appearing to listen while her mind was elsewhere. It also helped that she was slightly deaf. Bernard Merivale meant as little to her as he did to me. He was from another era; a time when my father had been in many respects quite different from the man she met and married.

* * *

For more than ten years Bernard Merivale was my father's literary agent, collaborator and close friend. It was a happy, fruitful partnership based on trust and affection. They wrote plays, scripts and stories, working so harmoniously together that afterwards neither could remember who had written what. It was Bernard who, following the success of *The Ghost Train*, suggested the idea for a second railway play, *The Wrecker*.

It was a troublesome production. The director, an American, who barely rehearsed the third act and was sacked after the first night, appeared to have no experience of the comedy-thriller genre and 'was desperately anxious to cut any line or situation intended to raise a laugh'. The rehearsals went badly and the technical effects were calamitous.

When *The Wrecker* opened at the Theatre Royal, Brighton, on a Monday night it was, as my father had feared, a shambles. 'Lights went on and off in the wrong places, bells sounded when they weren't required, doors stuck and couldn't be opened and what happened in the signal cabin defies description.' But, mercifully, at the final curtain the audience applauded and disaster was avoided.

It could have been so much worse.

Just before the start of the evening, Bernard Merivale and I discovered, to our horror, that William Pollock – then the drama critic of the *Daily Mail* and a man whose opinion mattered considerably in the theatre world – had come down from London to report on the opening. Bernard dealt with the matter in characteristic style. He met Bill Pollock in the foyer, dragged him off to the circle bar and succeeded in keeping him there for almost the entire evening, by which time Pollock was in a condition best described as 'a bit of a state'. In fact he was in such a state that he was glad to agree to Bernard's offer to phone through his notice to Fleet Street on his behalf. As could be expected in the circumstances, the notice that appeared under Pollock's name was magnificent. The opening line was, 'Let me put on record that *The Wrecker* is twice as good as *The Ghost Train*' – a slogan that was used for the entire run of the play.

* * *

Bernard Merivale was an accomplished master of the shadowy arts of influence; my father, by contrast, was his poor apprentice.

Recipe for Murder opened at The Theatre Royal, Glasgow, early in November. Just before the Sunday night dress rehearsal, I was told that I was wanted at the stage door. The visitor was a young man who introduced himself as the drama critic of the Scottish edition of a national morning paper. He asked if I could possibly allow him to attend the dress rehearsal of the play instead of the first performance. The Monday night opening clashed with his Old Boys' dinner and dance which he was most anxious to attend.

It didn't take me long to realise that I had a choice between two evils. If I allowed him in to the dress rehearsal, he would see a performance which might be full of bungles and hold-ups. On the other hand, if I refused him entry, he would be obliged to miss his highly-prized social engagement and, at the first performance, would be in a hostile frame of mind. I accepted what I thought was the lesser of two evils and let him in.

Actually the dress rehearsal didn't go too badly although, as I had expected, there were several delays. At curtain fall of the second act, the young critic approached me again and asked how long I thought it would be before the rehearsal ended. I said I hoped it wouldn't be too long but couldn't be sure. Certain scenes might have to be run through again on account of technical difficulties. He then said that he

143

was awkwardly placed as the last train to take him home left in twenty minutes' time. He supposed he would have to book in at a hotel for the night.

I quite thought I was pulling a Bernard Merivale masterstroke when I told him that, as he had seen the first two acts of the play – which he said he had enjoyed very much – and now knew what sort of a show it was, there was really no need for him to hang on for the third. 'I've had enough experience of this sort of play,' I told him, 'to know that the third act is usually a lot of bunk with everybody going round and round suspecting everybody else until it is finally discovered that the crime has been committed by the only unsuspected character, or that a crime hasn't been committed at all!' He seemed very pleased. 'You're sure you don't mind if I push off?' he enquired. 'Of course not,' I replied. 'Hurry up and catch your train and I hope you have a pleasant evening tomorrow.'

On the Tuesday morning I read his notice which appeared under the heading, 'Thriller spoilt by feeble last act'. The first two acts, he wrote, had been very good and then quoted me word for word concerning the third act which he hadn't seen!

* * *

'Bernard Merivale.' The name, the smile. Older and more worldly-wise, he seems to have introduced into my father's life a sense of fun and mischief that previously had been entirely missing; and which, after Bernard's premature death in May 1939, could not be recovered.

144

CHAPTER SEVENTEEN

Stage fright

We were all agreed – my mother, my father and I – that while the damage done to my father's confidence by Esme Filmer at Birmingham was a blow, the event that cut short my mother's stage career was a tragedy.

My father, we knew, was a competent actor but my mother was indisputably a star. She had that indefinable quality that sets an actor apart. As the theatrical saying has it, the lights went up when she came on stage. Long after her return to the West End theatre was aborted, she remained a leading actress.

It's only now that I find myself asking the question. Did we all – my mother, my father and I – underestimate my father's acting talents?

* * *

I arrived back in London shortly before D-day, heard that there was to be an audition for the Old Vic season which was soon to open with Laurence Olivier and Ralph Richardson sharing leads, went down to the Lyric Theatre, Hammersmith, where the audition was taking place and more or less 'gate-crashed'. I recited one scene only – the Prologue to the old mystery play, *Everyman*. I came away in high spirits. I had been offered three excellent parts in the Old Vic Company. Rehearsals for the season didn't commence until the middle of the week following my engagement and so I went down to my Caterham cottage to study my parts.

So much had happened. The collapse of his film company and financial ruin. The horrific evacuation from a beachhead in France.

A wearisome ENSA tour taking *The Ghost Train* to camps, garrisons and airfields throughout the British Isles. And now a new beginning.

I don't know if it would be fair to describe myself as accident-prone but I succeeded in being laid low by a flying bomb before I even knew that such weapons had been invented – in fact had I known of their existence I probably wouldn't have been injured.

One morning in June I woke at about 6.00 a.m. and got up to make myself a cup of tea. It was dull, misty and a slight drizzle was falling. I was just pouring boiling water into the teapot when I heard a rather unfamiliar noise and went out into the garden to investigate. There was a very odd-shaped aircraft hovering overhead which suddenly dived over the roof of the cottage as if it had been shot down. If I'd stayed where I was I should have been perfectly all right. I didn't. I ran round the thick protecting walls to see what was happening. The next thing I knew I was waking up at the base of an apple tree into which I had been blasted. I got up, went back to the cottage – in which not even a window had been broken – and found that my tea was stone cold. I must have been 'out' for some time. However, I seemed to have escaped serious injury although I was pretty sure I'd cracked a couple of ribs. But the pain wasn't acute and I decided there was no cause for alarm.

I returned to London on Monday, attended a costume measurement and commenced rehearsing in the basement of the National Gallery on Wednesday. On Thursday morning we started our first run through of *Peer Gynt* in which production Ralph Richardson was playing the name part.

I was just starting a short speech when, to my amazement, I found that I couldn't speak. Tyrone Guthrie, the director, asked what was the matter but I could only reply in inarticulate sounds and was trembling violently all over. The strange thing was that there were no bombs falling at that time and in any case we were in a place of comparative safety. Guthrie was most kind and suggested I should stop rehearsing for the day. Actually there wasn't much point in doing otherwise.

I crossed Trafalgar Square to the Savage Club with my nerve completely gone. The Savage Club steward took me down to the basement flat and sent for a doctor who, after careful examination, told me that the jelly in my spinal column had been badly jarred by the explosion that had blasted me into the apple tree and that I was suffering from delayed shock and spinal concussion.

A doctor in Bath confirmed this diagnosis and said that recovery would probably be delayed for weeks if not months; he wrote to the Old Vic to inform them that there was no possibility of my being able to open. It was a bitter blow.

From Bath I went to stay with friends in the Potteries. My speech was beginning to improve but I was still in a highly nervous state, hating being left alone and unable to cross a street unaccompanied. So, when I received an offer to join the White Rose Players at Harrogate for six weeks to play leading parts, I felt uncertain about accepting. However, I decided that being forced to do something might result in my pulling myself together and I set off for Yorkshire.

I was in pretty poor shape when I arrived in Harrogate, still finding slight difficulty with my speech and possessed by a terrible anxiety about my memory. Had it been damaged permanently? Would I be able to learn and remember words? Would I have black-outs and stand, a speechless figure of ridicule, unable to take a prompt?

* * *

The ghost of an actor walks round a rose garden in Harrogate. He is there in all weathers, his book in his hand. He sees nothing and what he hears is in his head. This is my father learning his lines. He said he would return in the afterlife to his Harrogate rose garden. A peaceful spirit, disturbing no one, describing his circle, mastering his part.

* * *

My father went to Harrogate for six weeks and stayed for eighteen months. During this period he played fifty-three parts. Harrogate was, as he described it, 'a comfortable engagement'. It was also exceptionally hard work. The cast of a weekly repertory company played one part in the evening, rehearsed the next week's part during the day and between times learnt the part for the week after that.

During my stay at Harrogate, I lived entirely in accordance with a timetable that I drew up for myself. I got up at seven and, after a cup of tea, studied until nine – nearly always out-of-doors. I bought a stout waterproof, a sou'wester and, whatever the state of the weather, strode around and around a nearby rose garden, learning lines. This enabled me to combine exercise with study. Breakfast was at nine followed by letter-writing, personal chores and more study. I left for the Opera House at 09.55 for the ten o'clock rehearsal. During the ten-minute coffee break at noon, I partook of a pint of beer – never more – at a local public house. Rehearsals ended at two. I had a snack lunch at a café opposite the stage door and went home to lie down and sleep. Tea was served to me at quarter to five, after which I studied for another two hours either circling the rose garden or walking on The Stray. When the curtain fell – usually about ten – I called it a day, walked over to my club, and drank a couple of pints, usually while playing a game of billiards or snooker. I left the club when the bar closed at eleven, went home to my main meal of the day, read the evening paper and was asleep within minutes. I adhered to this way of life strictly. Even on my wedding day, I studied and rehearsed in the morning and played a leading part at the Opera House the same night.

* * *

A later incident at Harrogate illustrates how an actor who is word perfect can still find himself unable to speak.

At lunch I swallowed a small bone which lodged in my windpipe causing continuous retching and coughing of the most unpleasant nature. A doctor diagnosed that, however disagreeable my state might be, I was in no danger of suffocation and sent me off to an eminent throat specialist, resident and practising in Harrogate. On arrival I learnt that the specialist was absent in Leeds performing an operation and that nobody knew the time of his return. I decided to stay put. In fact there was little else I could do.

The specialist arrived back shortly after five o'clock and I spent a very unhappy session with him until about six o'clock when he succeeded in removing the obstacle. 'Now listen carefully,' he said. 'This long delay has resulted in your throat getting into a really frightful state. You are to buy a slate and, for the next three days at least, write everything down. Then you're to come and see me again. In the meantime, you're not to speak a single word. Understand?' 'Quite,' I whispered, 'but I've got to play the lead at the Opera House at half past seven.' The specialist warned me that I was running a serious risk of the permanent loss of my voice and rang the theatre to inform the manager that I was appearing in defiance of medical advice and insisting that the audience be informed.

Our manager obeyed instructions in a front of curtain speech – laying it on a bit thick, I thought – with the result that on my first entrance I was greeted with embarrassingly rapturous applause. But within minutes I was being urged by someone in the circle – possibly a latecomer who hadn't heard the announcement – to speak up! That did it. The audience in the stalls rose in anger telling him to shut up, while the interrupter in the circle continued to insist I should speak up. It was not a pleasant evening. Fortunately the specialist's dire forebodings were unfulfilled although I must confess I've had a rather unpleasant rasp in my speaking voice ever since and for many years was liable to attacks of laryngitis.

The theatre is a testing profession; television, too, has its perils.

In the early days of television I was cast for the Bear in an adaptation of the famous French drama *Noah* to be broadcast live on Sunday evening from Alexandra Palace. It was a very pleasant part with no lines to be remembered and several pleasing mime scenes.

Rehearsals went quite smoothly until the costume rehearsal when I found the bear skin heavier and tighter than I had expected and the solid bear's head which fastened round my neck needed repair.

I also found that I was not the sole occupant of the skin – there was quite a large number of smaller ones! I reported this to the wardrobe mistress who assured me that this, together with the fastenings to the head-piece, would be thoroughly dealt with prior to the evening performance. It certainly was!

I must admit that in order to shorten the period of discomfort I delayed donning the bear skin for as long as possible. When I did, it stank of some violent type of disinfectant. But before I could do anything or even protest they were fastening the head-piece around my neck. Then I knew I was really in trouble. I was breathing disinfectant instead of air and a pretty lethal disinfectant too. I staggered onto the set with perspiration pouring down my face, legs failing, sight fading and a sudden thought rising in my befuddled mind: 'I wonder how many million people are going to see me die?'

The next thing I remember is lying on a seat in a cold wind outside Alexandra Palace with a first aid nurse assuring me that everything was 'all right'.

CHAPTER EIGHTEEN

Last cast

I was the only member of the family to appear on stage during the 1951 Festival of Britain.

When I was four, my mother enrolled me in a dancing class. I can't imagine why. I am the only boy, which doesn't bother me, and I show no aptitude for dancing which I don't remember bothering me either. It may have been unfortunate that, for the performance at the Festival Hall, we are dressed in buttercup yellow and also that we are required to skip in a line from stage left to stage right. The girls are good at skipping. I am not. Which must be why I am the last in line. We wait among the curtains and the snaking cables in the wings. And then we're on. A meadow of light, the rake of the stage, following the line of yellow tunics. My efforts at skipping must have provoked a ripple of mild amusement in the audience. I am not expecting laughter. I stop and look out beyond the footlights trying to identify its source. My expression of puzzlement and irritation produces more laughter. I don't attempt any further skipping. Instead I stare at the audience before turning on my heel and walking off the stage to a loud round of applause. I remember the applause, and I like it.

* * *

Ten years later. Half-term. My mother and I have taken the train to Bristol. We are here to spend a few days with my father who has been on tour for almost a year. It's good that he's in work but it's hard that he's not at home. Postcards, telephone calls and occasional Sundays in London aren't enough. What's so sad is that we have become used to it.

When we arrive, we are provided with complimentary tickets for the evening performance. (The management needs to fill the house.) We have seen the play several times before. The last occasion was in Blackpool where we stayed for five nights in theatrical digs, a jungle of bright plastic flowers with a painted plaster bust of the Virgin Mary on the landing. I don't want to see the play again.

I know it's irrational but in recent months I have become beset by anxieties. I feel a gnawing responsibility for the world around me and particularly for the people I love. Seeing my father on stage is now agony. What if something goes wrong? If he misses an entrance? If he fluffs his lines? I will be powerless to help. I know he plays the part every night without me but it makes no difference. I really don't want to be here.

I have tried explaining this to my mother but it's not something she understands. Yes, she says, things go wrong. Cues are missed, speeches skipped, doors jam, telephones stay silent when they should be ringing, lights come on too late or go off too soon, scenery falls down. But that's live theatre. It's what happens. Professional actors cope. They find a way through. In fact they enjoy it. The show goes on while the audience – cocooned in suspended disbelief – notices nothing. Besides, we could hardly refuse the tickets, she says.

The last scene of the first act. My father exits and I begin to relax. The actress who sits on the sofa centre stage is well-known to older members of the audience. There was a round of applause at her first entrance. The action revolves around her as younger members of the cast speak their lines. And then. A frozen moment. A missed cue. Prompt. Pause. A more audible prompt. The actress sits lifeless on the sofa. A sudden rush of energy left and right as the actors on stage take over the scene, delivering her lines, bringing the act to a close. Nearly there. Then she comes to life again. But it's a different life. She has lost her character. She recognises the lines being spoken around her. They are her lines. She wants to take them back. She interrupts. She contradicts. More energy. Frantic activity, stage left and stage right. The cast struggles through to the curtain. The audience applauds. Most have noticed nothing wrong.

An announcement at the end of the interval informs us that the actress is unwell and that an understudy will take over for the second act. There is sympathetic murmuring and light applause when the understudy – many years too young for the part – makes her first appearance. She has only recently joined the company and she exudes fear. She stumbles through the first scene but she is almost inaudible. It is clear, to me at least, that she doesn't know the lines. In the second scene – miserably, shamefully – she comes on with the book in her hand. The rest of the cast prop up her performance as best they can but the exuberance has gone and the desperation is evident. It's too wretched to watch. I can't close my eyes because this makes me more aware of the disaster that's being enacted on stage. I stare ahead blankly trying to will myself elsewhere. The play limps on to the final curtain. The audience has remained sympathetic but they are conscious of their generosity. The performance has continued with their permission. The illusion – the contract – that binds audience and players has been exposed as a fraud.

We sit in silence in my father's dressing-room while he takes off his make-up and drinks his after-show gin. Then we walk back to the digs in grim silence. It's as if we have been party to something indecent. The fear that I hoped was locked away safely in my imagination has exposed itself as an obscene reality.

* * *

I didn't see my father playing leading roles. There aren't many for elderly actors. While I was growing up, the parts he played were mostly small or very small indeed. *The Archers* (Doughy Hood, the baker), *Crossroads* (Guy Atkins, the vicar), *Coronation Street* (two brief appearances two years apart), *Carry On Girls* (Alderman Pratt), *Z Cars* ('gardener'), *The Avengers* ('elderly gent'). Not much to fill out the programme notes. But any part was better than none and often there was none. The acting profession, as I witnessed it, was a hand-to-mouth existence with great stretches of waiting. My father's agonising fear was that a time would soon come when there would be

153

no more parts and he would never work again. To his great surprise and delight this didn't happen.

*　*　*

If 'The Book' had been published, ardent fans of *Dad's Army* might have been disappointed. Fewer than three pages of the 206-page typescript relate to the series. There are no odd anecdotes or indiscreet revelations. There is nothing to titillate, fascinate or shock. There is simple gratitude.

> I learned that the BBC producer, David Croft, was planning a series
> connected with the Home Guard and I was invited to call at his office.
> He told me that there was a part that might suit me but he was a little
> worried by my age which he knew was fairly advanced. I countered that
> I was very fit and had survived two wars. David said he'd give it careful
> thought and let me know. Looking back, I'm surprised how little I
> concerned myself over the matter and it is just as well that I didn't
> realise how much was at stake and how much becoming a member of
> the cast of *Dad's Army* would change my status as an actor. Hearing
> from my agent that David had booked me for six episodes was good
> news. I received the batch of six scripts in due course and read them
> with great interest before coming to a conclusion which was as definite
> as I now know it to have been completely wrong. I was quite certain
> that Jimmy Perry and David Croft had written six quite excellent
> scripts which would delight the 'oldies' but wouldn't contain a shred
> of either humour or interest for the younger generation. How wrong I
> was, and how glad I am of it!

When I meet him forty years later, David Croft's own account of casting Private Godfrey differs little from my father's. 'Arnold first came into my orbit in the television series, *Hugh and I*. As usual, he gave a delightful performance playing a tailor and cutter with a Savile Row firm. In one scene his boss completely destroys the suit he has just completed after which Arnold says hopefully, "Otherwise satisfactory,

p left With the White Rose
ayers in Harrogate where
father played fifty-three
rts in eighteen months.
p right Playing Valentine
Twelfth Night with the
rmingham Repertory
ompany.
ove A range of poses as
oughy Hood in *The Archers*.
ght On tour with Phil
vers in *A Funny Thing
ppened on the Way
the Forum*.

My mother, my father and me, in Notting Hill Gate and Bath.

op left My father on location. 'Tell them to get on with it!' *Top right* A publicity picture f Private Godfrey for the *Dad's Army* film. *Above* The platoon between takes. A cigarette angs from his mouth, 'Godfrey is, recognisably, my father.'

A charity match at Hayfield Cricket Club, 9th August 1976. My father, 'an old cricketer, comfortable in pads and gloves', coming in to bat for the *Dad's Army* team

This Is Your life, 5th March 1976. 'My father is a true professional and perfectly happy to take part.'

Top My father's 80th birthday at the Shaftesbury Theatre on 7th January, 1976.
Bottom After the Royal Variety Performance at the London Palladium in 1975.

op left With his OBE at Buckingham Palace in 1982. *Top right* In *Jack and the Beanstalk* at
ne Theatre Royal Lincoln in 1978. *Above* With his last 'click-clicking Olivetti'.

My father at home in the sitting-room in Highgate.

My mother and father photographed in a garden, 'staged, posed, professional'.

My grandparents' grave in Bath Abbey Cemetery where my father's and mother's urns are buried.

Mr Miller?" I loved him from that moment on. When he came to see me about *Dad's Army*, Arnold was in his seventies. I told him I'd find it difficult to save him from having to trot about on occasions and asked him if he felt he could manage it. "Oh, yes," he said. "I think so." And he did.' David pauses. 'I have many happy memories of Arnold floundering around,' he says. 'There was enormous comedy to be had from the way he had to be lifted onto the back of the van and things like that. All his disabilities were an enormous advantage from the point of view of comedy. And the wonderful look of bewilderment on his face.'

A more down-to-earth version of events comes from Bill McLean who, as my father's new theatrical agent, was largely responsible for his change of fortune. 'Arnold had got a sniff of it. "There's this series coming along," he said. "It's full of old men. Keep your eye on it but whatever you do, don't lose it!" So, in agent's terms, I kept my eye on it by perpetually ringing David Croft and saying, "How far have you got?" and "There has to be a part for Arnold." As I remember it, David was very wary about using Arnold because he thought he wouldn't actually live long enough to complete the first series. *Everybody* had this impression about Arnold – that he wouldn't live long enough to complete whatever he was doing! That cuts the ground from under you a bit as an agent,' says Bill. 'Can't negotiate too hard here!' (This may explain why, for the first series, John Le Mesurier was paid £261.10s.0d per episode, Arthur Lowe and Clive Dunn £210, John Laurie £105, James Beck £78 and my father £63.)

When *Dad's Army* started, my father was seventy-two, the oldest member of the cast. While filming in a graveyard near Thetford, James Beck, who played Private Joe Walker, turned to my father, flashed his spiv's smile and said, 'Hardly worth your leaving, is it, Arnold?' A very good line, a most unhappy irony. Although he was among the youngest members of the cast, James Beck died at the age of forty-four from heart failure, renal failure and pancreatitis. The platoon was devastated but the show went on for three more series. By June 1977, when filming started again in Thetford, it was clear that this would be the last series. John Le Mesurier was suffering from cirrhosis of the liver, Arthur Lowe from narcolepsy and John Laurie from emphysema. My father, now eighty-one, was much less mobile than he had been. The writers, David Croft and Jimmy Perry, agreed that the best course was to leave the audience wanting more and bring things to a close. The final episode of *Dad's Army* was recorded on 29th July 1977 in Studio 8 at BBC Television Centre and broadcast on 13th November (Remembrance Sunday).

For some members of the cast, *Dad's Army* was a mixed blessing. John Laurie is said to have resented the fact that he would always be remembered more for playing the part of Private Frazer in a situation comedy that he faintly despised than for his long and distinguished career in film and theatre. For Ian Lavender, a highly talented actor at the start of his career, playing to perfection the part of the feeble Frank Pike meant that for many years after the series ended he would be virtually uncastable. Success can sometimes be as cruel as failure. But for my father, it was a contented, fulfilling period at the close of a long career. The final lines of 'The Book' read:

> I shall always be grateful to *Dad's Army*. One is supremely fortunate to be kept working busily amongst such comrades and true friends for ten years preceding and after one's eightieth birthday.

A happy ending? Very nearly. We will return to *Dad's Army* later. But, before that, two pantomimes.

* * *

After the 'incident at Bristol', I attended my first audition. I must have felt that a way to exorcise the terror of being a member of the audience was to join the cast. I played small parts in school productions, with the local amateurs, at university and later while working in Hong Kong. My father's advice to me was very simple. 'Try to keep out of the way of other actors and when it's your cue speak up.' I don't think I ever shone on stage.

New acquaintances have sometimes asked me if I ever considered following in my parents' footsteps and joining 'the profession'. I have a stock reply which mostly goes down well. 'I inherited some of the tricks of the trade from my parents but neither their talents nor their looks.' No one who has seen me appear on stage has ever been prompted to ask me about my theatrical ambitions.

My last part in Hong Kong was the Genie in *Aladdin*. It was, I think, the high point of a low amateur's career. I brought to the Genie a camp lisp, fluttering hand movements and a Welsh accent. The hands and lisp were an inspiration. The Welsh accent (or what the reviewer in the *South China Morning Post* invariably described as a Welsh accent) was my 'stage voice'. Its provenance puzzled me as much as anyone else but it accompanied me through a variety of parts from the Bishop of London to the Spanish Ambassador. (Had I felt a need to justify it I might have referred to a description by one of Henry Irving's contemporaries who wrote, 'His utterance was strange, often hollow, frequently staccato.')

The Genie's part had much to recommend it. Excellent entrances in a green cloak accompanied by a puff of smoke. A constant spotlight. Much more solo declamation than dialogue. Largely interchangeable lines with few cues. Memorable exits with more smoke. And finally a curtain call, on my own, with loud applause from parents and children, all the more delightful for being so richly undeserved.

But now, as always at this time of year, I am waiting in the warm winter sunshine at Kai Tak airport to catch a flight back to the winter gloom of an English Christmas. To be spent for once in Lincoln, not in London.

* * *

Dad's Army was not quite the end. My father's last engagement was to play the part of 'The King' in *Jack and the Beanstalk* in Lincoln.

My mother meets me at the railway station and we take a taxi to the theatre. Arriving at the stage door she leads me down some steps to my father's dressing-room. The steps worry me because I know from my mother's letters that my father has had a fall but, by the standards of a provincial theatre, the shabby dressing-room is comfortable enough. I take in his jacket and shapeless trousers hanging on a rail, his modest tray of make-up in front of the mirror, a folded copy of the local evening newspaper, a bottle of Gordon's gin and a tooth-mug on the shelf by the sink. My father is on stage, as he is for much of the show, but the tannoy has been turned down. Distorted dialogue, a shriek, laughter, applause. The end of a scene. My mother has been talking but jet-lag is catching up with me and I haven't been listening closely enough to realise she is trying to tell me something about my father. The door opens and a figure appears. He is dressed in a garish red costume adorned with bright buttons and brass bells. On his head is a cardboard crown. His face beneath the make-up is puffy and bruised. A line comes to me, grotesquely out of context: 'I know thee not, old man.' I am shocked beyond words by how much he has aged since I saw him twelve months ago. He greets me but his focus is on what he has to do next. Pantomime takes all his energy, mental and physical, and he has another scene before the end of the act and another act before the end of the show. I sit by the sink to keep out of the way. More laughter over the tannoy. I am trying not to weep. This is my father, the actor, playing his part. He climbs the steps again, wearing his cardboard crown.

* * *

Another dressing-room. A different theatre. Thirty years before.

My mother is playing the female lead. She has done exceptionally well to reclaim her place in the West End after the dark years of the war. It must be a matinée performance. I am two years old and we are waiting for the final curtain. My mother returns to her dressing-room, magnificent in her costume and stage make-up. My response is to burst into tears; inconsolable, insistent grief. I stand in the middle of the dressing-room and wail. My mother is distraught.

This is the afternoon she decides that, for a time, she must give up the theatre and be a mother. It's a story which she and my father tell and re-tell over the years to show how much they love me. Their intention is to assure me they will do whatever they can to make me happy and secure. They are – and remain for all their lives – completely unaware of the guilt I feel whenever I am reminded of the terrible sacrifice my mother had to make. The guilt persists throughout childhood and into adult life.

* * *

One memory fuses with another. The half hour, the quarter, five minutes, please. Beginners! The assistant stage manager's voice comes over the tannoy but there is no knock on my mother's dressing-room door. She and I are sitting together. I have a book and she is knitting. She is an understudy at the Piccadilly Theatre. She won't be playing tonight, or any night. The actress she is understudying is on stage, speaking the lines that should be my mother's. It is paid employment for a year. Not onerous you might say. But for my mother, who feels she is only fully alive when she is on stage, it is purgatory.

French's Acting Edition No. 90   4s net

YOU, MY GUESTS!

A Play

ARNOLD RIDLEY

SAMUEL FRENCH LIMITED

CHAPTER NINETEEN

Life and soul of the party

Most actors are gregarious; my father was not. He liked other people well enough and could sometimes pass for sociable, but he had limited reserves of social energy which, like many only children, he needed to refresh at frequent intervals by being alone. He didn't want to remain alone; he liked to engage with the rest of the world, but on his own terms. Above everything, he needed a ready exit.

His greatest fear was being 'tree'd'. This was a word of his own invention meaning trapped. (As with many family words, it was years before I realised it wasn't common currency.) The image is that of a cat sitting on a branch while a tiresome dog circles the base of the tree and barks unceasingly. Being 'tree'd' was for my father an ever-present threat which had to be guarded against at all times. This was why, whenever possible, he insisted on an aisle seat at the theatre or a place close to the exit in the stand so that, if he needed to leave early, he could. If, despite all his precautions, he found himself seated in the middle of a row, he would become – again in his own words – 'horse-eyed' and it would be difficult to persuade him to return to his seat after the interval. If he and my mother were there by themselves, they would both leave. If there were other members of the party – which wasn't often – he would exit alone.

'I'll be across the road in the pub,' he'd say, hurrying away before anyone could persuade him to stay. 'I'll see you after the show.'

* * *

If, as seems probable, we each have reserved for us our particular place in purgatory, my father's was a London hotel suite between the wars.

He had returned from wintering in Juan-les-Pins and was staying, as he frequently did, at Garlands Hotel when he came down with a sudden chill. This turned to pneumonia and he became very ill indeed. During the delirious stage of his illness he was attended by a nurse ('I have visions of a female in uniform subjecting me to indignities') but, once he began to recover, her place was taken by the hotel doctor who paid him daily visits.

He was efficient, shockingly expensive and the possessor of the most unfortunate bedside manner, at least as far as I was concerned. He was loud-spoken, boisterous and one of those people who seem to sustain their excess of energy by draining it from others. He would sit on my bed bouncing about and roaring with laughter at the stale joke with which he was attempting to cheer me. I remember a grave-faced hotel servant entering my bedroom one morning and announcing that the doctor had arrived. 'Tell him I don't feel well enough to see him,' I said.

Where the First World War and Spanish influenza had failed, the doctor at Garlands Hotel almost succeeded.

*　*　*

On my father's ladder of merit, 'the life and soul of the party' stood on one of the lower rungs; a rung above 'the smart Alec' perhaps but several below 'the bit of a bore' whose heart was in the right place. It didn't matter where the heart of 'the life and soul of the party' was located. It could be simple jollity that prompted him and his friends to their noisy antics; he was still impossible to forgive. 'The life and soul of the party.' I can hear the shudder in my father's voice as he utters the phrase. It was to him inconceivable that the description could be complimentary.

From this it can be gathered that my father was not, in today's parlance, 'a party animal'. It is a phrase I believe he would have adopted with grim relish to describe the occupants of the rooms on either side of his own at whichever provincial hotel he happened to be staying. These late-night revellers, whom he seemed unable to escape, invariably returned in the early hours in high spirits, their raucous laughter and discordant singing accompanying slammed doors and rattled handles, long after my father had retired to bed. In the morning my father would try to exact a measure of revenge with cheerful banging and bright clattering of his own, but I suspect this exercise was wasted and that the excesses of the night before permitted his neighbours to sleep though his protests undisturbed.

Among the party animals – if the laws of time and space had permitted it – might well have been my mother. By her own account her youth in New Zealand had been a vigorous round of dances, parties, galas and balls. The gaiety started again when she arrived 'home' in England to begin life in the West End theatre and continued through the early months of the war. Then she joined the ENSA tour of *The Ghost Train* where she met my father. After that, the partying ceased.

* * *

My father didn't mind touring, as long as the tour was measured in weeks and not months. A tour meant that he was in work and being paid. He missed his family, of course, but he wrote daily letters or postcards and telephoned us before the evening show to reassure himself that all was well. Touring also gave him an opportunity to be alone, although this wasn't always easy.

On a happy tour the company becomes a family. Each week a new town, new digs, new theatre, new audiences. They draw closer; they work and play together; they live in each other's pockets. This aspect of touring didn't suit my father at all. However much he liked individual members of the company, he had no wish to extend his family. (A wife and son were quite enough to worry about.) Inside the theatre he was fine; outside he had to tread carefully.

Which is why, at the beginning of each week, his first task was to seek out the darkest, dingiest, least welcoming pub in the town and occupy its most deserted corner for his lunchtime drink. By the middle of the week he would often find himself seated with a group of regulars because, although he had no small talk, in situations where he could relax he was able to give a very passable imitation of listening. At the end of the week the regulars would be sorry to see him go and, in a way, he might be sorry himself. But the people he met in pubs were people he could leave behind. They made no demands; they didn't pry; they left him alone.

Unlike certain members of the cast who – by an unlucky chance – might happen upon his pub and join him in his corner. 'Arnold! There you are!' Laughter, joviality, bonhomie. As soon as he could, with a show of regret, my father would announce that he had to return to his digs where he was expecting an important … But by now several conversations would be competing with each other and no one would hear him or notice his exit. Closing the door behind him, he would resolve next week to find a pub that was still darker, dingier and less welcoming.

* * *

I try to imagine how much my father would have loathed the mobile phone. Insistent ring tones and barked conversations in public places would have infuriated him. But his was a contrary world so overflowing with every kind of disturbance and obstruction that he might have scarcely noticed a new tribulation. The real reason for his loathing? The mobile phone would have denied him his best escape line.

Whatever the social occasion – a banquet, a christening, cocktails, a funeral – just before the door opened my father's last words to my mother would be, 'We won't stay long …' It tacked between a statement and a plea but whichever it was didn't matter. The door was opening and they were being admitted. 'We won't stay long …'

Amid the canapés and clink of glasses. Above the laughter and overlapping chatter. 'I'm afraid we won't be staying long …' Did anyone hear him above the noise of the party? (He didn't like raising his voice in public which is odd for an actor.) And if they did, would they have made any sense of what he was saying? At intervals through the evening – or the portion of it that he could manage –

like a fisherman tentatively casting his line, 'I'm afraid we won't be staying long. I'm expecting an important ...' While the tides of social intercourse swilled around him, lapping at his feet, washing over his head. Until he felt he'd done enough and could collect his hat and make for the door with a clear conscience.

My mother, on the other hand, would have welcomed the mobile phone. For her it would have been a godsend, a release. Whenever she had the telephone in her hand, my father hovered in the background. He didn't say anything. There was no need. Hovering was sufficient. His constant fear was that the line would be engaged when the 'important telephone call' came through. Most of my mother's conversations were therefore cut short. It must have been hugely frustrating although I don't remember her complaining. Or not very often. Did she subscribe to my father's belief in the 'important telephone call' that would bring them salvation? The West End show, the film part, the television series. Was it this shared faith that sustained them through their years of anxiety? Or did she simply accept that when the line wasn't free, my father fretted terribly?

If my mother had had a mobile, it would have been ringing constantly; friends, messages, gossip, invitations. My father's mobile meanwhile would have stayed stubbornly silent, the part that he'd hoped to be offered having been given to another middle-aged actor.

One actor in particular. Arthur Ridley.

*　*　*

As a child, it didn't strike me as odd that my father was so seldom with us on holiday or that, when he was, he joined us so briefly.

My mother might have liked his company but she realised that a houseful of children would have tested his endurance beyond bearing and that he needed time alone. And maybe she needed time when she was not alone, when she could laugh a little louder and talk a little longer than she could at home. Holidays were an opportunity to exercise her talent for fun and hilarity which for most of the year had to lie dormant.

165

My father was never conspicuously absent at family christenings, weddings or funerals because he was so seldom present. It was understood by my mother's family that 'Uncle Bear' was generally – well – somewhere else. By himself. On his own. No one minded. This is who he was and who he always had been. Which was fine.

* * *

Late in his life my father's social batteries recharged more slowly. He also began to lose the battle against encroaching guests.

For years he had successfully resisted them but my mother must have decided that the time had come to override his objections and invite people to dinner although no more than two or three at a time, which must have been a concession. My father's concessions were fewer. He would make his first appearance, gin in hand, several minutes after the guests had arrived and would expect to eat at once. At the dining-table he was a slow eater, but he didn't delay proceedings by taking any part in the conversation.

At a quarter past nine he would look at his watch; at half-past nine he would look at his watch again; at a quarter to ten he would leave the table; and at ten o'clock he would return to announce he was going to bed. Shortly after this it was not unknown for him to appear in his dressing-gown and stand at the door before my mother shooed him away.

There were guests who, unnerved by these proceedings and unconvinced by my mother's protestations that they should stay, left early. Such guests seldom returned. Others, more resilient, braved the first performance and became accustomed to the ritual.

'Good night, Arnold!' they would shout in unison from the table.

'Good night!' my mother would say firmly, and fill her guests' glasses with more of her homemade wine.

And my father, finding he had no further lines to speak, would go to bed.

* * *

Edgware, Middlesex. Many years later.

I am with Frank Williams, the Rev Timothy Farthing, the vicar from *Dad's Army*. He is telling me about the happy fortnights the cast spent filming in Norfolk.

'It was a wonderful time. Everyone enjoyed it. One of my great memories of Arnold is how devoted he and Althea were. Althea was absolutely marvellous. She would pack him into the car, drive him to the next location and produce two chairs from the boot. I can see the two of them sitting down together between shots with Althea saying, "Would you like a cup of tea, Arnold? Or a roll?"'

Listening to Frank, I begin to see it, too. A framed photograph on my mother's bookshelf. She and my father in Norfolk. The heavy tartan rug spread across their knees. The antique thermos flask leaning nearby. My father's *Daily Telegraph*; my mother's library book. Although I know she would have called him 'Bear' and offered him a 'bun'. For my mother, whether savoury or sweet, a roll was always a 'bun'.

After the day's filming and dinner at the Bell Hotel (where my father was always given a quiet room above the river and never one that overlooked the lively courtyard), the cast stayed at the table late into the night drinking and talking about this and that. But my father usually retired early to bed.

'I think Althea would have liked to stay down but she never did. She always went up with him when he wanted to go.' Frank pauses. 'I had a sense that Althea restrained her exuberance because she didn't want to eclipse him.' He pauses again. 'I was very fond of Arnold and Althea.'

French's Acting Edition. No. 2421

EASY MONEY

A COMEDY IN THREE ACTS

by

ARNOLD
RIDLEY

FIVE SHILLINGS
NET

SAMUEL FRENCH LIMITED

CHAPTER TWENTY

Even odds

For those of us who accept it, 'luck' is more than chance and less than destiny. Luck doesn't rule our lives but it alters them. It can frustrate or reward us, and there is no reasoning with it.

My mother had a rabbit's foot for luck. She kept it in a black tin box with her stage make-up. Although, as I try to picture it, I realise the 'foot' could have been any part of a rabbit, or any part of another animal, or no part of any animal at all. It was a dark, disagreeable, misshapen object with a covering of what must once have been fur, and it smelled of stale face powder. As a child, I was repelled by the rabbit's foot and refused all invitations to touch it. I'm not sure that the rabbit's foot brought my mother any luck but I don't think she expected any; she didn't have much time for 'luck'. However, actors are supposed to be superstitious and her rabbit's foot was therefore an essential prop.

My father believed in luck, both good and bad; and there are plentiful references to both throughout 'The Book'. On the mantelpiece in his bedroom he kept a china dog and a plaster cat while the oddly upholstered figure of Tim 'sat' on his mahogany chest of drawers. The dog had been his father's and the cat was his. Their names were, respectively, 'Dog' and 'Cat', which is a mystery because my father was a master of names and naming. The only explanation I can offer is that these were not their 'particular' names. Whether their true names were known to my father, I can't tell. And Cat and Dog say nothing. They sit with me here while I write; venerated, silent, omniscient. Tim isn't present. But I will return to Tim later.

* * *

My father felt he was most unlucky to have been born on January 7th. Children with birthdays close to Christmas run the risk of receiving one present instead of two. The least material of men, he nonetheless recalled this small injustice every year while he fumbled with sticky tape and wrapping paper – socks and handkerchiefs again because he could never think of anything he wanted – and insisted that he was too old for birthdays.

A particular injustice applies to children born on the day after Epiphany. Every year, my father remembered, the Christmas decorations were 'torn down' (not 'taken down' but 'torn down', with a measure of energy and glee) on the night before his birthday. The celebrations are over at last. The New Year can begin. But – what a nuisance! – tomorrow is Arnold's birthday. Could the decorations not stay up for one more day? No, they must come down on Twelfth Night or risk bad luck for the rest of the year.

* * *

My father's life was truly remarkable for its many ups and downs. He was not, I believe, lucky or unlucky more often than other people, but he may have been luckier and unluckier to a greater degree. By the time I was born, it could be said that he had used up a great proportion of the good luck in his life which meant that bad luck was in the ascendant through most of my childhood. His last modestly successful play, *Easy Money*, was produced in 1947, the year I was born. His later plays either failed or were not produced at all.

As a child, I remember the bright excitement surrounding two first nights: *Happy Holiday*, an improbable musical based on *The Ghost Train*, produced in 1954; and *Tabitha*, produced in 1955, a play that centred on the shocking poisoning of a cat. To my huge disappointment I was judged too young to attend the first night of either *Happy Holiday* or *Tabitha*. Tim, who it's true was much older than me, went instead, dressed in a dinner jacket (but no trousers) and a black bow tie sewn specially for him by my mother. He brought no luck to either of these productions.

With their failure, my father was forced to rely solely on acting for a living.

There are some middle-aged actors who are always in work, or so it seems. On radio, on television, in films. Their names appear towards the bottom of the cast list; a succession of anonymous parts that pay the bills. But for my father getting cast wasn't easy. Auditions he heard about too late; important telephone calls he missed; parts that should have been his but which went instead to other middle-aged actors. And one middle-aged in particular. Arthur Ridley. He didn't blame Arthur Ridley personally. Far from it. Arthur Ridley was a mild-mannered, working actor and may well have been among the misty figures we greeted amicably at rugby grounds on winter afternoons. But – and here my father would utter expressions of exasperated disbelief – Arthur Ridley was never out of work.

The explanation, my father said, was simple. The names 'Arthur' and 'Arnold' are easily muddled. A producer wanting 'a middle-aged gent' might as easily cast Arthur as Arnold. Which? (That is if anyone remembers that they are not in fact one and the same actor.) 'Arthur' is a name that springs more readily to mind. Yes, Arthur. Cast Arthur. Or, if you remember that there are two of them but can't remember which is which, or, if the part is so small that either will do, toss a coin. Arthur or Arnold? Arthur. Again!

* * *

Nobody can ever accuse me of being a compulsive gambler. I've never been interested in horse-racing, never played poker and, although I visited the casino at Monte Carlo quite a bit in the early 30s, it was merely as a spectator. I suppose my lack of enthusiasm is due to the fact that I experience more chagrin at losing money than joy at winning it.

But betting and gambling are not the same. My father may not have been 'a compulsive gambler' but this doesn't mean he didn't bet. During the war he would place bets on my mother, and on tour in the provinces he would bet on himself.

Wartime ENSA performances for the troops were usually followed by more entertainment in the mess. Entertainment mostly meant drinking with officers, or others, who had formed part of the audience. Each mess would have its champion whose proud boast was the speed with which he could swallow a pint of light ale. Many of these champions were 'pourers' who, through some freak of anatomy, were able to empty a pint down their throats without swallowing. Although my mother was not a 'pourer' (which both my father and my mother felt was certainly to her credit), she was a most prodigious swallower and – for a reason that was never entirely explained but may have been as simple as the diameter of her throat – my mother was able to swallow faster than any 'pourer' could pour. Before each nightly competition my father would – with very little show – move quietly among the champion's supporters accepting bets with the resigned demeanour of someone who felt he was likely to lose. My mother remained unbeaten throughout the war; my father was most grateful for his winnings.

The art of the confidence trickster is to set the scene without appearing to be the prime mover. My father had mastered this art. Although he didn't rate himself very highly as an actor, he had a range of well-practised stage skills. One of these was his ability to exit and – when he wished – to win a round of applause. Some nights he would exit with a round, some nights without, until the time came when some younger members of the company would offer to place bets on whether or not he would win a round that night. If they bet he wouldn't, he did. If they bet he would, he didn't. Members of the cast might try to upstage him at critical moments but an almost imperceptible pause would win him the round he required. The next night, his fellow players would fix their eyes on him as he moved upstage leaving a yawning chasm of silence after his exit, but somehow he contrived to be gone before anyone noticed and the audience stayed silent.

The money my father won in this way was a cause of quiet satisfaction.

* * *

'When we win the football pools ...'

It was my mother's refrain. An expression of dreams. The things she would like to do; the things she would like to have done. 'When we win the football pools ...' Words of wistful, distant defiance. It was not as if she believed she would ever win. Many weeks she failed to post her coupon, either because she forgot or she didn't have five shillings for the postal order. But my father completed and despatched his coupon religiously.

Ever since they started I've regularly participated in the football pools. I've never thought that any knowledge of professional soccer had anything to do with it. I've always regarded it as a form of state lottery in which the numbers are just as likely to come to you as you are to find them, and sending in the same ones each week saves a lot of trouble. I always felt that, having written a successful play about the pools, it was inevitable that my luck would continue and I should win myself. And so I did!

The play is *Easy Money*, a pleasing, well-constructed comedy with plot points that rattle about like dice in a beaker. Has the Stafford family won the football pools or not? Elation when they think they have; despair when it seems the coupon wasn't posted. After three acts of suburban tumult, calm is restored when it's discovered that the coupon that wasn't posted was last week's and not this. 'Well, this is a happy ending,' says Philip Stafford. 'No more money worries for a bit.'

My father's story was more complicated.

It couldn't have been at a better time for, financially, I was really terribly hard up and very worried about my bank overdraft and an income tax demand. Everything I'd touched had gone wrong. My radio appearances as Doughy Hood in *The Archers* had become very few; *Happy Holiday*, the musical version of *The Ghost Train* had had a disappointingly short run at the Palace Theatre and it had been the same with my latest play, *Tabitha*, at the Duchess. Every blessed thing

I touched seemed to go wrong and to say that I was in need of a break would have been a profound understatement. Then came that break.

On a Saturday night in the mid-60s I checked my coupon copy with the evening paper and found that I had an all correct column of eight draws. But there were a number of them that week and it wasn't till Sunday morning that I discovered that quite a lot of these drawn matches weren't on the coupon and that my dividend would be well over £1,000 which was quite a big sum in those days. I wired off my claim to the pools people. I faced the fact that my claim might not be accepted – I might have made a mistake on the coupon or it might have been lost in the post. There was nothing to be done except wait. So it was probably just as well that Monday was a busy day.

He recorded an episode of *The Archers* in Birmingham and then went on for a medical examination in Edgbaston. At the last minute he had been offered a small part in a film being shot the next day on location in Sheffield but this was dependent on a satisfactory doctor's report. It was therefore very worrying to find that his blood pressure was exceptionally high, but the doctor and he agreed that this was probably due to his anxiety about the football pools and that he should return later in the evening when he had had more news.

On leaving the doctor I dived into a telephone kiosk and phoned my wife. Yes, there was good news for me! A representative of the pools company had called, my winning coupon had been received safely, the dividend was between £1,250 and £1,500 – by no means a terrific sum but it would help me considerably in the situation at the time – and I should receive my cheque on Thursday evening. I revisited my kind doctor and was able to provide him with an interesting case of the ill effects of anxiety. My blood pressure was now perfectly normal!

For the next few days he played the part of a shirt-sleeved pigeon-fancier on the edge of a moor in a bitterly cold wind with driving squalls of sleet.

On Wednesday of that week I wrote to my bank manager promising a reduction in my overdraft and to my income tax collector promising a small payment on my return to London. And on the Thursday I phoned home again to confirm that my cheque had arrived from Liverpool. It hadn't. Neither had it come on Friday. Or Saturday. Before leaving Sheffield I telegraphed the pools promoters and on arriving in London the answer was awaiting me. The cheque had been sent to me on Wednesday and the matter would be investigated. After that – silence.

This was very worrying. Not only was I short of the cheque but the pools promoters protect themselves and when one signs a coupon one agrees that on all issues the decision of the promoters is final and with my usual impetuosity I'd promised a reduction in my bank overdraft and a payment of income tax. My situation was not a pleasant one but it remained unchanged for an entire fortnight. Then the missing cheque arrived. By then I felt I'd really earned it!

No vintage champagne. No celebrations of any kind. A payment to the bank manager and another to the collector of taxes. Back to the business of life.

And now? Put yourself in my father's place. For days he has been agonising over whether or not the cheque will arrive. Now it has. Not a large cheque, it's true, but the fact remains that he has won the football pools. After winning once, what are the chances of winning again? Isn't this the time to stop? But it's a difficult habit to break; a ritual that needs to be observed. Which is why he starts again. Or, more precisely, continues. He has used the same numbers for year after year. The odds against them winning in the first place were huge; the odds against these same numbers winning again are, surely, nil. (Let's not confuse the issue with statistical arguments.) But my father would not be convinced. The numbers were part of his ritual. To use different numbers would be to risk the disappointment of seeing his old numbers winning again. For another twenty years he completed his coupon as he had always done. He didn't win again. He didn't expect that he would.

* * *

Our pale blue book of Latin exercises was not designed to excite us. Dislocated sentences to be translated, empty of meaning. Word for word, dust to dust. Latin, we agreed, was a language as dead as French. But the blue book contained one illustration that intrigued me. A dark drawing of gloomy, shapeless figurines captioned, *Lares et Penates*. I studied it intently but it revealed nothing to me. After learning that *Lares and Penates* were a Roman's household gods, the obscurity of the picture was clear to me. From our own household gods I knew well enough that such entities could not be rendered with any sort of certainty.

Cat and Dog were mute. They had said everything they were going to say in a distant era. Today their role was to watch and wait upon events. They might pass judgement but they would not intervene. Tim was different. He was a functioning force, a power to be reckoned with. Above everything, Tim was not to be offended. And Tim was very easily offended.

Now I need to explain. Tim was my mother's very ancient teddy bear. But to describe Tim as a teddy bear is misleading. Tim was unquestionably unique. As a young bear he must have shared the attributes of other bears; in his later years, he did not. Certain particulars were missing. Multiple repairs had taken their toll and he had lost his figure. More bluntly, he had no shape at all, and, if he had once had fur, he had none now. With the passage of years the stuffing had been squeezed from his arms which now hung limp at his sides, but he still had the Steiff button in his ear and his eyes were bright, beady, calculating and unreadable.

In his youth, my mother said, there had been an unfortunate episode when a customs officer had suspected Tim of concealing smuggled gemstones within his person. It was only my mother's plaintive tears that prevented Tim from being cut open for inspection. She had saved his life but, she felt, he had been scarred by the experience and henceforward Tim viewed the world with suspicion.

My father recognised Tim's importance and treated him with wary respect. Tim took up residence in my father's bedroom and there he remained, monitoring him. Whether or not Tim could be appealed to or appeased was unclear. He gave us no clues. But we were well aware of his sensitivities. I have made no mention of Tim's other extremities because – there is no delicate way to put this – he had none. Visitors had to be warned not to speak of 'legs' or 'feet' in Tim's presence. They might well think us mad but we knew what we knew. Such references would cause Tim grave offence and this was to court disaster on a grand scale.

After my father's death, Tim returned to my mother's room; and he went with her to her tiny flat in Hampstead and then to her residential home.

When my mother died, I had the melancholy task of separating her possessions, boxing up what I thought I should keep, consigning the rest to the skip in the car park. Throughout, I was aware of Tim 'sitting' on her mantelpiece but I refused to look at him. I knew I wouldn't be brave enough to take Tim to the skip, but I had no wish at all to bring him home with me. I lifted the last box and closed the door of my mother's room behind me. As I reached the car, I became aware of someone running after me. I was being pursued by one of the carers from the home carrying Tim in her arms. She had been checking my mother's room. Did I know that I had left the bear behind? Avoiding Tim's eyes, I indicated that I did. If I didn't want the bear, would I mind if she kept it? She would like to give it to her grandchild. No, I said, I did not mind at all. In fact I would be very pleased.

As I drove away, the carer waved cheerfully; I tried not to look in the mirror; I didn't wave back.

Bartholomew's

Contour-coloured
World map series
with boundaries
roads and railways

AFRICA

Scale 1:10 000 000

Printed and Published
in Great Britain by
JOHN BARTHOLOMEW & SON LTD
EDINBURGH

CLOTH 7s 6d

CHAPTER TWENTY-ONE

Fathers and sons

I am at an afternoon audience in an over-furnished apartment in Bratislava. Huge fortunes have been made in the post-Socialist world. Once no more than a street hawker and still a young man, our host now presides over an extensive commercial empire and surrounds himself with toadies, bullies and occasional foreign visitors. We watch him drink tea; no one else is offered any. I'm not clear what my function is other than to be an observer. The nurse brings in his baby son who is dressed in a concoction of lace and leather. The child sits placidly on his father's knee while his chin is lifted and his head is stroked.

'He is going to be a great tennis player,' says the father.

The toadies beam and chuckle.

'Like his father,' says one crony.

There is a murmur of agreement.

'Better than his father,' says a second.

There's a hollow pause. Better than his father? Has this gone too far? Does the deep frown signal displeasure at the thought of this impertinent challenge or is this a father who is starting to shape a vision of his own immortality?

'Yes,' says the father. 'Better than his father. Much better than his father.'

All is well. The hole has closed over. There is a brief burst of supportive applause and the nurse comes in to take the child away.

* * *

Early evening on the airport bus at Paris Charles de Gaulle. A father and his young son have climbed aboard after me. They have their bags

179

with them. The father presents their tickets to the driver who nods them through. I sense that the father needs to ask a question but can't. There are other passengers behind him and he doesn't know whether or not the driver speaks English.

The father and son take their seats. The son is relaxed and confident in his father's company, but the father's anxiety is palpable. He clutches a much-folded map which gives him no comfort. While his son chatters away happily beside him, the father peers out of the window, straining for clues. He is lost, powerless, close to panic. What heroic impulse, I ask myself, has impelled him to travel to Paris with his son? I want to help. I catch his eye and smile. I have lived in Paris. It's a city I know well. He asks me where the bus stops and I show him on his map. Their hotel is close by. Relief floods through him. The fear of humiliation has receded for the present. He will not find himself exposed in front of his son. For the moment he can relax.

* * *

Timid or tyrannical, the father's task is to find the father he is; it is as simple and as difficult as that.

* * *

When we moved from Notting Hill Gate to Hammersmith, I found myself without any friends. Ladbroke Square – 'the gardens' – were lost to me and there was now nowhere else to go except deeper into my imagination. I'm not sure how much further I would have withdrawn if it hadn't been for Teddy Jones.

Teddy and I were very different, physically and temperamentally. He was outgoing, popular, glowing with health, while I was pale, withdrawn and intense. But we were both only children and knew how to share each other's worlds without trespassing. We began going home together on the District Line to West Kensington and found that we were comfortable in each other's company. The Jones' flat in Talgarth Road was within walking distance of ours at Palace

Mansions which meant that Teddy and I spent much of the weekend together. My world began to open out again.

Normally, at the end of the afternoon, Teddy walks home on his own. His announcement that this afternoon his mother and father will be coming to collect him seems to portend something.

Mr and Mrs Jones are standing in our hall. My mother greets them and my father is summoned. Mr Jones steps forward. He is wearing a smart sports jacket and there is an air of urgent vitality about him. There is no preamble.

'Teddy and Nicolas are becoming close friends,' he says, 'and I don't want them to be hurt. It's important that you see me so that, if you should decide you don't wish the boys to play together any more, you can say so now and not later when it will be more painful for both of them.'

At first my parents are mystified. And then suddenly they understand. Mr Jones – who we learn later is Teddy's stepfather – is 'Anglo-Indian'. It is London in the fifties and Mr Jones needs to establish whether or not the colour of his skin is going to be an objection. My father, whenever he recalled this moment, judged this to be an act of exceptional bravery. From that afternoon Mr Jones could do no wrong in my father's eyes. His faith – although tested – was always amply rewarded.

Mr Jones was an entirely different father from mine. He was young and vigorous and utterly fearless. He would take hold of Teddy or me or both of us together by the ankle and the wrist and hurl us into the middle of a swimming pool or lake. He would lead us on wildly extended bicycle rides from which we would return hungry, thirsty, exhausted and elated. He would bowl cricket balls at us at the greatest pace he could sustain, and we would duck his fearsome beamers and clout his long hops until it was time for tea. Mr Jones provided the physical adventure I couldn't have at home, and my father showed his own immense courage by watching from a distance and saying nothing.

* * *

January 7th. A bleak headline in *The Times*. A story to excite fear in any father.

FATHER AND SON DROWN WITHIN SOUND OF RESCUE
Lost on a fog-bound beach, a father lifted his nine-year-old son on to his shoulders to give the boy an extra chance of life as the incoming tide closed around them …

The father and son have walked out onto the beach at Ulverston looking for fishing bait. The fog has moved in and reduced the visibility to nil. The father has lost his bearings and become disorientated, and the tide has raced across the sands from Morecambe Bay. There are several phone calls between the father and the police who have been alerted by the local coastguard. Near the end the boy, sitting above the water on his father's shoulders, speaks on the mobile phone. 'My Daddy is all right,' he says. And then there are no more calls. Their bodies are found later.

Locals expressed surprise yesterday that people had ventured on to the beach during the winter despite signs warning about the dangers of quicksand, gulleys and incoming tides.

The wiseacres weigh in with their sanctimonious pronouncements about parental irresponsibility. After the event, it's all so clear to everyone. But why were they there, I ask myself. A father-and-son expedition, a taste of adventure, the two of them together, alone on the bleak winter beach. Isn't this what a father and his son are supposed to do? Unless, of course, it all goes terribly wrong.

I tear out the piece from the newspaper, fold it and slip it in my day-sack.

* * *

How remarkable that today should be January 7th – my father's birthday – and that I should find this clipping in my day-sack while walking the Pembrokeshire Coast Path.

It was to be our first proper walk together, father and son. Walking, I have told you – a little pompously as it seems to me now – is more than strolling through meadows in high summer. Proper walking means walking in all weathers: rain, wind, sleet or hail. (Although I hope it won't snow.) This is why I have planned this after-Christmas walk together. The two of us, a father-and-son adventure.

We will start at Fishguard and walk to St David's Head. Three days' walking in the mild Pembrokeshire winter. When we arrive at the Fishguard hotel, it's pouring with rain. At dinner, overcooked and tasteless, the hotelier, as seedy and shabby as his gloomy, empty hotel, asks me about our plans.

'We're walking to Trevine tomorrow,' I say.

'From here? That's much too far. Too far for the boy.'

We ignore him. More accurately, you ignore him. You have every confidence in me. What can this gloomy man tell your father that he doesn't know already? While you sleep soundly in the bed next to me, I lie awake listening to the rain, calculating and re-calculating distances and time. If we start earlier – but when is dawn? If we walk longer – but how long will the light last? And how far can I expect you to walk in a day at your age? Before it gets light I have decided the hotelier is right.

You are unaware of any change in our plans as we take a short cut up the narrow lanes to Strumble Head. It's pouring with rain but we are wearing waterproofs and it isn't cold. At midday we watch a lone seal swimming against the tide that rushes between the lighthouse and the rocky outcrop, testing itself for its own amusement, before turning on its side to be carried out to sea. We crouch in a grassy hollow and eat sandwiches, apples and chocolate. In the afternoon we return to the hotel where we have left the car. We are tired, wet, happy and safe. We drive to a sparkling clean bed-and-breakfast in Trevine – light blue nylon sheets and the smell of air freshener and window polish – where you lie on the bed and watch early evening television. We venture out a little later to a local pub, the Square and Compass, where we eat fried eggs and sausages at a small formica table while the juke-box plays music from the fifties and the drinkers crowd round the darts board. It's a glimpse of a world very different from our own. That night you and I are tucked up safely in our beds while the wind howls outside our window. I turn off the bedside lamp. We are warm and safe but we might be cold and wet, stranded on the dark cliffs. We might be, but we're not. I sleep soundly.

The next day we drive to Whitesands and walk round St David's Head. The wind is so strong that we have to flatten ourselves to the cliff in order to negotiate the headland while below us the waves roar round the rocks. We could stay another day if we want to, but we agree that it's time to go home. We drive back to London where we tell the story of the wind and the rain and the seal at Strumble Head. We have had our adventure and I have brought you back safely.

There are times when you recall our winter walk, and the eggs and sausages at the Square and Compass. I remember the roaring wind in the night but if I think at all about the hotelier at the Fishguard hotel, it's not for long.

* * *

There is usually a time when we find ourselves talking about our children. We ask about theirs. They ask about ours. Headlines only; recent news, little more. Enough to show interest. But this evening it's going to be difficult to talk to each other at all.

Friday night. We have arranged to meet at a gastropub. It's crowded with young people celebrating the end of another working week. The noise is surprisingly exhilarating but it's too loud to speak across the table. Before this evening he and I have only met as husbands but tonight our wives can't hear us and we can't hear them. We mime and smile and point at the menu, but that's all we can do. It's enough. Which is how, between successive waves of sound, he and I discover we have things we can say to each other and find ourselves talking about fathers and sons. The detail is drowned in the clamour around us but, with attentive listening, we each grasp the gist. Parents we agree – and fathers in particular – are certain to fail. The only question is how often and how much.

He tells me how he loved and admired his own father but that they were never close. He doesn't blame his father. It wasn't his fault. That's the way things were. But he's happy and proud that his relationship with his own sons is so much closer.

A second bottle of wine is brought to our table.

I tell him the story of our bike ride in Oxfordshire. How my son and I set out on our bikes with one my oldest friends. 'A short ride,' says my friend, 'between six miles and eight.' Being childless himself, he's unaware what distances mean for a seven-year-old boy on a bike. As six miles stretches beyond eight, and I see you tiring, my impatience grows as. At the bottom of the final hill your exhaustion overwhelms you. Your tears stoke my irritation and I erupt in fury. My friend is sent up the hill ahead of us. We follow him later. We reach the top of the hill without further mishap and pause before freewheeling home, our bike ride triumphantly completed. That night, when you're in bed, I apologise for my inexcusable rage. You tell me that it's all right. You mean it, and it is. I close the bedroom door and pause. Who is the father, I ask myself. Who is the son?

A loud burst of laughter from the bar. He smiles. He has understood. Our plates are cleared away.

There was one moment, he tells me, when his relationship with his father might have changed. A Sunday evening, as an adult, visiting his parents. Not something he did very often. He and his father find themselves alone in the front room. The moment seems right. 'Would you like to go out for a drink, Dad?' he asks. His father scarcely pauses. 'No,' he says. 'No, I don't think so.' And that was that. The moment has been lost and will not to be retrieved. He didn't feel any rancour, he says, but it was a pity and he didn't ask again. Shortly afterwards he moved to London, and soon after that his father died.

We stand outside the pub, our ears still ringing. A good evening, we agree. We say goodbye and walk home.

There are times when we should talk to each other; fathers and sons, fathers and fathers.

Saturday, November 23rd, for One Week
MATINEE WEDNESDAY at 2.30

Deirdre of the Sorrows

By J. M. SYNGE

Lavarcham (Deirdre's Nurse)	...	...	Mary Raby
Old Woman (Lavarcham's Servant)	...	...	Dorothy Taylor
Owen (Conchubor's Attendant and Spy)	...	...	Eric Ross
Conchubor (High King of Ulster)	...	...	M. Victor Tandy
Fergus (Conchubor's Friend)	...	...	Joseph A. Dodd
Deirdre	...	...	Maire O'Neill
Naisi (Deirdre's Lover)	...	...	William J. Rea
Ainnle (Naisi's Brother)	...	...	J. Austin Byrne
Ardan (Naisi's Brother)	...	...	Reginald Gaffy
First Soldier	...	...	Christian Morrow
Second Soldier	...	...	Arnold Rinsky

SCENE—
Act I.—Lavarcham's House on Slieve Fuadh.
Act II.—Alban. Early Morning in the beginning of Winter.
Outside the Tent of Deirdre and Naisi.
Act III.—Tent below Emain Macha.

Produced by JOHN DRINKWATER

Orchestra

Irish Folk Tunes—
Tunes (from County Derry) ....
(a) The Rakes of Mallow ....
(b) My dear Irish Boy ....
(c) Suantraidhe .... Grainger
(d) Kildare
(e) The Top of the Cork Road
Keltic Lament .... Foulds

Conductor - FRANK EDMONDS

CHAPTER TWENTY-TWO

With regard to women

When sons reach a certain age, fathers are expected to speak to them about sex. And about women, too, I suppose. It's not something you and I did. There was one time when I thought we should – I had nothing planned but I hoped it would come to me – but you thought we shouldn't and you were much more sure that we shouldn't than I was that we should. Which meant that we didn't.

* * *

My father doesn't look at me which, considering what he is about to say, is either odd or understandable.

'The fact is, old boy,' he begins, 'you're no oil painting.'

The only oil painting I can bring to mind is the one in our hall, a gloomy array of fruit or vegetables – it's not easy to tell which – lying lifeless in a bowl. Not being an oil painting doesn't worry me particularly.

'Not that there's anything wrong with you,' he continues, 'but you're no matinée idol, nor ever likely to be.'

I must have recognised the expression 'matinée idol' because Ivor Novello's creamy features appear in front of me. Not being Ivor Novello doesn't worry me either.

'What you must remember,' says my father, 'is that you are not, and you never will be, "God's gift to women".'

I nod – it seems the right thing to do – which encourages my father to proceed.

'That's why if a woman – or a girl – invites you to her bed the first time you meet her, you should be very, very careful indeed.

(Pause.) She may be mad, she may be drunk, she may be terribly unhappy. Or she may be all three. In any case, it will be everything to do with her and nothing to do with you. (Pause.) She probably doesn't know what she's doing. She may have had her heart broken and want to break yours. (Pause.) Or she may have mistaken you for somebody else. In which case you'll both be terribly embarrassed the next morning.'

I nod again – although less certainly.

'You see it's not the loud girls who shout about sex the whole time you need worry about. They're generally fairly harmless. The ones to watch are the quiet ones who'll corner you in a broom cupboard before you know where you are.'

My father sits for several moments looking thoughtful.

'Yes,' he says. And then, after further reflection, 'Yes.'

And that was how our conversation ended. I think I must have been eight or nine at the time.

* * *

Whether my father's advice was sound or not, I still don't know. I would have liked to put it to the test a little more often, but I don't seem to have been troubled much by 'the quiet ones', in broom cupboards, or anywhere else for that matter. Which is just as well really because I'm pretty sure I would have muffed it.

An instance. While working as a publisher in Hong Kong, I had the opportunity to travel to other countries in the region. These were business trips although I wasn't quite clear what business I should be doing. I didn't let it worry me unduly because by now I had discovered expenses. Expenses were very liberating as, among other things, they allowed me to entertain potential authors.

To be truthful, it was most unlikely that my Singapore author would ever produce a publishable manuscript, but he was excellent company with a fund of disgraceful stories which I happily heard repeated on every visit. He had an old colonial's well-practised capacity for bottles of Tiger beer which, gamely, I did my best to match. My evenings with the author were immensely enjoyable; the mornings which followed were like wading through sewage.

Picture me now in the departure lounge at Singapore airport waiting to catch an early flight home to Hong Kong. I am wearing, as I did in those days, my round, wire-framed, National Health Service glasses but I am in no state to read the latest version of my Singapore author's manuscript which I have in my hands. I know from a recent visit to the airport lavatory that my face is puffy and the colour of putty. I take off my glasses and shake my head but this makes me feel worse. I put on my glasses again and look up. The girl behind the desk – as beautiful as the Singapore Girl on the billboards – is looking in my direction. I look down again at the manuscript. A mistake. My head rolls about like a buoy in the tide. I look up. Singapore Girl is still looking in my direction and smiling. Then she beckons. I look behind me to see who she is smiling at. The seats behind me are empty. Hesitantly I point to my chest. Me? She nods. She is still smiling as I approach the desk. She beckons me again and I lean forward to hear her.

'You look so cute in your glasses,' she says, in a light Asian-American accent.

You must believe me. This isn't a scene I could invent. But what does your father say? What does he do? How does he respond to sweet Singapore Girl with whom he will be flying to Hong Kong where she might like to be shown the delights of Wanchai, Tsim Sha Tsui, Aberdeen Harbour, The Peak? At first words fail him completely. Nothing comes out. She looks at him expectantly, still smiling.

'Oh,' he says. 'Thank you.'

And he returns to his seat, sheepish, limp, undone and still horribly hung-over.

* * *

It often surprises people to learn that my mother was my father's third wife. The theatre is full of philanderers and failed marriages, but my father was simply not the sort of man you would expect to have married more than once. On the other hand, it surprised no one to hear that my mother had had a string of exotic boyfriends – rich, handsome, titled, foreign – before she finally found my father. She enjoyed telling us about them and we enjoyed listening to her. I think we both felt how fortunate we were that she'd found and chosen us and not them.

*   *   *

It's hard to imagine my father doing much finding or choosing. This isn't to say that women didn't interest him. They did. Greatly. But, as a boy, his experience of the opposite sex was limited to school and his restricted contact with girls – at Miss Silversides' Seminary and at Bath City Secondary School – can have done nothing at all to prepare him for future encounters. It was while he was a games master at Torquay Secondary School that the first of these occurred.

During the winter of 1917–18 I was very happy. The boys seemed to like me, my health was improving rapidly and my landlady couldn't have looked after me with more care had I been her son. Then, in the spring of 1918, two disasters overtook me. First I caught measles and bronchitis and nearly died, and then, immediately after my recovery, I fell in love. The second of these misfortunes proved to be the more serious.

People are apt to scoff at the pangs of first love but they can lead to very real and acute suffering. This was certainly true in my case. War service had taught me nothing about women, either mentally or physically. I don't remember ever kissing the girl. In fact I'm sure I never did. Such a memory could not have been forgotten.

She was Yorkshire-born, handsome rather than pretty, two years my elder, a 'trials' hockey player and accomplished pianist. We met at a staff party and I fell in love at first sight. Within a few weeks, I proposed marriage. She said she would like to think it over. She thought it over and said 'No'.

My world was in ruins. I gave notice that I would be leaving

Torquay at the end of the summer term and, oddly enough as we had not discussed the matter, she did likewise. We exchanged our last goodbyes on a crowded school staircase, amidst the turmoil of end-of-term scurryings. It rather spoilt the Arthurian farewell.

After this first painful experience of love in Torquay, he seems to have been content to admire women from a distance.

Towards the end of my first season at Birmingham Repertory I made a brief appearance with the famous Irish Players who arrived from Dublin to present *Deidre of the Sorrows* with Maire O'Neill in the name part. On the journey over one of the company had been taken ill and I was selected to fill the vacancy. The part was tiny consisting of one two-line speech only. Maire O'Neill didn't attend the rehearsals and the first time I saw her was when she made her entrance. 'They call me Deidre. Deidre of the Sorrows.' She seemed the most beautiful woman I had ever seen, but as a junior member of the company I dared not speak to her. I was obliged to worship from afar.

To adore but not to address. So much safer than conversing about nothing in particular or 'going on one or two walks together'.

I was married at Bradford-on-Avon Parish Church in January 1926 shortly after my thirtieth birthday, my bride being a Bath girl I'd known for a very long time and to whom I'd been engaged for four years. We'd first met at the time I was newly-discharged from the army and wandering around Bath suffering from shell-shock. She was then a shy and unhappy teenager who used to accompany her mother, a keen bowler at a local bowling club of which my father was a member. Sometimes we used to sit together and converse about nothing in particular. Then I went to Torquay.

Some years later we met again and went on one or two walks together. There the matter would probably have ended had not her father issued an ultimatum forbidding her to see me again. This had the effect of angering me so much that I went to see him and demanded

a reason. Why wasn't I fit to consort with his daughter? It ended
with him allowing that, provided there was no question of an early
marriage, we might become engaged. And that was that!

Although we remained married until the spring of 1939, it would be
useless to pretend that the union was ideally happy, even in the early
years. There were too many things against success. The most important
reason for the failure was that neither of us – both only children –
had the remotest experience of the other sex. A long engagement in a
provincial city in the '20s could certainly prevent the opening of the
doors of passionate exploration! We had drifted through this long
engagement and then into marriage without actually being in love with
each other.

* * *

After the death of his father, there followed an ugly, angry battle with
whisky. My father recovered, but his domestic life remained wretched.
He needed to escape. In a drawer he found the first two acts of a thriller
he'd written and abandoned several years before because he couldn't
finish it. He decided to write a last act ('a very short and, as I now
realise, a very bad last act') and to finance and direct the play himself.
In 1932, *Recipe for Murder* opened at the Theatre Royal, Glasgow.

During the first week of *Recipe for Murder* at Glasgow an incident
occurred which, although it seemed trivial at the time, was to have
a vital influence on many years of my life. After the first night
performance, I went around the dressing-rooms inviting members of
the cast to an informal party at the Central Hotel. Soon after it had
started I noticed that our young stage-manageress – it was her first
professional engagement – wasn't with us. On making enquiries, I
discovered that her dressing-room was in a different part of the theatre
from the others. The reason she wasn't present was that I hadn't invited
her. My stage-director volunteered to take a taxi and fetch her but
returned to say that she had already left the theatre before his arrival
and hadn't written the address of her digs in the stage door book.

On the Tuesday I sought her out to apologise for what must have appeared rudeness or unkindness on my part and invited her in reparation to have supper with me that night. It was the beginning of an association which was to lead to our marriage in September, 1939.

The years of marriage without love were followed by years of love without marriage, and then a second marriage.

I find it difficult to report that this short period of marriage broke up in tragic circumstances. I don't think either of us was really to blame and I'm absolutely certain that she wasn't. Circumstances were against us for too long. She had to encounter family objections and my divorce from my first wife was long delayed – at one point a legal mistake deferred it for an entire further year. A few months after I was legally entitled to re-marry, we parted by mutual consent, but well-meaning friends – unwisely perhaps – brought us together again. I'm quite sure she married me from a sense of loyalty rather than a keen desire to do so. We both did our best, but it didn't work. I suppose it was ridiculous to expect that it could. In his comedy, *The Constant Wife*, Somerset Maugham puts such a situation in one bitter but frighteningly truthful line: 'My dear, no one can make yesterday's cold mutton into tomorrow's lamb cutlets.' I provided the evidence enabling her to divorce me. I'm glad to say that some time afterwards she married again most successfully.

* * *

When we lived in Notting Hill Gate, a slim black female cat inhabited the communal garden that we shared with the other residents of Lansdowne Road. She visited us daily to be given a saucer of milk. My father named her 'Marie Stopes' because, he explained, she had no kittens. I didn't understand but he was so pleased with the name, which also amused my mother, that I was perfectly content to use it. Once our tabby cat, Thomas, joined the family, Marie Stopes' visits ceased abruptly.

* * *

It's a warm summer afternoon and my father and I are sitting together on a bench outside the local pub, the Duke of St Albans.

'Your mother is a remarkable woman,' he says.

As he gets older, this happens more often. My father's statement has appeared from nowhere. Like a fish that leaps in a pond. You see it in flight and then it's gone. Will it leap again?

A bus arrives from Kentish Town and sets down its passengers. Another bus leaves.

'A remarkable woman,' he says again.

I know he's right. My mother is a truly remarkable woman but I know he's saying more than this. I retrace the arc of his thought. My father has married other women. He knows how fortunate he is to be married to my mother. My mother is unlike other women; other women are not like her. I would be fortunate to find myself married to a woman such as my mother. But – my mother being unlike other women and other women being unlike my mother – the chances aren't good. Although I may be lucky. I think this is what he's saying …

We sit with our beer and I wait to see if the fish will leap again. It doesn't.

* * *

In 1941 my father, who had been invited to take *The Ghost Train* on an ENSA tour to entertain the troops, was attending a casting session at Drury Lane.

> I was standing just inside the stage door when I saw a tall and handsome young woman approaching and held open an inner door for her to pass through. She swept on her way without even a murmured thank-you. 'Snooty bitch!' I muttered to myself, unaware that, when not wearing her spectacles, Althea was very nearly blind. The 'snooty bitch' and I were married at Knaresborough on October 3rd 1945.

They stayed married. I don't think my father had planned to marry again. He may have felt he wasn't good at marriage. But, like many sound decisions, it was taken for him.

* * *

Your mother and I will remember the particulars differently but my version doesn't stray too far from the truth.

'I could never marry you,' she tells me suddenly one morning. 'Your children would be much too ugly.'

This surprises me on two counts. First, when I was a boy my mother always told me that I was good-looking. Although I may not have entirely believed her, the demure girls in the bars of Roppongi, kneeling to pour beer into iced glasses, had – with shy smiles – said much the same thing. As had a willowy lady-boy in a *katoey* bar in Patpong and a languorous sculptor in Rome who wanted to read poetry to me in his attic. Could it be that they were wrong? Secondly, no thought of marriage had occurred to me. Not remotely. I had only known your mother for two or three weeks and I didn't plan to marry anyone until I was thirty-five. Although, as I thought about it, I couldn't remember precisely why thirty-five had seemed the right age to marry.

'Oh,' I said.

Which I think was all I was required to say at the time.

* * *

A family christening. It's a family I don't know. A family that, at the time, I have no need to know. Your mother's family.

'I'm not good at that sort of thing,' I say.

But your mother is keen I should accompany her and I find that I've agreed. Although with the condition that, whenever I choose, I can leave. Without any argument or fuss. Without protest or commotion. I can go.

It is, if anything, worse than I'd feared. The family is larger and louder than I could have imagined. Herds of relations, intent on jollity, rear up at us from all directions. The service itself is a merciful interval of peace but I know the reception is going to be dreadful. I drink a glass of sparkling wine, eat something on a stick and then tell your mother that I'm going. This is the test. Will I be allowed to leave? I'm not sure I expect her to pass it, but she does. In fact she tells me she is coming with me. This wasn't our arrangement, and it seems to me a pity because she is clearly enjoying herself. She is insistent and I feel a tweak of guilt. Although not enough to make me stay.

We don't say much in the car. A disconcerting quiet after the roar of the reception. Your mother is driving – faster than I would be driving myself – and I am sitting in the passenger seat interrogating myself. Is my behaviour unreasonable? How guilty should I be feeling? Is my shyness real or do I use it as an excuse? I'm so busy rehearsing my questions and answers that, momentarily, I can't be sure whether what I think I've heard is your mother speaking or me talking to myself. I replay the words.

'I suppose this means you won't marry me?'

I may have paused but I don't think I did.

'No,' I said. 'It doesn't mean that.'

* * *

Your mother hasn't changed her mind about my looks, but she admits she was wrong about my children. Our children. As she claims she always knew she would be.

CHAPTER TWENTY-THREE

Late, lost, the boy who travels

My father attributed his anxiety to his childhood. He inherited it, he said, from his mother, although the cause was his father.

My parents' exceptionally happy marriage was a perfect example of the successful union of opposites. During their partnership of nearly forty years, I doubt if they ever seriously exchanged a cross word. Yet, apart from their deep affection for each other and a common bond of fortitude, few married couples could have been more different in temperament. My father was a cheerful optimist, always ready for the next adventure and content to let troubles look after themselves, whereas my mother was the possessor of an incurable anxiety complex.

The rheumatic fever which had ended my grandfather's athletic career damaged his heart and lungs irreparably. To outward appearance he looked young and vigorous. At the age of fifty-nine, shortly before his death, 'there was no sign of grey in his red hair and he walked with the stride of a sergeant major'. He was, as my father describes him, 'a living lie', or, as he described himself, 'a damn fine watch with a broken mainspring'. It was a watch that might stop at any moment; a spring that could suddenly snap.

My grandmother stands on the step of the family house at 14 Manvers Street. She is watching my grandfather – late as habitually he is – sprinting at full pace in the direction of the railway station to catch the morning train that takes him once a week from Bath to Bristol. My father, a boy of five or six, stands beside his mother. It's not something that either of them will say out loud, but they are wondering if he will be coming back to them this evening.

* * *

An ordinary weekday evening. My father is standing at the window of our second-floor flat looking down at the path below. For most of its length – from Highgate West Hill, a short walk from where the buses terminate beside the Duke of St Albans, to a branching path that runs up a slight slope to the steps at the entrance to our block – it is concealed from his view by a tall, trimmed hedge. My father watches the path, stiff with anxiety and irritation. His anxiety is for my mother who is returning from her typing job in West Kensington; his irritation is with himself.

My mother has said she will be back shortly after six o'clock. This is what she says every day, but she is generally a little later than she says she will be. My father has, as usual, been standing at the window since five. He holds up his wrist so that he can look at the dial of his watch without entirely taking his eyes from the path. (His watch is always fast.) Next, he turns to look behind him at the grandfather clock in the living-room – my mother's larger, louder, Parker clock. Then, when the tension becomes too great, he leaves the window and goes out into the hall to check the other grandfather clock – the smaller, quieter, Morrish clock. (My father rewinds both grandfather clocks on Sunday mornings and resets them five minutes fast to allow for any time they might lose during the week.) He paces up and down the hall for a while, trying to control his anxiety, before returning to the living-room and his position at the window.

As occasionally happens, at the moment my mother comes into view, my father is checking the clock in the hall. This means that he has returned to his position at the window by the time she puts her key in the front door. Hearing the door closing, he leaves the window and hurries into the hall to greet her. No mention is made of my mother's time of return or my father's wait at the window. It is only by seeming to ignore it that either of them can cope with my father's anxiety complex. It tests my mother's patience sorely – she has tangible, practical worries to occupy her – and it doesn't help that he is so humbly apologetic about his condition.

198

'An anxiety complex is a disease like any other,' my father explains to anyone who will listen. (In practice this is me because my mother has gone to the kitchen.) 'It can't be cured. There's no logic to it. No reasoning with it. There's nothing to be done about it. It tyrannises those who love you because – however irritating it may be – it's difficult to be too angry with someone whose only crime is worrying about you.' He sighs and smiles. My mother is home and safe; he is, for the present, placid, at ease.

'Blessed are the unpunctual,' he reflects, 'for they shall never be kept waiting.' This is his favourite saying when the crisis has passed. He seems not to hear my mother crashing plates in the kitchen.

* * *

I would prefer to be walking to Hammersmith with Neil Anderson but instead I am waiting outside the High Master's door beside a gold-lettered board that lists head boys, prefects and club captains. (It is not a list on which my name will appear.) Pupils leaving the school at the end of the year are granted an interview with the High Master in the last week of the summer term. I have been allocated a time; I have no choice in the matter.

Before being offered a place at St Paul's, I was interviewed, along with my father, by the High Master's predecessor, the Olympian Mr Gilkes. In my first year, while I was still in the very lowest form of the school, Mr Gilkes taught us Divinity. To me it seemed a most appropriate subject for the High Master to teach. His habit of punctuating statements with a rhetorical 'Don't you know?' I found endearing. When Mr Gilkes retired, I felt something was lost.

My career at St Paul's has been undistinguished. The school and I have disappointed each other. I've had no reason to meet Mr Gilkes' successor who, by comparison, strikes me as a small figure. The High Master's door opens and I am admitted. Whereas my father and I were interviewed by Mr Gilkes in a turret room, three chairs by the window, the present High Master occupies an oak-panelled room the length of two cricket pitches. His desk is at the far end and, until I reach it, he does not look up. Although a high-backed chair stands in front of his desk, I don't sit down. It seems to me that neither of us knows what should happen next. The High Master studies the piece of paper in front of him, and then looks up.

'Ah, Ridley,' he says. 'The boy who travels.'

'Yes,' I reply.

We eye each other awkwardly.

'Do you plan to continue travelling?'

'Yes,' I say.

Although 'plan' isn't quite the right word.

* * *

As a child, I yearned to travel. It was a longing stimulated by my mother's stories of New Zealand. Swimming, sailing, camping, horse-riding; mountains, geysers, beaches, fiords. Tauranga, Wanganui, Waikato, Rotorua; Maori names she pronounced so fondly. As far away from our dark Victorian flat opposite the grey edifice of Olympia as it was possible to imagine. One day, she said, she would travel again. There were the countries we should visit; Italy, Portugal, Greece, Spain … But these were dreams. Only well-off families could afford to go abroad.

In time this changed. One summer, my mother and I watched the cousins departing for a two-week coach tour of the Tyrol. I tried not to mind. It had been arranged that my mother and I would stay behind in the cousins' house in Southbourne and, as on other summer holidays, most mornings we walked down the zig-zag to the chilly beach, swam in the sea, wrapped ourselves in our towels and shivered while we waited for the sun to re-appear from behind the clouds. We brushed the sand off our sandwiches and, once a day, we bought ice-cream cornets. My mother read her library books and I read *The Eagle* or watched the clouds. I'm sure we enjoyed ourselves. We usually did. As if by agreement, we didn't talk about the cousins on their coach in the Tyrol and we caught the bus back home to London before they returned from Austria with their stories and souvenirs.

My father wasn't interested in foreign travel. He had been to France to fight. Between the wars he had spent several winters writing on the Riviera. He had toured Germany with *Easy Money*. I think he felt that was enough. There had once been an opportunity to sail to New York for the Broadway opening of *The Ghost Train* but his first wife hated ships and she was too jealous to let him go to America alone. He sometimes said he regretted this but I'm not sure that he did.

Although he wasn't interested in travelling, he liked timetables and maps. He enjoyed locating place-names on the page – his head bent intently over the table, a cigarette burning in a saucer – and tracing routes from here to there, from place to place, from page to page. Fictional itineraries to pass the time.

* * *

When I was seventeen and still at school, I was invited to join a party travelling overland from London to Dar-es-Salaam. This was such amazing good fortune that I sometimes find myself asking if it really happened. But here are the letters and postcards that I sent home. Here is the envelope of black-and-white photographs. Here, too, is my stained map of Africa.

AFRICA
Scale: 1:10,000,000
Contour-coloured with boundaries,
roads and railways
Printed and published in Great Britain by
JOHN BARTHOLOMEW & SON LTD
Edinburgh
Cloth 7s 6d

I'm not sure why I bought my map from Stanfords in Covent Garden or what purpose I thought it would serve. It must have been symbolic more than practical because the AA had provided us with our route through Europe, the Middle East and Africa. The route through Europe was detailed; through the Middle East the details became fewer; in Africa we were to be guided by little more than lines linking place-names. Port Said → Cairo → Aswan → Wadi Halfa → Khartoum → Juba → Kampala → Nairobi ... These were the names I rehearsed while I worked in the bread factory at Cadby Hall, Hammersmith, during my Easter holidays, earning the money I needed for the trip.

I queued up for my visas and had my inoculations. I bought khaki shorts, sunglasses, insect repellent and an ex-army water-bottle. The school raised no objections. Everyone agreed it was a chance not to miss. My parents were provided with a list of *poste restante* addresses. I said I would write whenever I could and my father opened up the atlas on the dining-room table.

I am humbled to remember my parents' courage. To put no obstacles in my way. To conceal their fears so successfully that I could allow myself to be unaware of them. Watching their only child climb aboard the ten-year-old Land Rover parked at the bottom of Highgate West Hill. Waving good-bye as we drove off towards Kentish Town and Dover. Returning to the flat to wait for my return.

If calamity had ended our journey in Calais, I would have been quite content. I had crossed the English Channel, seen the pastel houses on the French shoreline, had my passport stamped.

I am abroad at last.

Our journey goes well through Europe and the Middle East. Impressions and sensations overwhelm me. I receive post from home and write cards and letters to my parents but they are bland affairs. It is all too much to share in words. We reach Beirut with a day to spare before our Land Rovers are hoisted onto the ship taking us to Port Said. It takes forty-eight hours to clear customs. The Suez invasion is still fresh in the Egyptian memory and the British are unpopular. From Cairo we drive to Giza to see the pyramids. (Here is a photograph of us sitting in a row on a wall, happy, smiling, our arms round each other, the Sphinx in the background.) The next day, at the British embassy, we are advised that our journey is over. Fighting in southern Sudan has closed the border and travel between Aswan and Juba will be impossible. Elsewhere we learn that if we return to

Port Said we should be able to find a ship to take us through the Suez Canal and on to Ethiopia. I sit in the grounds of the Gezira Sporting Club, where we have pitched our tents, and write a letter home to outline our change of plan.

In Port Said we book a passage on the *Jelsa*, a Yugoslav merchantman, that takes us through the Suez Canal and round the Red Sea calling at Jeddah, Aden and Djibouti before landing us at the Ethiopian port of Massawa. From here we will drive to Addis Ababa and south to Kenya and Tanganyika. My Bartholomew's map shows very few roads. The route looks straightforward enough.

Most of my letters from Europe have been received safely and my father, sitting at the dining-room table in Highgate, has plotted our progress in the atlas. The postcard I sent from Beirut arrives in London in three days but my letter mailed in Port Said is never received. There are six weeks of silence.

We drive through the Borana region of Ethiopia, where we boil our soup on primus stoves watched by local tribesman who live on the milk and blood of the camels they herd; and on through the Northern Frontier District of Kenya, where the *shifta*, Somali bandits, are attacking villages and ambushing convoys. This is a different story for another time but there comes a point during our journey when it seems likely we'll die.

We are utterly alone in a grey, featureless desert. I regret it, of course – I don't want to die – but I'm calm. The memory of the thought is as sharp as the sunlight, as harsh as the landscape. It would have been so much worse to die sooner. Because now I have travelled. I have drunk bottles of raw red wine in Sarnico and woken up in a field of cabbages with spiders in my hair. I have drunk slivovic in Ljubljana and sung 'Oh, my darling Clementine' in Serbo-Croat while the rain poured down on the corrugated roof. I have slept in a police station in an Anatolian village and been shown the nearby springs where Alexander the Great is said to have bathed. I have seen Krak des Chevaliers in the distance, ridden a horse through the Siq into Petra, and visited the Dome of the Rock. I feel I have lived which means dying seems bearable. I am seventeen and wholly self-absorbed. I give no thought at all to the effect my death will have on my father and mother sitting together in the kitchen in Highgate.

*   *   *

LOST IN THE DESERT. Arriving in Nairobi we find we are news. Nothing has been heard from us for six weeks and we have been reported missing. If we have been driving through the Borana region or the Northern Frontier District we are – in the view of the Foreign Office, London – dead. Our hosts show us the newspapers. We're bemused by the attention. We give newspaper interviews in Nairobi and later in Dar-es-Salaam. Our photographs appear beside shockingly inaccurate stories; my first experience of journalists and the press. A week later I board a turbo-prop to fly to Luton Airport where my mother meets me with a Masonic friend of my father's. My father is rehearsing in Manchester and won't be back for a day or two. We drive home to Highgate where the friend declines an invitation to tea. My mother and I sit together in the kitchen. It's a muted homecoming; only now do I begin to understand the effect my disappearance has had on my parents. For a fortnight they were called by journalists asking how they felt about their only son being lost in the African desert. My father was forced to take the telephone off the hook; it hasn't yet been replaced.

*   *   *

I go back to school. The bus to Kentish Town from Parliament Hill Fields, the Northern Line to Leicester Square, the Piccadilly Line to Barons Court. I walk down Gliddon Road, in through the side gate, past the chemistry block and the grimy, unheated swimming pool, down some stone steps to the basement and up the stairs that lead into the main school building. Cream and grey corridors filled with scuffling, scuttling schoolboys from whom I now feel an unbridgeable distance. Not that I felt very close to many of them before.

Later in the week the editor of a local newspaper believes he may be able to squeeze a last drop of news from the LOST IN THE DESERT story and sends a photographer to the school. A group of 'classmates' are encouraged to cluster round me for the purpose of the picture. When the photographer puts away his camera, the classmates disperse. Only Neil Anderson is left. Neil, my laconic lunchtime companion, has successfully avoided appearing in the photograph. Most days he and I walk down to the Adana café in Hammersmith where we drink mugs of tea and smoke cigarettes. The café is owned by a Turkish couple. I would like to tell them that I have passed through Adana on the way into Syria. It's not something many people can say and I think they may be interested, but lunchtimes are busy in the café and the Turkish couple don't have much time for two schoolboys who take up a table, drinking tea and smoking cigarettes.

'What was it like then?' Neil asks, after a second cigarette.

'Good,' I say. 'Yes.'

My reply satisfies him; Neil doesn't want a travelogue.

*   *   *

We wait for my father to return from Manchester before I tell the story of my trip. I sit with the atlas at the dining-room table – my mother on one side and my father on the other – tracing the places I have passed through page by page. They listen attentively but they don't press me with questions. When I reach Addis Ababa, my father says, 'During the war I used to travel up to London with Haile Selassie on the train from Bath.' But this is my narrative and besides the idea is preposterous. When I reach Dar-es-Salaam, there's a pause and my father stands up. 'Good night, old boy. It's good to have you home.' Although I don't admit it, I am disappointed. This is not how I had imagined it would be. I had expected eager excitement; I have encountered a form of exhaustion. It takes me a long time to realise what has happened. My parents have faced their worst fear. A tragedy they had not allowed themselves to imagine. Their son is dead. There are some losses that cannot be confronted twice. This is one of them. My childhood and adolescence have ended. My father and mother are preparing to let me go.

* * *

Years later, researching another topic, I come across a reference to Haile Selassie's five-year exile in England, much of which was spent at Fairfield House, a property he bought in Bath. My father's story that he used to sit opposite the Lion of Judah, the direct descendant of King Solomon and the Queen of Sheba, in a first class compartment on the train to Paddington proves to be true.

CHAPTER TWENTY-FOUR

Foodstuff (and drinkstuff)

I can eat anything (except fufu). For this I must thank my mother. Cookery was for her – like sewing, decorating, upholstery and plumbing – a practical problem to be solved and not an art to be perfected. She had never been taught to cook. She hadn't expected she would need to cook. When she met my father, she set about learning how it was done. She found inspiration in *Mrs Beeton's Book of Household Management* and the recipe leaflets published by the wartime Ministry of Food. The key ingredient in my mother's cooking was urgency. What she didn't boil was likely to be fried.

* * *

I am back at our kitchen table in Highgate. This evening we are eating 'curry'. My mother's curry is a personal interpretation of the Anglo-Indian dish she must have remembered her own mother asking their cook to prepare. The chief ingredient is the khaki curry powder that comes from a square tin with a corroded lid and a faded violet label. My mother favours the heaped tablespoon above the level teaspoon which means that other ingredients in the curry are incidental. My father and I are perfectly happy with my mother's curry. I have grown up with it; my father has grown used to it. Neither of us would dream of suggesting that it was anything other than first-rate.

My father has been reminiscing about the fashionable restaurants he once frequented in the West End; lunch at the Savoy or the Carlton Grill, after-theatre supper at Rules in Maiden Lane. Although he was no gourmet, he had – in his wealthy days – greatly enjoyed the surroundings and there must have been moments when he missed them.

I have recently returned from Japan and am keen to tell my parents about fugu restaurants where blowfish, parts of which are one thousand times more poisonous than cyanide, are prepared by licensed chefs for rich Japanese diners addicted to risk. But now that I'm back home, my mother and father are not especially interested in Japan.

I tell them anyway. My father isn't listening to me. I'm not listening to him. And my mother, whose thoughts are far away, is listening to neither of us. We are perfectly content, sitting together as before, at our kitchen table in Highgate.

* * *

During my childhood, we didn't eat in restaurants. I remember only one occasion when we ate out. In the dining-room of a respectable hotel in Bath my father ordered rissoles, peas and boiled potatoes. We were served by three waiters with white napkins and silver forks and spoons, and it was very grand. But the breaded orange rissoles were little different from those we had at home.

In the afternoon we went to Wellsway to visit Granny. My father and mother, Granny and Rose, sit drinking tea. I have a glass of orange squash. Granny is, as usual, picking the currants out of her currant bun. This always exasperates my father although he says nothing at the time.

'Why doesn't she ask Rose to buy buns without currants?' he asks my mother, on the train home to London.

'Perhaps currants add to the flavour of the bun,' my mother suggests, without much conviction.

My father snorts but, as the fields slip past the carriage window, I think I can understand how soothing it must be to pick currants from a currant bun.

* * *

My father ate what was put in front of him. If he had been asked to express a preference, he might have mentioned lamb chops or haddock. But he might not. At teatime he liked bloater paste. My mother – remembering her father's partiality for *Patum Peperium* – would sometimes buy a jar of Gentleman's Relish. This my father spread with due care on buttered toast. But I think he preferred his bloater paste on brown bread.

In some unguarded moment he must once have extolled the virtues of tripe and onions. Whatever it was that he said served to convince my mother that he harboured a particular passion for the dish. She herself loathed tripe and preparing it disgusted her but, at intervals, it was something she felt she should do. As my mother and I survey the tripe in the pan – pale and pulpy – we find it difficult to believe that anyone can bring themselves to eat it. But, we agree sagely, people are different and have different tastes. The French eat most peculiar things and so, it is said, do some Africans.

I don't know whether or not my father really liked tripe; or, if he did, whether or not he liked the tripe that my mother cooked for him. If he didn't, he would never have said anything. He knows what my mother's tripe means. He eats it sitting by himself in the kitchen. My mother and I can't stand the sight or smell of the appalling mess and we eat our water-logged poached eggs in front of the television.

* * *

GODFREY My sister Dolly won't have drink in the house except parsnip wine which she makes herself. I tried it once. (Pause.) I fell over.

– *My Brother and I, Dad's Army Episode 73*

* * *

'I am an alcoholic,' my father would declare. Nothing in particular would prompt him to say it although he often had a glass of wine in his hand at the time.

Were my mother and I expected to respond by assuring him that he wasn't? If we were, we didn't. We knew what came next.

'I'm not saying that I'm a roaring drunk,' he'd continue, 'but I am to some degree dependent on alcohol. And therefore – technically – I am an alcoholic.'

The thought seemed to give him some satisfaction. Whether to prove or disprove his assertion, he would periodically go 'on the wagon'. This was a serious undertaking which was not ventured upon lightly. His weeks 'on the wagon' were trying periods and we were all heartily relieved when his bout of abstinence came to an end.

My father's alcoholism wasn't entirely a myth. After the death of his father he had – in his words – 'thrown over the traces' and started drinking whisky. Whisky didn't suit him. It changed his personality, destroyed his sense of humour and clouded his judgement.

'Gin pickles your innards but whisky's the killer.' (Pause.) 'The problem with whisky is the whisky hangover. One thing cures the whisky hangover and that's more whisky. You wake up with a whisky hangover and you begin again. That's why whisky is the killer.' (Pause.) 'Today I only drink whisky for medicinal purposes.'

Whisky was one thing but beer, gin and wine were another. Beer, gin and wine were friends.

'Wine,' says my father, 'delights all the senses.'

(I say something similar myself.)

'The sense of taste and the sense of smell, and also the senses of sight and sound.'

(I know what's coming next.)

'The colour of the wine, the label on the bottle; the sound of the cork, the wine being poured into a glass.'

(The sense of touch is trickier and is sometimes omitted.)

'The wine on your lips, the shape of the bottle in your hand.'

('Hold wine bottles by the neck,' says my father, on other occasions, 'and women by the waist.')

'The Phoenicians used to bathe in wine and so, I believe, did the Mesopotamians.'

(Did my father say this? It sounds more like me.)

My father and I sit and reflect upon the life-enhancing properties of wine. However, he's been speaking theoretically. Neither of us moves to open the unlabelled bottle that stands in front of us at the centre of the kitchen table.

My mother began making wine as an economy measure; and because she thought she could. In fact she couldn't. The wine that my mother made was virtually undrinkable. She certainly didn't drink it herself and, if I could avoid it, neither did I. Whenever my father knew I was coming to supper, he would make a special effort to bring home bottles of Guinness from the Duke of St Albans. I was grateful, but he himself knew where his duty lay.

It seems a pity that now, when he can afford a bottle of Burgundy again, he has to drink my mother's wine, but the habit has become established and acceptance is a virtue that my father embodies. Besides, he has already drunk a pint or two of bitter at the Duke of St Albans and an 'actor's gin' before he draws up his chair to the kitchen table.

Beer was, for my father, beer. Nothing more. At Sunday lunch he drank light ale; in the pub he drank bitter. He didn't distinguish between keg and cask. The cause of real ale didn't concern him. The watery, flavourless 'bitter' that he and his companions drank at the Duke of St Albans they cheerfully referred to as 'Pond', a homage to the Highgate ponds nearby. He drank beer, my father said, for volume. His body needed liquid and beer supplied that need. If he hadn't disliked the taste of London tap water, he said, he might have drunk more of it. Unlike Birmingham water which, coming from the hills of Wales, was sweet and pure. From time to time he spoke of bringing back bottles of water on the train home from Birmingham after recording episodes of *The Archers*. He never did. And I'm sure he drank as much beer in Birmingham as he did in London.

Gin was Gordons, and an 'actor's gin' was a ritual. It involved pouring a hefty measure into a 'tooth-mug' and then a fraction more to be sure there was sufficient. The 'tooth-mug' was a glass which, while not actually dirty, was not noticeably clean. There was no question of adding tonic, lemon or ice to an actor's gin. The correct procedure was to leave the cold tap running for a minute (allowing some of the lead in the pipes to go down the drain) and then wave the tooth-mug in the general direction of the flow. There was no need to let much – or indeed any – of the water enter the glass. An actor's gin lasted as long as it took my mother and me to lay the kitchen table for three.

* * *

Although not strictly medicinal, gin could be restorative. Bill Pertwee – Hodges, Chief Air Raid Warden in *Dad's Army* – recalls an afternoon filming in Norfolk when my father had to tell the director, David Croft, that he was feeling unwell. David, who was always exceptionally solicitous, at once arranged for a car to take him back to the Bell Hotel to rest. 'When we arrived back in Thetford,' says Bill, 'we saw Arnold walking out of a nearby pub. "Shouldn't you be resting?", we asked. He replied, "Well, I had a gin in the hotel and I felt so much better that I thought I'd go out and have another one."'

* * *

Being cast away on a desert island would have suited my mother's practical skills. She would have enjoyed constructing a shelter and finding food. But very soon she would have become horribly lonely, and perhaps with no one to take care of, she might not have bothered at all. In any case, it was my father who was invited to become Roy Plomley's guest on *Desert Island Discs* in November 1973.

The cassette recording reminds me that for the show my father adopted the higher-pitched actor's voice he employed when playing Doughy Hood in *The Archers* and Private Godfrey in *Dad's Army*. He was, in effect, in character and playing Arnold Ridley, the actor. His choice of music was – probably still in character – quite dreadful and included the Palm Court Trio playing *A Little Love, a Little Kiss* and John McCormack singing *I Hear You Calling Me*. His choice of a book and a luxury to accompany him on the island were more personal.

For his book he chose *Bradshaw's Railway Timetable*. This would, he said, allow him to plan an infinite number of railway journeys from one part of the British Isles to another. It was, I think, an eminently practical choice. After all, the Bible and Shakespeare are enough for most people.

His choice of luxury struck me at first as bizarre. What on earth could my father do with a wine-making kit? He would have no idea how to use it; he would make no attempt to find out. If wine was what he wanted, why not ask for a crate of Burgundy? Did he want not to seem to be imposing on the BBC's generosity? Or was this a private token of appreciation addressed to my mother? Was he saying that although the peace and solitude of the desert island – no barking dogs, no loud laughter, no transistor radios – would hold many attractions for him, he would miss her terribly and would like to be rescued – please – as soon as possible and returned to the kitchen table in Highgate?

* * *

Two other members of the *Dad's Army* cast were Roy Plomley's guests on *Desert Island Discs*. For his luxury Arthur Lowe ordered 'claret', while John Le Mesurier's request was for 'a small distillery'.

Radio4

Private Godfrey gets posted . . . Arnold Ridley: 7.2 pm

2.0
Weekend
Woman's Hour
Introduced by Judith Chalmers
The week in *Woman's Hour*.
What the European papers say.
Entertainment Round-up: by
GORDON GOW.
What's New for the Home:
SALLY HOLLOWAY reports.
Fit for Work?, advice on
keeping healthy for women at
work. 5: The single woman in
a bed-sitter.
The Walking Shadow
by JEAN STUBBS
abridged by MYRA SKATON
Read by MICHAEL MCCLAIN

3.0 News

3.5
Afternoon Theatre
The Bringer of Bad News
by MIKE STOTT
with Alan Downer as
Det-Sgt John Smith
'They say ' The bringer of bad
news is not loved.' When Det-
Sgt John Smith agrees to act
as a private-eye for very personal reasons he finds out just
how true that saying is.
Det-Con Phil Breech
                    PETER MESSALINE

6.15
Letter from America
by ALISTAIR COOKE
(Friday's broadcast: repeated
again on Sunday, 9.15 am) ‡

6.30
Sports Session
A nationwide look at the stories
behind the day's sporting headlines.

7.0 News

7.2
Desert Island Discs
Arnold Ridley, actor and playwright, discusses with ROY
PLOMLEY (in a recorded programme devised by him) the
gramophone records he would
take to a *desert island*.
Producer RONALD COOK
(Repeated: Monday, 12.27 pm)

7.30 *Stereo*
These You Have Loved
Records introduced by
Richard Baker
(Shortened edn: Thurs, 9.5 am)

8.30
Saturday-Night

CHAPTER TWENTY-FIVE

Touching fame

This is what it means to be famous, however modestly.

We are sitting in the departure hall at Southampton docks – an almost empty cavern – my mother, my father and I. It's a grey day. Storms have been forecast. This is a scene we have played out before but it hasn't become any less painful. I'm going away again. I am taking up a job in Spain; not far from Barcelona. Not far away at all. But the question that hangs over us is still the same. Is this the last time the three of us will be together? There is no suggestion I shouldn't go but the fact remains that when I first started travelling, my father was ten years younger than he is today. He is now seventy-eight. He's in work. All is well. But I will be away for nine months. There is nothing to be said or done except to sit together and wait until it's time for me to pick up my bags and leave.

On the other side of the departure hall is a large family group. Mother, father, children, uncles, aunts, friends. I don't notice them until two members of the party approach. I ignore them as they start to circle us.

'It's not, is it?'

'Yes, it is.'

'Is it?'

'It's him.'

'Who?'

'The old one.'

They go away and return with another member of the party.

'Yes, that's him.'

'What's his name?'

'Godfrey.'

'Is it?'

'Yes.'

'Private Godfrey!'

It's as if we're not really here. As if we're on display at an exhibition. Animals in a zoo. One of them tries to poke us into life.

'Private Godfrey! Private Godfrey! Do you want to be excused?'

I find I'm on my feet. I don't shout. I don't need to shout. My rage is too terrible.

'Why – don't – you – fuck – off!'

They're shocked. Dumbstruck. I'm shocked myself. My parents, still lost in their misery, register nothing.

'We just wanted to …'

His words trail away. They are hurt and aggrieved. There'll be no confrontation. I resume my seat and they slink back to their group. I feel bad. I have punctured their jollity.

'It wasn't him anyway,' I hear one of them say.

We continue our wait in silence.

*   *   *

I thought my story about fame ended in Southampton, but now I find that it doesn't.

On the ship to Bilbao, I find the bar and some boisterous company. A storm has blown up in the Bay of Biscay and the evening is becoming more riotous.

'You know who that is, don't you?' says my drinking companion, pointing to a figure in a flying jacket standing at the bar.

I admit that I don't.

'That's Ginger Baker.'

'Oh?'

The name is familiar but nothing more.

'Ginger Baker. Cream. The drummer. Or rather he was.'

I know that Cream is a group, but they may have come to prominence while I was out of the country because I don't know their music. However, I study Ginger Baker – if this is who he is – with interest. He is surrounded by a group of drinkers and seems to be holding court.

'He's started his own group. Ginger Baker's Air Force. He's on his way to Africa.'

I find I am storing away these facts as if they mattered to me.

Later in the evening I am standing at the bar myself. The ship is bucking and rolling and we need to empty our glasses quickly to avoid spilling our drinks. At some point I find that Ginger Baker has linked arms with me. He has mistaken me for someone else – an old friend called Buster or Dusty – and I don't disabuse him. We've all drunk too much to make explanations easy. Besides, I don't mind being Ginger Baker's friend. Not in the slightest. In fact I feel privileged. The group around us has grown and the volume of noise and laughter has swollen to fill the entire bar. A lewd story has exploded in a barrage of expletives when a middle-aged man in a dark blue blazer and regimental tie approaches our group.

'Would you mind moderating your language,' he says. 'My wife is sitting over there.'

It's plain the blazer doesn't know that he is addressing Ginger Baker, ex-drummer of Cream. We wait to see what will happen.

'She is, is she?' Ginger Baker replies, unlinking his arm from mine. 'And that's my old lady sitting over there. What about it?'

The blazer sees there is no answer to this and wisely retreats to his table. He and his wife leave the bar shortly afterwards.

'Old fool!' we think. 'Ginger Baker told him.'

The night continues; the storm rises; bottles and glasses start to fall to the floor. We stagger to our cabins. A Japanese boy in a lower bunk is feeling ill and pleads for someone to call the ship's doctor. We ignore him.

We arrive in Bilbao eighteen hours late. I have missed my train connection to Barcelona and must hitch a lift. I don't see Ginger Baker again, although what may be his Land Rover – a row of jerry cans on the roof – roars past the point where I'm standing.

I spend my first night in Spain on a mattress in someone's flat. Lying awake, I replay the previous evening in the ship's bar. I see that I have been party to a piece of boorish bullying. I have brushed against celebrity and been found wanting. I feel tainted by the contact and more than a little ashamed of myself. In the morning I learn that the stain on the mattress is where, last week, the cat haemorrhaged and died.

I put the episode behind me.

* * *

In the course of a long life my father encountered a bewildering variety of famous names. Some that he referred to in passing would catch me by surprise – George Bernard Shaw, 'too much charm to really be offensive', Noel Coward, 'a sprightly and uninhibited actor' – but, while I was a truculent teenager, I maintained a studied indifference. Very few of them receive any mention in 'The Book', and those who do seem to be there for no better reason than that their names came to mind as he sat at his typewriter.

> I saw *Juno and the Paycock* at the Royalty Theatre in company with the author. Beyond the fact that we were both newcomers to the London scene Sean O'Casey and myself had little in common but we saw quite a bit of each other. When he was in London we often went drinking together in the Charlotte Street area. I remember him as a quiet man, lacking in conversation. Or perhaps I did too much of the talking!

The fact is that as a showbiz autobiography 'The Book' is a flop. It has no tinsel, no tittle-tattle, no scandal, no sparkle. While my father is touchingly frank about himself, he is absurdly discreet about other people. Whenever there's a hint of a misdemeanour, the protagonists' names are disguised as 'X', 'Y' and 'Z'. This does not make for exciting reading.

I will illustrate what I'm saying with some extracts. Here, for example, is what my father writes about the classical actor, Henry Ainley, whose name means nothing to me although further research reveals that he was at one time a member of Herbert Beerbohm Tree's company and that his professional debut was in *Henry V* (although not as the king). But Henry Ainley must have been a figure of importance for my father. Why else would he appear in 'The Book'?

> Garlands Hotel was much patronised by bishops and lesser clergy and Henry Ainley was one of the permanent guests. He was in badly failing health at the time and, although I sometimes passed him in the hall or on the stairs, I don't remember any conversation between us.

This isn't illuminating. And neither is this extract about the film director, Alfred Hitchcock.

> While working at Elstree, I got to know Alfred Hitchcock quite well. He had just started on the road to world fame by making one of the greatest successes of early talkies: a drama entitled *Blackmail* which became a landmark in British pictures. 'Hitch' had a small car and often drove me back to the West End. Sometimes I had tea with him and his wife at their flat which, if I remember correctly, was somewhere near St John's Wood.

Nor another about the crime writer, Agatha Christie.

> On the morning of the first rehearsal [of the stage version of *Peril At End House* which my father had adapted for the theatre] I met Mrs Christie by appointment at the Richmond Theatre. I must admit she didn't answer my preconceived picture of a world famous novelist in the least. She possessed an air of great dignity and always suggested to me the wife of a rural dean. Her head had by no means been turned by success. That day she had actually brought some sandwiches for her lunch.

There are many more examples in 'The Book' but I'll leave them where they are. It's enough to say that in the world of celebrity my father was for the most part an innocent.

* * *

Fame, like youth, passes. And, although, like youth, we know it must, it's difficult to believe it will. Unlike youth, however, fame sometimes returns.

I am mildly surprised to find that my father proposes to travel with me as far as Kentish Town on the 214 bus. My mother normally drives him wherever he wants to go or, now that he can afford them again, he takes a taxi. I am more surprised to find he has acquired a pair of dark glasses which he now takes from the side pocket of his jacket and puts on before we cross Highgate West Hill at the zebra crossing.

My mother tells me later that he has taken to wearing dark glasses whenever *Dad's Army* is showing on television. To protect his anonymity, she explains. An elderly man catching the 214 bus at Parliament Hill Fields is unlikely to attract much attention. An elderly man wearing dark glasses and a panama hat on a dull day in March almost certainly will. Outside the Duke of St Albans two women pause in their conversation; a middle-aged couple looks up and then looks away again rapidly. On the top deck of the bus huddling schoolgirls giggle and nudge each other. My father affects not to notice them but I am not persuaded. It amuses me to find that he is enjoying his modest, late-flowering celebrity.

* * *

Wednesday, 7th January 1976. My father's eightieth birthday.

I have been teaching cheerful Brazilians in Malet Street but Wednesdays are a half-day and I finish at lunchtime. I decide to walk to the theatre to see my father before the matinée. The stage show of *Dad's Army* has been running at the Shaftesbury Theatre for several weeks and there will be a matinée this afternoon and an evening performance tonight. We have decided not to celebrate my father's birthday until Sunday when he can relax, but it would be good to wish him happy birthday on the day itself.

What I didn't expect was the crowd of fans around the stage door.

They are waiting expectantly with autograph books and souvenirs to be signed. This isn't a world I know. The fans are of every description. They have nothing obvious in common except their need to be here. I am out of place. I am a son who has come to wish his father happy birthday but I feel I am trespassing. Which is why, when the taxi pulls up, I don't push to the front of the crowd.

'It's …'

'Godfrey!'

'Who …?'

'Private Godfrey!'

'Which …?'

'Private Godfrey! Arnold! Over here.'

'Not now!' says my father, flapping a folded copy of the *Evening Standard*. 'Not now!'

He is wearing a kindly smile but his fixed intent is to reach the haven of the stage door.

'OB,' I say, not very loudly. 'OB!'

His gesture with the *Evening Standard* is a mixture of a gracious acknowledgement and swatting a fly.

'Not now!' he says. 'Not now!'

The stage door opens and he disappears inside. I press through the crowd again and present myself to the doorkeeper.

'That was my father,' I say. 'I think he'd want to see me.'

When my father hurries back to the stage door, I tell him – with not a little relish – that he has just brushed aside his only son in the crowd. I am amused, but he is mortified. I assure him that it doesn't matter at all, but to him it does. I follow him down the passage to his dressing-room and listen to another apology. The only way I can make him feel better is to stay for the matinée performance. It's not what I want to do – I have other plans for the afternoon – but I seem to have no choice.

I sit on my own in the stalls, uncomfortable and out of place. The show itself is infused with a wartime nostalgia that leaves me cold and, having seen very little of *Dad's Army*, nothing means much to me. We are approaching the interval when my father – in the character of

Arnold Ridley more than Private Godfrey – steps forward with the spotlight to recite *Lords of the Air*. His eyes are fixed on the dress circle, utter concentration, exemplary verse-speaking. The chorus, singing *a capella* in the background, moves slowly downstage to surround him. A moment of true theatre. Which dissolves. And we return to music hall and period comedy. I sink back into my seat.

At some point the band plays *Happy Birthday* and a cake with eighty candles is brought onto the stage. Whether this happens during the show itself or after the audience has left the auditorium, I don't remember. By this time *Dad's Army* and real life have become disturbingly intertwined. I escape from the theatre as soon as I can and, with some relief, find myself back on Shaftesbury Avenue.

*　*　*

The researcher and I don't like each other. She reminds me of a tin fairy my mother used to hang on our Christmas tree. It seems likely I remind her of something worse, but she has been forced to buy me lunch. Her task is to persuade me to recall, and then relate, an amusing incident revolving around my father and me. This is to be my contribution when the show is recorded. I am not being cooperative and have told her that I have no intention of telling stories to a television audience.

'If you don't,' she says, 'I'm afraid you won't be in the show.'

This is her trump card.

'I have no wish to be in the show,' I say, 'and it wouldn't surprise me if my father did a Danny Blanchflower and refused to take part.'

The researcher looks disbelieving, then aghast.

'He's a very private person,' I explain. 'We both are.'

She concludes I'm deranged, but we continue with lunch and resume negotiation. Finally I agree to appear on the show on condition that I am not required to utter a single word.

I wasn't at my best that afternoon ten days after the run of the stage version of *Dad's Army* had completed its longish run at the Shaftesbury

Theatre. For one thing I was still annoyed at having lost a record of which I was very proud. Until the penultimate week of the play, I hadn't missed a single performance or show – stage, radio or television – since October 1918 when I had been struck down by Spanish influenza at Birmingham. Now, only a fortnight before the end of the Shaftesbury run, I was again suffering from 'flu and my doctor had said that it would be madness to go to the theatre in my state of health at my age. I only missed four performances, but the record was gone. Now my afternoon nap was to be interrupted. 'Be at Marylebone station at three o'clock sharp! Report to the old dining-room on Platform 1 where your dresser will be waiting for you with your costume.' Apparently we were to make a short publicity film. A bit annoying, to say the least of it.

On arriving at Platform 1, I found Arthur Lowe and members of the platoon with the usual dressers changing in the dining-room which had been reserved for us. I was told by one of the technicians, who seemed to be in command of the operation, that the actual filming was to take place on one of the centre platforms and that I wouldn't be required for the opening shots. Apparently the script had it that the platoon was going off by train and were waiting for Godfrey who was late. As I wasn't wanted immediately and only just recovering from my influenza bout, it would be better if I remained in the warm until actually wanted. So off everyone went leaving me alone.

About five minutes later one of the technicians appeared, said they were waiting for me and that he would conduct me to my starting point. He picked up my kit bag and escorted me down Platform 1 and around to the gate of one of the centre platforms on which, some way down, I could see the platoon in a group with Captain Mainwaring looking in my direction and waving.

'Right,' said the technician, handing over my kit bag and off I stumbled along the platform, acting like mad the part of a worried latecomer. A little short of breath I was approaching Captain Mainwaring and the rest of the platoon. But before I reached Arthur Lowe there was an interruption. 'Arnold Ridley,' said Eamonn Andrews, handing me the red book. 'This is Your Life.'

I am proved entirely wrong. My father is a true professional and perfectly happy to take part. The show itself skips through his life innocuously enough and everyone is pleased with it.

I watch the programme when it is transmitted, and see myself sitting beside my mother, saying nothing, looking like a lemon.

The researcher doesn't speak to me at the after-show party which is a surprisingly lively affair. The producers have arranged for a group of vigorous old rugby club boys to come up from Bath by train and they set about the business of enjoying themselves with the rather prim BBC catering staff. When the beer runs out, they decide to make a night of it in the West End and almost persuade my father to join them. Towards the close, a very senior BBC executive joins the party, a gin-and-tonic in his hand.

'What would you say,' he asks my father, with no preamble, 'if I called you "Arthur Ridley"?'

The question is one of such startling inanity that momentarily my father is lost for words.

'I'd ignore you,' he replies. 'Unless, of course, you were offering me a job.'

* * *

An advantage of living on Hong Kong Island is that every morning I can take the Star Ferry to Kowloon where I catch a bus or taxi to the office.

It's a beautiful day in December – bright sun, blue sky – and the harbour is postcard perfect. Life is good. The Hong Kong Stage Club production of *Aladdin* is half way through its run and I am enjoying my part. A week of late nights may catch up with me but I will be able to sleep on the overnight flight on Sunday when I return to the UK for Christmas.

Why is that child staring at me? I return to the *South China Morning Post*. And then look up again. The boy is improbably blond, as are many expatriate children born and brought up in Hong Kong. He tugs at his elder sister's sleeve and she too stares in my direction.

The sister taps her mother on the arm. She looks up briefly from her magazine and nods. The two children approach and it dawns on me that, although I am not wearing green make-up or gold glitter, I have been recognised. A piece of paper is put in front of me – I have to provide my own pen – and with a flourish I write, 'THE GENIE'. I know it isn't me they're interested in but the part I'm playing. They thank me politely and return to their mother who doesn't look up again. (I notice she is reading the *Hong Kong Tatler*.) I try to decide whether I feel irritated or gratified. On balance I find I'm gratified.

The next morning I look out for more *gweilo* children on the Star Ferry. I see several but none of them asks me for my autograph. Can I bring myself to admit that I am disappointed?

CHAPTER TWENTY-SIX

'Dear Arnold'

Sunday, 11th May 2008. We have been to the *Dad's Army Day* at the Bressingham Steam Museum and now we are sitting in the courtyard of the Bell Hotel, Thetford, where the cast used to stay while they were filming in Norfolk. A good moment to talk to you about your grandfather. The grandfather you were too young to know. Private Godfrey and Arnold Ridley. Arnold Ridley and Private Godfrey. I feel sure it must be easy to confuse the two.

Dad's Army lives on; an unlooked-for, mild-mannered immortality. Forty years after the show was first broadcast, the ghosts and shadows of the Walmington-on-Sea platoon remain on parade. In the front row stands Private Godfrey. *Click. Play* ▷ You can see him whenever you choose.

A family photograph is a single image, to be studied, interpreted, brought to life by narrative and imagination. But a television character is somehow complete, a living reality, a fictional fact. It must be difficult to dispel. Which leads me to ask you my question.

'When you picture your grandfather, do you see Private Godfrey? Can I put it another way. Do you ever feel that you're Godfrey's grandson?'

When we arrive at Bressingham, we park in a field. Thin wisps of brown smoke are rising above a line of trees. The smell of steam trains catches at my memory. Paddington station; Sunday mornings with my father. Three thousand *Dad's Army* enthusiasts have come to celebrate the fortieth anniversary of the show. It's a gentle event in the sun. Speeches, stalls, celebrity signings. This isn't a world where you and I belong but we're perfectly content to be here for an hour or two. As we're about to leave, we are asked for our autographs. Why?

We know the answer, of course. We are Godfrey's son and Godfrey's grandson. But it doesn't seem enough. Shyly we sign the programme that has been proffered and we are warmly thanked.

We drive on to Thetford and try to follow the *Dad's Army* walking trail which takes in many of the locations used in the show. But because neither of us has watched more than a handful of episodes, it means very little to us. When we find ourselves at the Bell Hotel, we study the *Dad's Army* plaque in reception and the display of photographs on the wall before taking our drinks outside.

'Godfrey's grandson? No, not at all. Godfrey was a part OB played on television.' (It touches me that you use my father's 'particular' name so comfortably.) 'I feel amazingly proud of him but he was an actor. I'm more impressed that he was a playwright.' (Do you sense I need further convincing?) 'So, no. I don't see Godfrey. The way I picture OB has been shaped by the stories you've told me about him. Not by television.' (You could have said nothing better.)

And now it's plain. The question I should be asking – not you but me – is why do I find Godfrey so troubling?

*   *   *

When I was very young, powdery old theatricals would bend down, look me full in the face, and tell me how proud I should feel to be the son of the author of *The Ghost Train*. To be told this disturbed me. There were so many ways I was proud of my father but the fact that he had written a famous play wasn't really one of them. I felt I must be letting him down although I didn't know how.

I have the same sense about Private Godfrey.

Nine years. From 1968 to 1977. Eighty television episodes, the West End stage show, the provincial tour, the Royal Variety Performance. The *Dad's Army* years were, for my father and mother, a happy, hard-working time. Regular television fees gave them a degree of financial security that they hadn't known since our early years in Notting Hill Gate. The show's success restored my father's faith in himself and my mother's faith in everything. For this I am immeasurably grateful.

But I wasn't there.

My relationship with Private Godfrey has remained distant. For many people he is a much-loved figure, a national treasure, but I feel no kinship with him, no affection for him, nothing. On the occasions when we have come face-to-face (such as those excruciating moments when I have been introduced to strangers as 'Godfrey's son') I am – more than is necessary – brusque, sullen, aloof. Why? What am I defending? Who am I protecting? My father or myself? Am I the son tenderly shaving the back of his father's neck with a dry razor, or the child at Lord's, mistaken for a grandson, engulfed by a painful rage that he can't explain or share? In either case, it's a poor reward for blameless, bewildered Godfrey, in whose debt I know I am; and about whom – it now strikes me – I know very little.

* * *

In a box of my mother's unsorted possessions I find *Dad's Army* books and videos. I have no recollection of deciding to keep them but I seemed to know they were there.

I let the books fall open at random. Mellow anecdotes, potted biographies, histories, lists. I skim them quickly. I don't know what I'm looking for. My eyes pass across the photographs. Pictures taken on location, scenes from the show. Here is Godfrey. And here. Anxious, puzzled, guileless. In his Home Guard uniform with a tin hat and rifle, wearing his medical orderly's armband and carrying his first aid bag, dressed as a Morris dancer, dressed as a Pierrot. I see Private Godfrey but I don't see my father. Another photograph. My mother and father taken together in a garden. (Whose garden?) My father is wearing his Savage Club tie; my mother has her arm round his shoulder. It is staged, posed, professional. The actor, Arnold Ridley, and his wife. It's not them. I turn back a page. This is a picture I didn't expect to see. The framed photograph that always hung in my father's bedroom KEEPERS OF YOUTH. His name in lights in St Martin's Lane.

As a child, I would stand in front of this photograph for minutes at a time. Here was the evidence of my father's career at its peak; my

229

father, the successful West End playwright as I never knew him. It's unsettling to find it here in this book. I pick up another book which falls open at a picture of the platoon in a break between takes. Godfrey, Pike, Mainwaring, Jones, Wilson, Walker. They are resting on a grass bank, plastic beakers in their hands. A cigarette hangs from Godfrey's mouth, as it did when he sat by his bed playing cards or, at the dining-room table, frowning over his accounts. Godfrey is, recognisably, my father. I'm not sure if this pleases me or not.

*　*　*

I set myself the task of searching out Private Godfrey although what I am hoping to find isn't clear to me. I send letters to the writers of *Dad's Army*, Jimmy Perry and David Croft, and to two surviving members of the cast, Bill Pertwee and Frank Williams. They respond kindly and we arrange to meet. I don't know what I'll learn – their stories have been recounted so fully and so well that there can't be much to add – but I'm hoping that by talking to them I will breathe life into whatever it is I'm doing.

I watch several episodes of *Dad's Army* and become better acquainted with Private Godfrey. But I don't warm to him. His deference irritates me, as do his requests to be excused and his tendency to fall asleep. I have an irrational urge to protest. This isn't my father. This isn't how I want him portrayed. (I know I'm becoming muddled.)

Godfrey's weak bladder was a fiction. Although, when I think about it, on rugby afternoons, after his pre-kick-off drink, we very seldom passed a Gents. 'Never miss an opportunity,' my father advises me, 'as the Duke of Wellington used to say.' (I can find no record of the Duke of Wellington having said this.) But my father's need for sleep was a fact.

I find it terribly difficult to keep awake between 2.30 and 4.00 p.m. and the matinee performances of *Twelve Angry Men* at the Queens and Lyric Theatres in Shaftesbury Avenue were torture for me. Not only was I on stage from the beginning to the very end of the play but, for nearly all the time, I was sitting at a table with long intervals between speeches and lines. There were times when I found the greatest difficulty in stopping myself from sliding off my chair onto the floor of the stage.

I read later that my father took his own folding chair to rehearsals and, in the afternoons, when he wasn't on the set, he would drop off to sleep. A production assistant would be sent to wake him very gently. 'Excuse me, Arnold, but we're just coming up to your scene.' And he would open his eyes and say, in character, 'Oh, I'm terribly sorry.'

Branded – the episode in which Private Godfrey lets it be known that he was a conscientious objector in the First World War – catches me off-guard. Godfrey is ostracised horribly by the rest of the platoon before an act of heroism and the revelation of his true war record redeem him in everyone's eyes. My father gives a well-judged performance in a part that has been crafted for him. I watch the episode again. But then the closing credits: *You have been watching* ... The members of the platoon advance, rifles in hand. Mainwaring, Wilson, Jones, Frazer, Walker ... The camera reaches Godfrey. Why, I wonder, must he look so gaga?

I visit the British Library at St Pancras and sit at a desk in the humanities reading room in front of a collection of *Dad's Army* biographies, autobiographies, memoirs, scripts, guides, companions. Most are amiable, bland, unchallenging. One or two include sharper traces of truth. The pedant in me begins to detect minor inconsistencies, inaccuracies and contradictions but they're not important. The story remains the same. A happy time, fondly remembered. Incidents are generously embellished, anecdotes swell with the re-telling. The actors and the characters come together and draw apart as in a dance. Captain Mainwaring's fussy pomposity and Arthur Lowe's insistence on Craven 'A' cigarettes, Mr Kipling cakes and 'swim-about kippers'. Sergeant Wilson's well-bred courtesy and impossible vagueness and John Le Mesurier's practised helplessness. 'This heat is really exhausting. Could someone wind up my watch for me, please.' Private Frazer's doom-laden predictions and deranged soliloquies and John

Laurie's undisguised disdain for many of his colleagues – 'I'm the only actor here!' – and for the show itself. Everyone is invested with his own mythology.

'Dear Arnold.' My father is remembered with affection as a disciplined actor who knew his lines and learnt his moves quickly. On location, he had a habit of walking up and down during filming muttering, 'Tell them to get on with it!' – this sounds very like my father – but no one seems to have minded. When re-telling his history there are mildly inflated claims for the sporting achievements of his youth, and sympathetic (if frequently inaccurate) accounts of his financial travails. It is all very kindly meant.

There is only one discordant note: my father's relationship with John Laurie. Tales of rivalry and professional jealousy sound so unlike my father that I'm inclined to dismiss them, but the story reappears which means there must be a basis for it.

There are, or so I suppose, two ways to confront old age – to go gently or to rage – and we must choose which suits us best.

David Croft was a considerate director. He did not forget that two members of his cast, my father and John Laurie, were septuagenarians and he made every effort to look after them. John Laurie, an acerbic, independent character, seems to have rejected any special treatment and to have been keen to put a distance between himself and my father. 'Poor old boy. Look at him. He's falling apart.' My father, by contrast, accepted whatever was on offer and his gratitude was rewarded. In Thetford he was spared those shots that demanded too much physical exertion. In London his scenes were rehearsed first so that he could go home early. And at Television Centre he was fussed over agreeably by make-up girls, dressers and production assistants.

'Dear Arnold' was, I'm sure, a part to be played as much as Godfrey; although, like Godfrey, he borrowed heavily from himself to play it. 'Dear Arnold' helped him survive.

* * *

A story which I'll borrow from the stock of *Dad's Army* anecdotes.

My father had had a serious fall and torn a muscle in his calf. This meant that a few days before filming was due to begin in Norfolk, he was lying in bed at the Royal Masonic Hospital. His agent, Bill McLean, telephoned the BBC. 'I told them that Arnold had had a mishap. What I didn't tell them was that his leg was in plaster from toe to thigh. But it all worked out. They laid on a car to take him to Norfolk and he sat in the back waving out of the window like the Queen.'

The final stage of the journey was along a bumpy road. By the time the car stopped, my father had slipped down and was lying prone on the floor. David Croft opened the door and shook hands with him. 'He smiled bravely and I said I hoped the journey wasn't too hard for him. John Laurie, who was spying from the make-up caravan, seeing me shaking Arnold's hand, shouted out, "Look! Look! They're pumping him up! They're pumping him up!"'

'We propped him up against a tree,' David tells me, 'and photographed him looking left, right, up and down, wearing the worried expression he did so well. They were the only reaction shots I needed for what we were filming for the next week or two. After that I sent him home. He came back to us later as game as ever.'

David Croft shares another memory of my father.

'Your father had a dressing-room in the Shaftesbury Theatre just below the stage. There was a broken-down armchair in it. The chair must have been almost as old as Arnold. When he wasn't on stage, he would be poured into this chair like a blancmange. Wardrobe assistants would take off his trousers and dress him for the next scene and then help him onto the stage. And he never complained. Not once.'

I thank David for casting my father and tell him how much the part meant to him. I then ask him about my father's talents as an actor, mentioning the lifelong damage done to his confidence by AE Filmer.

'He was very good at being Arnold Ridley, marvellous at being Arnold Ridley,' says David.

This isn't, in all honesty, the answer I was expecting.

'Just as John Le Mesurier couldn't possibly have been anything else except John Le Mesurier,' David continues. 'John Le Mesurier used to say to James Beck, "You're far too versatile. If possible you should try to play the same part and – whenever you can – you should wear the same suit."'

* * *

It is one of many similar tributes.

'Private Godfrey was a wonderful invention and perfectly cast for Arnold Ridley because he was so sweet and gentle.'

Sweet and gentle? The remark is so graciously meant but I find it grates. How can I explain the compulsion I feel to prise them away from each other; Godfrey from my father, the actor from his part.

'Sweet and gentle as long as everything was going fine,' says Bill McLean, 'but he didn't stand for fools and could more than hold his own.'

We are sitting opposite each other in rattan chairs in Bill's office in Putney. Bill has a fine view of the river; I haven't been here before. Why is this? He was such an important part of my parent's life. It was after Bill took over as his agent that my father's career – then at a particularly low ebb – began to look up. But Bill and I don't know each other. We sometimes speak on the telephone – he is jovial, businesslike – but the last time we met was at my father's funeral. Or was it my mother's? Neither of us can remember.

'He was rehearsing a show in Manchester. All the actors were on time (as actors usually are) but the director arrived late and, without a word, started the rehearsal. Arnold called the whole rehearsal to a halt and demanded that the director apologise for being late before they continued. Which he did. This is a sweet old man? Don't count on it!'

Bill began life as an actor and, like most actors, he has a fund of well-rehearsed stories that he enjoys telling and tells well.

'I remember attending the first night of a revival of *The Ghost Train* at the Old Vic with Arnold and Althea. We sat down in the stalls, the curtain went up and Arnold promptly disappeared from the seat next to me. I didn't see him again for the rest of the production. Come the end of the performance the producer stands up on stage and starts to say they're very honoured to have the author in the audience and would he like to stand up and take a bow. Upon which a spotlight starts to sweep over the auditorium towards what is still an empty seat beside me. Althea doesn't bat an eyelid – maybe she's been through this before – but I am sitting there wondering what to do when the spotlight arrives at the empty seat. Can I stand up and pretend to be Arnold? I'm not required to say anything. I only have to wave. But, just as the spotlight hits the seat, so does Arnold – I've never seen such good timing – and he stands up as if he's been there throughout the whole performance. Later on, in the bar, having a drink, the director came up to him and asked him what he thought. It was always a mistake to ask Arnold this unless you were sure what the answer was going to be. "Well," he replied, "perhaps one day you'll write a play and I can bugger *that* up!" This is a gentle old man?'

Yes, Bill, I think. That was my father.

He pauses.

'But I never knew him to be nasty about anyone. Quite the contrary in fact.'

I ask Bill about my father's rivalry with John Laurie.

'I don't think there was anything serious. I always understood it was because they could never decide who was the oldest. Arnold used to celebrate his birthdays at least one year early in case he didn't make it to the next one. *I* was certainly confused about how old he was and I strongly suspect that *he* was confused, too!'

We talk about the studio recordings at Television Centre which he always attended with my mother.

'As an agent, I have a tendency to sit quietly at the back and try to be unnoticed. Which was not Althea's way of doing anything. She sat where the spotlight was and usually insisted that I came and sat next to her.'

I like my picture of them sitting together, my mother and Bill; a surrogate son. I went to none of the *Dad's Army* recordings myself.

*   *   *

The year of events, 1968. The Prague Spring. The Tet Offensive. Riots in Paris. Protests in Grosvenor Square. A year of historical change. The post-war era is ending and all things are possible.

In the summer I leave university; I have to decide what happens next. I see an advertisement in *The Times*. Berlitz is recruiting teachers to work in Japan. I've no knowledge of Japan but I remember that James Joyce taught for Berlitz in Trieste and I want to travel.

I attend an open interview at the Park Lane Hotel, Piccadilly, and am surprised to find so many other applicants queuing at the table in the lobby. I join the queue, complete an application form and – an hour or two later – I am interviewed by a man in a sharp suit. I don't know whether the interview goes well or badly. I am asked questions and I answer them. I leave the hotel and think no more about it.

That evening I am back in the kitchen in Highgate. My parents and I are eating supper when the telephone rings. I leave the table to answer it. When the call ends, I remain alone in the hall. In the dark. In shock. I have been offered a job in Japan and I find that I have accepted it. I replace the receiver and return to the kitchen.

I haven't prepared them; I haven't prepared myself. This isn't the way to say it but I find I'm saying it anyway.

'I've taken a job in Japan.'

I sit at the table. But it is now a different table. I can't bring myself to look at my parents. I know I've been brutal but I don't know why. Not much is said. A question or two, which I'm not yet able to answer. And that's all. My mother and I start to wash up and my father goes to bed. 'Good night, old boy.' Life – it seems – goes on as before.

Except that it doesn't, but I am too wrapped up in my preparations to notice what has begun to happen. A readjustment, a fractional realignment, a drawing together. For comfort, consolation, protection. Our family arithmetic is altering. Three is separating into two and one.

My parents are releasing me.

* * *

I watch, for the first time, the final episode, *Never Too Old*. The cast knew, while they were recording it, that this was the end of *Dad's Army*. The mood on the set is said to have been sombre but steady, although a member of the production team had to leave the studio in tears. And then, while I'm watching, among the guests at the wedding of Corporal Jones and Mrs Fox, resplendent in a period hat and lilac dress and 'reacting' vigorously, is my mother. A complete surprise.

* * *

Rehearsals, filming, recordings. In 1968 I was unaware of *Dad's Army*. My father was working and I was grateful for that. It seemed for now their money worries were receding. (My father was able to lend me £200 to travel to Japan.)

I saw none of the first series broadcast in the summer. I was working on the pea harvest in Norfolk. And when, next year, a second series was broadcast, I was teaching in Akasaka, living in Jingumae, making my own life.

Dad's Army wasn't part of it.

Japan, Morocco, Hong Kong. Working, travelling, living abroad as I had promised myself I would. But this doesn't explain enough. There were many months that I spent in England. When I had supper with my parents in Highgate. When I told them where I had been and where I planned to go next. Why didn't I ask them about the television show that was changing their lives?

I have talked about my jealousy of my parents' youth. My father as a young man. My mother as a West End star. How can I now explain my stony incuriosity about *Dad's Army*? Why did I try to shut it out? I recall Southampton docks, the Shaftesbury Theatre, *This Is Your Life*. My fury, my exasperation, my alienation. Was it a different jealousy that made me unwilling to accept that my father and mother were living their lives without me?

We know, as parents, that we must learn to let our children go. They have their own lives. Lives which aren't ours. And now a second lesson, learned very late. As children, we must do the same. We must let our parents go. As painful as such separations always are, we must allow them to return to a life without us.

I must release my parents as they released me.

* * *

I haven't found Godfrey; nor his shadow, 'Dear Arnold'. They've gone. But looking for them has been helpful.

It's not as Godfrey that I remember my father. It's not how I want to remember him. It's not how I would like him to be remembered. But this isn't in my gift. I may continue to insist that my father was much more than Private Godfrey but I must accept that – although this is how I knew him least – he was Private Godfrey, too. And I must also accept that it's as Private Godfrey he will be most often remembered.

CHAPTER TWENTY-SEVEN

The last wave by

Two incidents from the Great War illustrated for my father the fragility and tenacity of life.

In a forward trench a young subaltern is making his way along the line when he suddenly falls dead at my father's feet. Death is now numbingly familiar but the subaltern's death is abnormally abrupt. Lying in the mud, he appears completely unmarked. A close examination shows a single spot, the merest blemish, above his hairline where the needle of shrapnel has entered his skull and killed him instantly.

At a makeshift dressing-station my father, wounded for the first time, watches as a soldier is brought in, screaming, on a stretcher. He recognises him as a comrade from his own company. The soldier's guts are spilling out of his tunic and the orderly is endeavouring to push them back and hold them in. A medical officer attends to my father – the less seriously wounded are always treated first – and he is returned to the front line. Twelve years later my father encounters the screaming soldier walking towards him along Jermyn Street.

From this he concluded that our lives hang by a thread which may snap or may hold and that death cannot be foretold or forestalled.

* * *

'I'm just checking to see if I'm dead,' says my father, turning to the obituaries in *The Daily Telegraph*.

When I was a child, my father frequently talked about his own death. It wasn't a topic I wanted to hear him discuss but he appeared unaware of this.

'I was perfectly happy before I was born,' he used to say, placidly, 'and I expect I will be perfectly happy after I'm dead.'

This statement seemed to give him some blithe satisfaction; it gave me none. Thinking about it afterwards – as I often did – equating happiness with unconsciousness seemed particularly bleak.

As an adult I might have discussed mortality with my father but he didn't raise the subject and neither did I. At times he talked about his funeral arrangements but not about death itself. I don't want to suggest that he began to fear death or dying but, in his later years, some of his earlier equanimity had deserted him. What had once seemed cheerful acceptance was now a passive submission.

* * *

I have listened to *Under Milk Wood* on the radio but this is the first time that I have read any poetry by Dylan Thomas. It's the last period on Friday afternoon and cyclostyled copies of the poem are being passed round the class. 'Take one and pass them on.' 'Take one and pass them on.' Silence as we read.

Do not go gentle into that good night,
Old age should burn and rave at close of day;
Rage, rage against the dying of the light.

I put down my copy. I don't want to read this again. Not here. Not in public. Don't ask me to talk about it. Not in class. I need to take it home. To read it and re-read it on my own.

In my heart I knew that my father was already too weary to rage. It would be asking too much of him. Better that he should go gentle and leave me to rage.

* * *

Over the years my father suffered from a range of ailments – arthritis, bronchitis, laryngitis, tonsillitis, neuralgia, lumbago – and often several of them together. There were times when he had to lean against the scenery or be helped in and out of his costume. And there were performances when the cast needed to ad-lib while he struggled for the breath to speak his next line. But he was always there for the show; this was what he was paid for. He said his wish was to break a contract when he died. By this he meant that he wanted to miss a performance with the best of all possible excuses. That he was dead.

There are actors who have died on stage but it's not an exit my father would have enjoyed. Too dramatic; too theatrical. He might have liked not to wake up from one of his afternoon sleeps; or to be found at the close of play sitting in his turret at Lord's, his field-glasses and scorecard by his side. But it's not what happened.

*   *   *

Generously supported by the profession, Denville Hall, the home for retired theatricals in Northwood, is a comfortable, caring place where actors end their days in the company of colleagues who have shared the life of the theatre. Plush carpeting, fresh flowers and polished furniture. Playbills and portraits, photographs and busts; venerable shadows, worthy props. An interval in which to rehearse and reminisce. A well-stocked bar which opens at lunchtime and again in the evening. A good setting, you would say. Except it wasn't where he wanted to be.

This is how I would like to picture it.

Early evening. My father retires from the bar. His 'actor's gin' in his hand, he waves vaguely at the group of cooing ladies in the corner who are trying to entice him to stay. In the passage, he pauses to take a drink and then proceeds towards his room. Does he forget for a moment that he isn't at home? A step. An unexpected piece of furniture. He trips and – still holding the tooth-mug – falls. That's it. That's all. Exit. Farewell. Fade to black.

But his fall was in the morning.

*   *   *

In his final year my father became increasingly frail and there was less that he could do for himself. It was my mother's friends who decided that my father should go to Denville Hall. My mother was exhausted, they said, and she could no longer be expected to look after him. Whether or not they were right, they prevailed. My father's wish was to remain at home but this was judged to be selfish and, at the age of eighty-eight, he was too tired to protest. A taxi transported him from Highgate to Northwood and that was that. He had no reason not to be happy at Denville Hall, said the friends, and my mother was now freed from the burden of looking after him. A sensible solution, they agreed. Except in practice.

However much my father missed my mother, my mother missed my father more. Every morning for two months she drove the fifteen miles from Highgate to Northwood to be with him. And each evening, before it grew too dark, she drove home, exhausted. After he watched her drive away, my father made his way to the bar for an 'actor's gin' which he drank in his room while waiting for her telephone call to say she'd arrived home safely. After that he went to bed. Although he wasn't in his own home, he would see my mother the next day; and he had stayed in many digs much less agreeable than Denville Hall.

The morning of my father's fall my mother wasn't there. It may have been one morning when she was finally too tired to drive. I don't know. I wasn't there either; at the time my home was in Paris. There are always reasons for guilt.

When my father fell, he didn't die. For a day or two in hospital it seemed he would regain consciousness. But he didn't. He may have felt there was no longer a strong enough reason to make the effort.

* * *

The compulsion to say something – anything – is, it seems, irresistible; I lose count of the number of people who say it.

'He had a good innings.'

So you say, I think, but who are you to give him out?

After the funeral service at St Anne's, the vicar and I go together to Golders Green. My mother was to be spared the cremation. These were my father's instructions. He was right. It is a grim and mechanical business. The doors open, the coffin slides forward and tips away to be burnt. The doors close. Finish. I'm stunned. When we leave, a small family group is waiting outside. Another coffin in another hearse. On the way back to Highgate, I wonder if the vicar is going to engage me in comforting conversation. Thankfully he doesn't.

Returning to the flat I find the party has moved on from solemn condolence to social pleasantry. I'm not yet ready for this myself. I collect a drink, pull aside the curtain in front of my father's bedroom door and sit on his bed for several minutes. When I reappear, the noise level has risen appreciably. My father couldn't have stood it. I'm amused to think that he would have had to leave his own funeral to find peace in the Duke of St Albans.

As I stand in front of the bedroom door, a cousin approaches, a drink in his hand, swaying very slightly. I have always liked his shy smile but we see very little of each other. At once I have a dreadful premonition. I know what he's going to say. I hope – I pray – he won't, but I'm sure that he will. It's his standard opening on such occasions.

'It's the only time we all see each other, isn't it?' he begins. 'At christenings, weddings and funerals.'

It's what he always says on such occasions. Before, it's been fine. But not today, and not to me. Not at my father's funeral. He hears what he's said. He's aghast. I try to smile. I want to make things better but I don't know how. We stand there together.

'I'm very sorry,' he says.

Which is, of course, the right thing to say.

* * *

I had known that my father wished to be cremated. It was the constant topic of his conversations with the vicar in the kitchen in Highgate. What he didn't say was where he wanted his urn to be buried.

The Bath Abbey cemetery was, at that time, neglected and overgrown but my grandparents' grave was well-sited with a pleasing view towards Widcombe and the parish church of St Thomas À Becket. A tall, austere priest came up from the Abbey to say some simple prayers. My father's urn was interred at the foot of his parents' grave and we drove home to London.

In the years that follow I sometimes find myself near Bath. Parking the car in the city, I walk up the hill to the cemetery and locate my grandparents' grave.

In Loving Memory of
William Robert Ridley
Born May 12th 1871   Died August 10th 1931
He hath fought the good fight. He hath finished his course.

It feels right standing here in a light drizzle. A peaceful spot, fine *feng shui*. 'He hath fought the good fight.' A just epitaph.

Also Rosa Caroline Ridley
Wife of the above
Born June 2nd 1870   Died August 16th 1956
Re-united

Again the right words. After twenty-five years. 'Re-united.' Below my grandparents' inscriptions, a generous space had been left for my father.

Also their son
W. Arnold Ridley O.B.E.
Actor, Author and Playwright
Born 7th January 1896   Died 12th March 1984

Father, mother and son. The family complete. A satisfying tableau, although not quite perfect. Look carefully and one can see that the monumental mason has had to make a small correction to my father's year of birth. His habit of adding a year to his age always caused confusion.

* * *

When, as a son, your father dies, you know you're the next man in. And although you may have had your pads on for some time, it's a while before it feels real.

I picture myself walking with friends in the hills. I sit down and lean back against a rock. I don't loosen my boots; that will come later. I hear a girl's voice, indescribably sweet. She is singing a lullaby on a damp morning in a campsite in Ljubljana. I am in Istanbul, in Petra, in Fes, in Camprodon. The scent of sandalwood, steamed dumplings, wild basil. I am with my father at Lord's. And now my mother is sitting on my bed reading to me, the flowered summer curtains billowing in an evening breeze. My father comes in to say goodnight. Goodnight, old man. Good night. They'll be there when I wake.

What I know now is that, like most people, I would like to die with my family nearby; knowing that they're there.

* * *

My mother liked the company of theatricals. She should have been happy at Denville Hall. Perhaps, for a time, she was. But she hated being old and, after my father's death, she was never quite happy again.

We have come to visit her, my elder daughter, Catherine, and I. But my mother is not in her room. We find her sitting alone at the far end of the bar. It's not where I'd expect to find her. Three residents – actresses – sit in a group at a short distance from her. I don't know them but they greet me. My mother doesn't. Catherine and I sit down on either side of her and she smiles at us absently. I see suddenly that she doesn't know who we are.

'It's Nic,' I say. 'Nicolas.'

'Do you know my son, Nicolas?'

'I am Nicolas.'

'That's my son's name, Nicolas. Do you know him?'

'I am your son. I'm Nicolas.'

245

'Tell him to come to see me. He never comes to see me. I never see him.'

The three residents have been listening to our dialogue.

'I'm Nicolas,' I say. 'I'm your son.'

There are the clucking sounds of gleeful sympathy from nearby.

'Such a shame,' say the actresses.

'Yes, isn't it?' they agree.

They continue to listen.

I don't know who my mother sees in front of her but it's not me. I have a terrible, senseless urge to spell out my name. N-I-C-O-L-A-S. I don't but I try one more time. Then I give up. Catherine and I sit with her in dumb misery. There is nothing we can say or do.

'If you see Nicolas, tell him to come to see me,' says my mother, as we're going.

I say that I will.

One of the carers says a cheerful goodbye and closes the front door behind us. By the car Catherine turns to me and bursts into tears. We hold on to each other. I know that she is crying for Granny. She is also crying for me. And – whether or not she knows this – she is crying for herself. For the time when she will lose her own mother and father. This is what it's like. This is how it is going to be.

* * *

I was in St Louis when my mother died. The last leg of an extended business trip, I'd arrived late at night after a series of connecting flights from Mexico City. A free day before the start of the conference. A chance to explore the city. I am about to leave my room when I receive a message from Denville Hall. My mother is ill and not expected to live. Am I going to fly home? I don't have to decide right away. There are no flights until the evening.

I walk down to the Mississippi. A dull, grey stretch of water. A disappointment. The Gateway Arch, a famed tourist attraction, leaves me cold. I walk on and find a small church by a square. I would like to remember its name but I can't. It's simple, pleasing, empty and I'm grateful it's there. I sit on a straight-backed chair. It's not difficult to hear what my mother is saying. 'Don't be absurd, darling. Do what you came to do. Try to come back for the funeral if you can.' This decides me. When I return to the hotel, there's another call. My mother has died. I stay on in St Louis as she would have wanted.

This is during your gap year. You're in Chile but you send an email from Patagonia. A simple message: 'Granny has joined OB.' I know that you're right but it's good to have you remind me. My father will not have minded having some time alone but he has been by himself long enough. Now he's waiting, pacing the platform, checking his wristwatch against the station clock. He's early, of course, and inevitably my mother's train is late.

* * *

Back at Bath Abbey cemetery. A second simple service. There was no space for my mother's inscription on my grandparents' stone. She has her own bold tablet at the front of the grave. The position seems right. The words are mine.

ALSO

ALTHEA HELEN RIDLEY

née PARKER

WIFE, MOTHER

ACTRESS, FRIEND

MUCH LOVED

AND GREATLY MISSED

BORN 13TH SEPTEMBER 1911

DIED 27TH FEBRUARY 2001

* * *

This is an extract from a letter that I found among my father's papers. It's a letter I hope you'll find among mine and wish to keep. The envelope is addressed 'Arnold' and the initials 'RCR' are written on the back. The handwriting is firm, flowing and well-formed.

My darling Arnold

I feel I should like to write this letter to you to give you some guide as to what I should like you to do when I am gone. First I must tell you how I love you & Althea & Nicky, & then how grateful I am for all your love and help. You have been such a good son, & I pray we may meet again an unbroken family in our Father's house, never to part again ... Do not grieve for me but pray we may all meet again. If possible lay me with Daddy & put on [the] stone re-united ...

Mother

I try to picture my grandmother. Will she be the tranquil figure in black sitting in the front room in Wellsway picking currants from her bun? Or the young woman helping her sister look after a house full of lodgers? Will my grandfather be the 'handsome red-haired athlete' or the husband who 'fought the good fight' with such courage and 'finished his course' so many years before her? Will her son be the small boy playing with tin soldiers who hears the Widcombe bell tolling for the death of Queen Victoria, or the successful West End dramatist wintering in Antibes? Is this where I will find my father, young, confident, vigorous; and my mother, the glamorous actress, pursued by a string of suitors?

To 'meet again an unbroken family in our Father's house'. A simple wish. A prayer to be shared with everyone whose life has been touched by love. The strength of a faith beyond theology.

Re-united.

CHAPTER TWENTY-EIGHT

In the end, a beginning

Writing is a hidden business. It happens, when it happens, out of sight. Much the same can be said of not writing.

I'm alone in a room at the top of a house. I have written in other rooms in many houses, but now the room is mine and the house is ours. Which makes everything both easier and more difficult.

'What are you doing, Daddy?'

My younger daughter, Lottie, is standing at the door.

> *Click ▶* ♥3 → ♥4
> *Click ▶* ♥4 + ♥3 → ♥5
> *Pause   Deal!*

'Daddy? What are you doing?'

> *Click ▶* ♠Q + ♠J → ♠K
> *Click ▶* ♠K + ♠Q + ♠J → ♠A
> *Pause   Deal!*

She's waiting.

'Oh. Thinking. Just thinking.'

The family is under instruction not to disturb me when my door is closed. Unless, of course, it's an emergency. Some members of the family take a relaxed view of what constitutes an emergency. I compose my features into tolerant irritation. And close the program. *Click ▶*

'I'm really sorry, Dad, but …'

I listen patiently while my body language tries to say that I've been interrupted, although I'm not sure that my body language is telling the truth. I respond to her request in the affirmative as she knew I would.

'Thanks, Dad.'

She knows she should leave but there are questions she'd like to ask me. They hang in the air on invisible strings. Her father doesn't talk about whatever it is he's doing at the top of the house. 'Later,' he says. 'When the time is right.' It's strange. And irritating. But parents often are. Particularly fathers.

We smile at each other and she closes the door behind her. (Softly. So that she won't disturb me.) But I have been happy enough to be disturbed. I know where I am heading. I have a sense that I am being guided home.

*   *   *

We are taught to distrust our memories. We are instructed to find evidence. Documentation to substantiate the insubstantial; letters, notes, photographs, diaries. Some sort of corroboration.

For a full year, as a schoolboy, I kept a diary. A light-brown cover, one ruled page per day. I was a disciplined child and wrote in it punctiliously before going to bed. The diary came with a thin lead pencil that was awkward to write with. For the first week I remember that I found it difficult to fill each day's empty page. After that, it became much easier. I didn't have any more to write but I wrote in greater detail. After a few months I must have lost the pencil because I started using a pen. What I wrote in pencil is faint and illegible today, but my penned entries have survived. Here they are. A painstaking record, a wearisome task. At the end of December, I stopped and I haven't kept a daily diary since. Re-reading it as an adult, I am dismayed by my fact-full, page-per-day diary. Can it really have been such a dreary year?

*   *   *

When I'm overtaken by restlessness, I walk. I follow my boots. I go where they take me. And this evening, without knowing how, I find myself in Notting Hill Gate on an early autumn evening. A happy accident.

I walk up towards Lansdowne Road and cross over to the pillar box on the corner. Except that there is no pillar box. There must be. This is where it was. The pillar box where my father used to come; his change loose in his trouser pocket, a letter to the bank manager in his hand. But there is no pillar box. My memory has misled me.

Puzzled, I walk up Lansdowne Rise and begin a discourse with myself on the frailty of memory. I'm wrong. It's unarguable. But here I am again. At the pillar box. Exactly where it should be. The explanation is simple. I wasn't where I thought I was. This is where Lansdowne Road crosses Lansdowne Rise. Here not there. I look at the pillar box more closely and notice that it leans sharply to one side. This isn't something I remember at all, but it's not important.

I walk up to Ladbroke Crescent and turn left. At the end of the crescent is where the Bulls used to live. Mary Bull, my mother's close friend, who died from leukaemia. Joanna Bull, her daughter, with whom I went to dancing classes. I can see Joanna's golden hair, the yellow tunic she wore at the Festival of Britain. I smell the paraffin heaters in their first floor flat. The father was a drunk, or so it was said, but I liked Mr Bull. He played cricket with the other fathers and sons in Ladbroke Square. Bowling underarm, Mr Bull could spin the tennis ball ferociously. We children could never believe how sharply it turned.

* * *

I came across my 'blue diary' by accident. I wasn't looking for it. If I hadn't found it, I wouldn't have remembered its existence. It starts six months after your mother and I were married, twelve months before you were born. But after five blank years without an entry it ends:

Wednesday, 20th December 1989 – Kent Road, Chiswick. Isn't it time to put this notebook out of its misery? The new decade approaches and this poor account of very little adds nothing much, I think.

I was wrong. Although the entries are very uneven, I'm pleased to be able to re-read my blue diary. There are details here I might have forgotten. It isn't something you'll want to read yourself. I will try to remember to dispose of it and not leave the task to you.

* * *

At the end of her life my mother had so little left and yet she seemed to leave so much behind. Ornaments and trinkets, remnants and remainders. Sorting through these possessions after her death was a brutal occupation. Separating what had value for her from what might have meaning for me. Throwing away the evidence of a life. My patience wearing thin with guilt, time running short. Skip – car. Car – skip. Arbitrary. Awful.

Her books are easier to deal with. Religion, fiction, poetry, history. Yes – no. No – yes. I find I am holding my mother's copy of Kahlil Gibran's *The Prophet*. I have my own copy but I will keep hers, too. I can hear her reading out a passage she has marked. I am packing, preparing to go away. I'm only half-listening as I sort through what I need to take with me. She reads it only once. Then sits, the book open on her lap, watching me pack. A piece about parents and children. I look for it. (I shouldn't be doing this. I don't have time.) I sit down on one of the boxes and find the passage.

> *Your children are not your children.*
> *They are the sons and daughters of Life's longing for itself.*
> *They come through you but not from you,*
> *And though they are with you yet they belong not to you.*

How much did I understand this when she read it to me? Less than I understand it now with children of my own. I read the passage again and close the book. I sit for a moment before continuing to sort through her papers.

Receipts, instructions, guarantees, unidentified photographs, empty envelopes, scribbled notes. Here are her pocket diaries, held together by rubber bands. Many are stamped with gold lettering: 'The Duke of St Albans.' Christmas gifts from the landlord. There are years missing. Is this by choice or by chance? Should I keep them? Will they mean anything to me? Not really. Not much. One or two words per day. More blank days in the later diaries. More blank pages each year. Names, places, times. Dentist, bridge, church. Enough perhaps to remind her what she will be doing next week, what she did the week before. Meaningless to me. But then I notice other entries.

– *N gone away*
– *Letter from N*
– *Telephone call from N*
– *N back home*

Through the years of my adult life, each contact carefully noted. A simple record. No detail, no commentary. The more poignant for being so spare.

*　*　*

My father wasn't present at my birth. It wasn't an era when fathers were. If it had been, he would have found a reason to absent himself. He had mastered the art of not being where he didn't want to be. As it happened, he didn't need an excuse. At the time of my birth, my father had mumps. A painful condition for a man in his fifties but not uncommon among first-time fathers.

My father and mother were lodged in different wings of the same sanatorium in Bath. This meant that my father's first view of his son was when I was held up out of my mother's ground floor window while he looked down from his window above. This sight, my mother asserted firmly, thoroughly delighted him and justified her decision to bear a child. Although I'm unclear how she can have known this with quite such certainty when, for three weeks, she and my father were separated from each other by two floors. Today an enforced quarantine might be seen as regrettable but, in my father's case, it was providential. It gave him time to accustom himself to the reality of fatherhood which would otherwise have come to him as a considerable shock. As it was, when his period of isolation ended, he was able to emerge – prepared – to take on the role.

* * *

If I had given any thought to it, I would have cast myself in the role of the Ealing comedy father, pacing the corridors of the maternity ward until the time that a beaming midwife invites me to see the mother and child, both doing well. I would find myself the proud father of a baby boy. Or baby girl. Either would have been fine; I wasn't thinking that far ahead. In the scene that follows I would retire, as is customary, to the local hostelry to celebrate my success with disorderly friends and freeloading strangers. But by the time of your birth, fathers were no longer allowed to wait in the wings.

> *Tuesday, 18th May 1982 – Chiswick. Antenatal classes. Deep breathing and the mysteries of childbirth in the company of several very earnest couples.*

I didn't take in very much at the antenatal classes. Anatomical diagrams, stages of labour, centimetres of dilation. It seemed so medical.

The breathing exercises and singing were closer to what I felt I could cope with. Lying on pillows on the carpet, breathing in and out. This was something I could do; and your mother and I had decided on the song we'd sing during labour.

> ♪ *Ten green bottles, hanging on the wall*
>> ♪ *Ten green bottles, hanging on the wall*
>>> ♪ *And if one green bottle should accidentally fall …*

We are practising our song on the way back from class when we hear the news from the South Atlantic on the car radio. *HMS Sheffield* has been sunk. The first British losses in the Falklands War.

We drive the rest of the way home in silence.

* * *

I have no memory of writing any of this, but I find I did.

254

Wednesday, 16th June – Chiswick. Our friends everywhere are having children and I am beginning to panic. The whole idea of fatherhood and a child in my life alarms me. I'm sure – I think I'm sure – it will alarm me less when it actually happens.

Marriage has meant change. I drink less but eat more. My health has improved but I have put on weight. The occasional game of squash is no longer sufficient. I start running again. I find that my shorts don't fit and that my feet have grown fatter. I buy tracksuit trousers and new trainers and look for a route. I settle for a local park with a perimeter path where I can run at night. I build up slowly. One lap running, half-a-lap walking, half-a-lap running. And home. Over time I walk less and run more. At six laps I feel I have found my distance. Six laps of the park becomes my routine

Tuesday, 27th July 1982 – Chiswick. In fact Wednesday, 28th July 1982 – 1.00 a.m. Just returned from an evening run completed with something like ease. The night suits me and is my proper time to run. Strange to find no Joç asleep in bed. I took her into Queen Charlotte's at 3.00 p.m. as arranged. No drama. No sign of labour. Which means she will be induced. Tomorrow will bring what?

Saturday, 7th August 1982 – Chiswick. To which the answer was a son. At 15:16 hours on Wednesday 28th July. A Leo. Weight 3.4 kilos or 7lb 8oz. Very average. Quite exceptional. A telephone call from the hospital at just before 5.00 a.m. to say that Joç was asking for me. Chiswick deserted at this hour in the morning. Straight up to the labour ward on the fifth floor. The labour wasn't complicated but it was long. We had all the help and support we could ever have hoped for. Even the slightly fussy student midwife had her heart very much in the right place. Doctors, tutors, sisters – they were all keen to allow us to give birth in the way we wished. An overwhelming experience. And the result is xxxxxxx William Ridley – still unnamed.

* * *

I return from the hospital a father. Physically and emotionally I am drained but I know I won't sleep. I put on my tracksuit trousers and my trainers and walk to the park. The gate isn't locked which means I don't have to climb over the fence. I take this to be a good omen.

I run my first lap and my second. In the background I hear the fading hum of the traffic on the Great West Road. My third lap. My fourth? I normally know precisely which lap I'm running but tonight I've lost count. It's not important. Tonight I can always run an extra lap. There's no one waiting for me at home. My fourth lap? My fifth? And then I'm not counting any more.

> ♪ One green bottle, hanging on the wall
> > ♪ And if one green bottle should accidentally fall
> > > ♪ There'll be no green bottles, hanging on the wall.

We've done it. It's over. A baby lying on his mother's stomach. Fulfilment, achievement, wonder and love. My child. My son. More beautiful than anything I could have imagined. (Subsequent photographs show that you looked like a frog but your mother and I didn't see this.) I run on, another lap. It's difficult to take in the wonder and impossible to express the joy. I am a father. More laps and a light snow falling in the dark. This is how my own parents must have felt. How they have continued to feel. And how I will always feel myself. I was wanted. I was loved. My birth was a gift. I've no need to feel any guilt, no need to be weighed down by obligation. My mother returning to her dressing-room, her son bursting into tears. My father bowling his first 'tweaker' of the morning, hiding his grimace. I am not – I have never been – indebted. What I owe my parents is what I have chosen to owe them. I feel years of guilt lifting, releasing me. I'm free to run on. Lap after lap. Until, when the snow has stopped falling, I go home to sleep.

But there was no snow. You were born at the end of July. There can't have been snow. I have mixed two memories – maybe more than two – and made them into one. It's still true. The dark night, the falling snow, running lap after lap, a moment of supreme happiness. As true as anything can be.

256

Author's acknowledgements

I am very grateful to the following who, at different times and in different ways, have – knowingly and unknowingly – provided me with support, guidance, encouragement and accommodation.

John Aldridge, Caroline Allen, Kevin Ancient, Alan Beaton, Cath Bruzzone, Jo and Julian Chisholm, Christine Cox, David Croft, Chris Dick, Paul Donovan, Jo Elsworth and the Bristol Theatre Collection, Anna Farthing, Ruth Gairns, Ronnie Grainge, Rachel Hunt, Brian Jackson, Jerry and Sue Johns, Laura Longrigg, Dot McCall, Bill McLean, Davy Nougarede, Liz Nuttall, Jimmy Perry, Bill Pertwee, Nick Pollard, Robin Price, Stephen Probyn, Stuart Redman, Catherine Ridley, Christopher Ridley, Jocelyn Ridley, Lottie Ridley, Charlotte Rolfe, David Roper, Alison Samuel, Bénédicte Scholefield and the Ammerdown Centre, Andrew Simon, Harold Snoad, Richard Van Emden, Ray Vost, David Wallace and Frank Williams.

Thank you all. (And everyone I have forgotten.)